The Women's Orchestra
of Auschwitz

Also by Anne Sebba

Samplers: Five Centuries of a Gentle Craft

Enid Bagnold: A Life

Laura Ashley: A Life By Design

*Battling for News: Women Reporters from the Risorgimento
to Tiananmen Square*

Mother Teresa: Beyond the Image

*The Exiled Collector: William Bankes and the Making
of an English Country House*

Jennie Churchill: Winston's American Mother

That Woman: The Life of Wallis Simpson, Duchess of Windsor

*Les Parisiennes: How the Women of Paris Lived,
Loved and Died in the 1940s*

*Ethel Rosenberg: The Short Life and Great Betrayal of an
American Wife and Mother*

The Women's Orchestra of Auschwitz

A Story of Survival

ANNE SEBBA

WEIDENFELD & NICOLSON

First published in Great Britain in 2025 by Weidenfeld & Nicolson,
an imprint of The Orion Publishing Group Ltd
Carmelite House, 50 Victoria Embankment
London EC4Y ODZ

An Hachette UK Company

The authorised representative in the EEA is Hachette Ireland, 8 Castlecourt Centre,
Dublin 15, D15 XTP3, Ireland (email: info@hbgi.ie)

3 5 7 9 10 8 6 4

Copyright © Anne Sebba 2025

A CIP catalogue record for this book is
available from the British Library.

ISBN (Hardback) 978 1 3996 1073 5
ISBN (Export Trade Paperback) 978 1 3996 1074 2
ISBN (Ebook) 978 1 3996 1076 6
ISBN (Audio) 978 1 3996 1077 3

Typeset at The Spartan Press Ltd,
Lymington, Hants

Printed in Great Britain by Clays Ltd,
Elcograf S.p.A.

MIX
Paper | Supporting
responsible forestry
FSC® C104740

www.weidenfeldandnicolson.co.uk
www.orionbooks.co.uk

In memory of those who cannot tell their story

CONTENTS

INTRODUCTION
The Women's Orchestra of Auschwitz

One evening in early 1944, four emaciated young women, attempting to rouse themselves from their grim prison conditions, began a secret performance of Beethoven's *Pathétique* sonata in the cold and cramped barrack that also served as their dormitory, practice room, eating place and parcel depot. Although the piece was originally written for solo piano, it had been transcribed for three violins and a cello by a recently arrived French nightclub singer who had studied music at a conservatory before the war.

The four women, three of whom were Jewish, were all inmates of Auschwitz, the Nazis' most notorious extermination camp outside the southern Polish city of Oświęcim. They were part of the only entirely female orchestra in any of the prisons, camps and ghettos established by the Nazis before and during the Second World War. Throughout the orchestra's brief existence, from April 1943 until October 1944, most of its members were teenagers, one as young as fourteen. Remarkably, almost all of the forty or so core players survived their time here and avoided being deliberately gassed, although their main conductor did not survive.

The women's orchestra, separated from their fellow inmates in a special block, was required by their Nazi overseers to play jaunty marches every morning and evening so that other female

1

prisoners kept in step as they were sent to work outside the camp. Playing on a grassy mound located to the side of the so-called 'French gate' of the women's camp, they had only twelve or so marches in their repertoire and if they reached the end and had played them all they simply started again from the beginning. The orchestra also performed regular weekly concerts from an approved repertoire for the other prisoners, for sick inmates in the infirmary and for guards as well as occasional visiting Nazi dignitaries. Yet on this evening, the four women – a German, a Pole, a Belgian and a Frenchwoman – were playing Beethoven's masterpiece, clandestinely since Jewish musicians were not considered worthy of playing such magnificent German works and were doing so just for their own pleasure. The informal concert had to be done with extreme caution, with a designated 'lookout person' to warn of impending danger in the form of an SS man.[1]

Anita Lasker, eighteen at the time, passionate since childhood about the cello, recalled the occasion as 'one where we were able to raise ourselves high above the inferno of Auschwitz into spheres where we could not be touched by the degradation of concentration camp existence'.[2] On another occasion she described it as 'a link with the outside world, with beauty, with culture, a complete escape into an imaginary and unattainable world'.[3]

Auschwitz has become a byword for the mass murder and bestiality of the Nazi regime. It was a place where 1.1 million men, women and children, mostly Jews, were gassed to death while others died as a result of various forms of ill treatment, torture and starvation. It was not a place anyone would naturally associate with music at all, let alone Beethoven, the great German composer whose music offers a profound rallying cry to freedom. Not surprisingly, the other female prisoners who faced a daily offering of brutal labour and punishment as they worked, had every reason not to share Anita's feelings about the elevating power of great music. Yet the most beautiful music is often a manifestation of deep pain, and what may seem a disparity – sublime music expressing great emotional strain – is often at the heart of musical genius.

Charlotte Delbo, a French Communist resister who arrived at Auschwitz in January 1943, was one of the other prisoners. She recalled in 1995 that it was 'intolerable' to hear the women's orchestra playing Viennese waltzes while 'naked men reduced to skeletons' exited their barracks to go to work, 'driven by blows that make them reel'.[4]

Pearl Pufeles, deported in March 1944 to Auschwitz with the rest of her family, wept more than four decades later when she remembered what she believed was the cruel deception of the orchestra greeting the latest Jewish transport as they stepped off the train from Czechoslovakia with music by Dvořák and Smetana. 'I said to my sister Helen, "Gosh, this can't be that bad if they play music here." Our whole family was very musical. Helen and I played violin, my other sister had a beautiful voice.' But as she and Helen were twins, volunteering for the orchestra was not an option. They were selected instead for grotesque medical 'experiments', supervised by the infamous SS mass murderer Dr Josef Mengele.[5]

Irene Zisblatt, just thirteen when she arrived in Auschwitz in the spring of 1944, remembered being forced to listen to the orchestra that autumn:

> We'd just come in . . . after four hours in the rain, and they brought us back close to the crematoria so that the ashes were falling on the ground where we were, and they ordered us to sit on the ground, there were hot ashes like drizzles of rain on us. And they told us they were going to give us a concert to celebrate the holidays. And so 32,000 [sic] women more

3

or less sat on the ground on the hot ashes, all the crematoria were burning away, the stench from the bodies... it was a grey day, it was like nighttime so dark.

And there in front of us on a platform were these beautiful women in crisp uniforms with makeup and lipstick and blonde, long hair and these SS men, young men, strong and well fed... laughing... having a great time.

And then the band came up on the platform.

We sat for hours, it was torture, we just wanted to die. We will never enjoy this band or have the hair and the lipstick. It was another way of killing us.

Like Pearl, Irene was reduced to tears when she recounted this memory of the orchestra in an interview in Florida in 1995 for the Shoah Foundation. 'This was not music for our souls,' she declared emphatically. 'I was thinking of my parents and brothers and people burning.'[6]

Although some former prisoners did look back on their time in Auschwitz-Birkenau, the largest section of the overall camp where most prisoners were held until they died or were deliberately gassed, and recalled hearing music as soothing or at least something which offered a chance for them to take their minds off the grim daily realities they faced, these conflicting testimonies illustrate why the story of the Auschwitz women's orchestra does not belong to any one individual or even exclusively to the players themselves. Their audience of fellow prisoners matters, as well as the responses of the various male orchestras who occasionally looked on enviously as they had to work as well as play music. Szymon Laks, conductor of one of several male orchestras at Auschwitz-Birkenau, vehemently refuted the notion that music was helpful to anyone in the camp. 'In no case did I ever meet a prisoner who found courage in our music, whose life our music helped save,'[7] he commented. Laks was clear-eyed about the role of his and other orchestras being entirely a propaganda tool for the Nazis and was fully aware of the unfairness of these 'privileges' granted to the small number of prisoners eligible, just one of the many moral conundrums at the heart of this story.

In 1976 the French singer who had transcribed the *Pathétique* sonata for the impromptu quartet published the first book about the orchestra. Fania Fénelon was at least a decade older than most of the other girls in the so-called music block and, by all accounts, had an unusual musical memory if a less reliable one for events. She had arrived only in January 1944 but was much welcomed as 'one of the few accomplished musicians in the group',[8] transcribing and arranging being an essential skill for the officially sanctioned orchestra to operate successfully.

Yet her book, first published as *Sursis pour l'Orchestre*, translated as *The Musicians of Auschwitz*, was a novelised and sensational account which appalled almost all the other members of the ragtag band. It was later turned into a film which roused several of the women to write their own memoirs of the orchestra. Among them was Anita, who went on to become the renowned musician Anita Lasker-Wallfisch, ninety-nine and living in London at the time of writing.

Anita and other surviving orchestra players felt especially that Fénelon, who died in 1983, had betrayed the memory of Alma Rosé, the Austrian Jewish professional violinist who had held the orchestra together as conductor before her own sudden death in April 1944 at the age of thirty-seven, probably from accidental food poisoning. In their view, Fénelon's harshly negative portrayal of Alma ignored the degree to which Alma's sometimes ferocious discipline enabled all the players under her baton to survive; for as Alma regularly reminded them, if they left the orchestra, they too would 'go to the gas'.

Alma's warning is the leitmotif which runs through this book, the first attempt using new information to collect the oral and written memories of the orchestra as well as other prisoners into a single narrative. There is a vast body of literature on many aspects of Auschwitz in general, and many individual accounts and memoirs of those who played in the 'girls' band', as it was called at the time. But in writing about the orchestra now, I have tried to reflect not only the perspective of other prisoners who were forced to listen to the music while being denied privileges granted to the players – the most precious of all being the players' fragile protection against being dispatched to the gas chambers – but also to make clear the views of the musicians themselves, some of whom had been forced to join under compulsion. They suffered during their captivity not only from the same hunger, cold and fear endured by the camp's prisoners but, long after their release, from a different kind of nightmare and depression based on rage and despair as they agonised over their impotence. What else might they have done? What choices did they really have?

The essence of the conundrum was: 'Should we protect our lives and play or refuse to play and doom ourselves to a harsher life, or even to death?' as one of the non-Jewish Polish musicians expressed it.[9] Other prisoners imagined that the musicians were so-called '*prominenten*' or 'big shots'[10] who were shown favours and lived in 'silky conditions'. The truth was that in practical terms they had very little beyond a bunk and a blanket, both of critical importance, to differentiate themselves. But, as long as they played well and were therefore useful to the Nazis, they had an identity beyond a number and with it a chance to survive. This alone was enough to ensure they were despised by others.

The Nazi use of music in the death camps has many explanations. The Germans saw themselves as a cultured people and yet during the war they used music as an additional tool of torture.

6

In Nazi nomenclature, the women of the orchestra were a work kommando, or squad, whose job was to make the other prisoners march faster out to work and back in again in rows of five, thus making them easier to count. If the women's playing or practising near the station platform had the effect of calming arriving prisoners into a false sense of security as they clambered off the train, that was an additional benefit. And if their playing also had the effect of sowing discord among other inmates who saw these relatively well-dressed women as collaborators, the Nazi guards did not object.

Clearly, the Nazis also wanted to humiliate the musicians in their use of music as a further tool of violent assault. The female musicians, because they were excused work in other kommandos and were always practising in their block or performing at the entrance gate, witnessed the arrival of thousands of desperate people, the cries of children mingled with the shouts of SS men, wild barking of dogs and snatches of sentimental songs. In this way they were forced to provide the backdrop to murder. Lily Mathé, one of the orchestra's best violinists, vividly remembered being made to play jolly tunes in the SS officers' mess at Auschwitz every evening while the guards ate their dinner. Adolf Eichmann, one of the chief perpetrators of the Holocaust, was a regular witness to the mess during his frequent visits to Auschwitz in 1944 to check on how the mass extermination of inmates was progressing. 'Eichmann used to drink a lot and would delight at waving chicken bones before our hungry eyes and contemptuously throwing one at us to grovel for,' Lily remembered.[11]

It is plain from their post-war testimonies that Lily and all the other orchestra players despised their captors. The fact that there were also frequent internal arguments between different musicians and factions within the orchestra should not obscure this important point. Indeed, it seems a fitting prelude to this complicated, often discordant story that both aspects of the orchestra were on display that evening in early 1944, a few months before Lily arrived at Auschwitz, when the quartet launched into the first bars of the *Pathétique* sonata. The mere act of playing this sublime music for their own delight was also an act of defiance against their SS guards.

However, the quartet never finished the piece. They stopped when the Polish Aryan* violinist, Helena Dunicz, playing among three Jews, suddenly refused to continue. Recalling the moment in her 2014 memoirs when she was almost ninety-nine, she could no longer remember the precise circumstances. She simply remarked how unhappy she was that the private performance had ended so abruptly, because it had reminded her of her pre-war life in Lwów, when she had played chamber music with her brother and mother.

In 1996 Helena wrote more candidly to Anita of her deep regret at how the other Polish women in the orchestra did not want her to associate so closely with the Jewish girls who were players. Helena had to choose between the strong support she derived from being part of the Polish Christian group within the orchestra, with their small privileges as non-Jews, or mixing with the Jews for the sake of the quartet. She lamented to Anita that she had not felt strong enough to argue with her fellow Poles. 'Because of the solidarity with others I had to stop . . . I felt very unhappy to behave in such a style. As I was very timid since my birth and horrified in the camp, I didn't feel strong enough to intermediate[sic].'[12] Anita, reflecting on the debacle today, still shakes her head in sorrow.

Yet when they performed together, the Poles and the Jews did

---

* The Nazis promoted the idea that the German people were members of the 'Aryan Race' and Jews were non-Aryans.

put aside their differences to present a common orchestral front against their jailers, playing to the best of their varying abilities to save each other's lives.

I had long been aware of the existence of the women's orchestra through my professional research into other Holocaust stories.* But I had never connected the orchestra with my own father's wartime story. Yet as I read more about the women's experiences and learned how some of them had been transferred at the end of 1944 to another camp at Bergen-Belsen in northern Germany, I decided it was time to research the role of my father, who had been part of the British forces liberating Belsen a few months later.

As the Allies advanced across Europe, the Germans destroyed what they could of Auschwitz and other camps, burning documents and hoping not to leave a trace of their atrocities. With the imminent approach of the Russian army, the Nazis force-marched survivors out of the camps on what are now known as the death marches. Weakened stragglers were shot or simply collapsed and died on the road.

On 1 November 1944, the Auschwitz women's orchestra suddenly stopped performing, on Nazi orders. Its Jewish musicians were transported by train to Bergen-Belsen while two and a half months later the remaining non-Jewish players were sent to the only all-women camp at Ravensbrück, 90 kilometres north of Berlin, marching in freezing winter conditions with no food.

My father was a thirty-two-year-old tank commander who had crossed to occupied France shortly after D-Day, fought in the savage battle for Caen and then on through northern France. In April 1945 he and his regiment reached Belsen shortly after its

---

* Specifically visiting Ravensbrück for *Les Parisiennes*.

liberation. Even though he had been in uniform for seven years, having joined the Territorials in 1938, nothing my father had seen could have prepared him for this horror. Thousands of skeletal creatures were lying on bunks unable to move, while dead bodies were piled in heaps all around the camp, reeking of putrefaction.

Recently promoted to major with the role of quartermaster general, my father was in charge of all procurement. He was also responsible for keeping the official regimental diary in which he discussed the position of 'displaced persons', as they were now described – specifically, those camp survivors who had no homes to return to and were not allowed, or were unwilling, to go to Palestine, then run by a British mandate.

When I was growing up in England in the 1950s and 1960s, I could never talk to my father about what he had seen because he would immediately shut down any discussion of Belsen, feeling it was too gruesome a conversation for a young family. All that remains for me are memories of whispered conversations between my parents involving the strange word 'Belsen'.

Yet one day in January 2022, long after my father's death in 1997, I found a thin little file in Britain's National Archives – the Regimental War Diary, with his unmistakable signature, Maj. Eric Rubinstein, 31st Armoured Brigade. Against the date of 24 May 1945 he had written: '7 R Tanks with Crocodiles burning BELSEN camp'.[13]

What did this mean? Once all the prisoners had been moved out of their huts and housed in other accommodation in the camp, the disease-ridden buildings were razed to the ground using powerful flamethrowers fired by Churchill Crocodile tanks to prevent the spread of further infections. The tanks could throw roaring jets of flame more than 100 metres, much further than a man-carried flamethrower, supplied by an armoured trailer which was towed behind carrying 400 gallons of fuel.

No wonder that Anita Lasker-Wallfisch still vividly remembers this day of destruction. She was in that crucible of hell along with a handful of other Jewish survivors from the orchestra when my father also witnessed the flamethrowers at work. In her 1996 memoir, Anita recalled watching the flamethrower tanks destroying the huts and described her many interactions with British officers. One such officer, she wrote, had made it his duty 'since he is in charge of the stores' to get Anita and her sister Renate properly outfitted for their work as interpreters. Could that possibly be my father, whose job it was as brigade QMG to procure provisions?

Apart from Anita, other remnants of the women's orchestra who had been removed from Auschwitz to Belsen included the Hungarian violinist Lily Mathé, her compatriot the singer Eva Steiner, the Dutch pianist Flora Jacobs and the music copyist Hilde Grünbaum, a close friend of the conductor Alma Rosé, and the two Greek sisters, Lili and Yvette Assael. On 24 May 1945, the same day that the flamethrowers went into action, Lily and Eva performed in a Red Cross concert at Belsen, presumably in the evening after the destruction. It seems possible, even likely, that my father attended. Tantalisingly, I shall never know, but ever since I discovered my father's proximity to these events, I have been gripped by a need to understand more not only about the women in the Auschwitz orchestra, how they survived and at what cost, but also what hearing music in this inferno meant to the other prisoners and how we should think today about this additional attempt to degrade what it means to be human.

I

We did not feel pain anymore

On 1 September 1939 German troops marched into Poland. Two days later Britain and France declared war on Germany as the invasion triggered the guarantees they had given to Poland, which was also attacked from the east by the Soviet Union, which in August had signed the Nazi-Soviet pact. Poland, an independent state since 1918, was swiftly partitioned, resulting in around one-third of the country's estimated three million Jews finding themselves under Soviet rule. Thousands of Polish Jews fled eastwards to avoid the Nazis and were mostly sent to work in labour camps in Siberia. Although conditions were brutal and anti-Semitism the norm, the Soviets saw the internees as useful forced labour in forests, mines and farms and did not follow the Nazi policy of deliberate genocide. Most of these relatively fortunate Polish Jews survived the war. Later in the war some Poles managed to enlist in special units such as the Polish Independent Carpathian Brigade, which went on to fight the Germans in North Africa. Other Poles in exile made substantial contributions to the Allied military effort throughout the war, fighting on land, sea and in the air in a variety of different theatres of war including the well-documented 145 Polish pilots flying under British command in 1940 during the Battle of Britain.

Meanwhile, the rest of Poland's Jews under Nazi rule were in mortal danger. The extermination of the Jews, while not yet an official Nazi war aim, began as soon as Hitler's troops crossed the Polish border. SS operational units roamed through newly captured Polish towns, lining up groups of Jews for execution, indulging in random killings and setting fire to Jewish-owned businesses.

These random killings rapidly escalated into systematic mass murder. By the end of 1941, following the invasion of the Soviet Union, the Nazi killing squads had succeeded in exterminating tens of thousands of Jews in eastern Poland and the Baltic states of Latvia and Lithuania, often aided by local communities with long-standing anti-Semitic hatreds. At the same time, the Nazis exported Germany's existing concentration camp system into the conquered eastern territories to hold Jews destined for the gas chambers, as well as a vast range of other perceived enemies of the Third Reich across occupied Europe, from gypsies and Communists to nationalists and homosexuals.

Auschwitz – the German name for the medieval Polish city of Oświęcim, home to many Jewish families – was the hub of this vastly expanded concentration camp network. On 27 April 1940 SS Commander in Chief Heinrich Himmler gave orders for the founding of a camp complex on the site of a former Austro-Hungarian army barracks just outside the city centre, near to a disused tobacco factory. The work of clearing and building was undertaken by prisoners sent for the purpose. This original camp, called Auschwitz I, or Stammlager, remained the nucleus and administrative centre of the vast camp complex, its infamous gate proclaiming *Arbeit Macht Frei* ('Work Makes for Freedom') becoming the ultimate symbol of the Holocaust.

Auschwitz gradually evolved into a web of concentration and extermination camps as well as factories as the Jewish Holocaust gathered momentum. The network was situated in the southern

Polish region of Upper Silesia, which was newly incorporated into Germany at the juncture of the Vistula and Sola rivers.

Logistically, Auschwitz's location was ideal for the Nazis' purposes, because it stood at the centre of major road and rail networks which would facilitate transporting large numbers of people there from multiple points of departure around Europe. Yet it was also to some extent isolated from the outside world, despite its good connections with the now German-run General Government of Poland and proximity to the former states of Austria and Czechoslovakia.

The first commandant of Auschwitz I, Rudolf Höss, was an experienced thirty-eight-year-old SS officer who previously worked at the Nazis' first concentration camp at Dachau, near Munich, and then at Sachsenhausen, which he headed from 1938 until his transfer to Auschwitz in May 1940. He was officially named commandant on 4 May. At Auschwitz, Höss, his wife

Three SS officers socialise at Auschwitz (from left to right): Richard Baer (commandant of Auschwitz), Josef Mengele and Rudolf Höss (the former commandant)

Hedwig and their four children lived in a comfortable two-storey house with prisoners as domestic servants and a pretty garden within sight of the first crematorium.

For the first two years, Auschwitz was not in fact a concentration camp specifically for Jews. The original inmates were largely a mixture of male political prisoners and professional criminals drawn from across the greater German Reich, including Austria, Czechoslovakia and the annexed regions of western Poland. The first mass transport of prisoners, comprising 728 Polish men from Tarnow prison, arrived in Auschwitz on 14 June, immediately after the Fall of France. They included Jews and Catholics, many of whom were arrested attempting to cross the southern Polish border to reach the newly formed Polish army in exile in France. As the influx of prisoners increased during these early months, Höss swiftly oversaw the establishment of Auschwitz II or Auschwitz-Birkenau, almost two miles from the initial camp. To make way for Birkenau, the village of Brzezinka and several surrounding smaller hamlets were demolished, evicting the local population of Poles and some Jews who still lived in the area.

Birkenau, which took its name from the birch tree groves in the area, was in operation by March 1942, even though the camp was far from finished. It would become the site of the main crematoria and so-called gas 'chambers', rooms disguised as shower rooms and called morgues by the SS on their building plans. By now, the Nazis no longer needed to rely on slow and cumbersome mobile gas units to kill their victims, having perfected a method of rapidly slaughtering large numbers of people, predominantly Jews, with canisters of Zyklon B gas, a cyanide-based pesticide.

Until 1942 the early Auschwitz camps were for men only. The first women began to arrive at the end of March 1942, soon including mothers with children who were dispatched immediately to be gassed. The surviving women were treated as slave labour and sent directly to work, mostly on demolition squads to clear space for expansion of the camp, without being quarantined or undergoing 'selection', the euphemism for the Nazi system of deciding on arrival in the camp who was fit enough to work and who should be immediately gassed.

There were rapidly proliferating sub-camps, some within marching distance of the main Auschwitz railway station. Many prisoners at these sub-camps were 'sold' as slave labour to German industry, aiding the war effort. The largest of these Auschwitz slave factories, which eventually numbered forty, was the Buna synthetic rubber plant at Monowitz, established in October 1942 and known as Auschwitz III. It was run by the chemical conglomerate I G Farben and although the working conditions at Buna and other Auschwitz factories were brutal, prisoners who could tolerate the regime were at least safe from being selected for extermination.

For Auschwitz had become by the end of 1942 the largest of all the Nazi extermination centres, whose camps and sub-camps covered an area of approximately 40 square kilometres, the whole described as an 'interest zone' by the Germans. In the summer of 1941, Himmler had informed Höss that Auschwitz had been chosen as a key location for the mass extermination of the Jews and by January the following year the plan that the Nazis came to describe euphemistically as the Final Solution was formalised by a small group of senior Nazi officials, including SS Lt Col. Adolf Eichmann, who specialised in 'Jewish Affairs'.

Meeting at an impressive lakeside villa a few miles outside Berlin, the conference agreed that the remaining Jews in Europe would no longer be allowed to emigrate; they would instead be exterminated. The Wannsee Conference was chaired by thirty-seven-year-old Reinhard Heydrich, who used the event to assert his own authority over the process of systematic Jewish annihilation, which from now on was to replace randomised killing. This had been a fundamental plank of Hitler's worldview and manifesto. In less than a day it was agreed that the entire population of Europe, whose Jewish contingent was estimated by Heydrich to stand at about eleven million, including countries which Germany did not then occupy such as Britain and neutral nations such as Switzerland, Ireland, Sweden, Spain, Portugal and European Turkey, would be made free of all Jews – *Judenfrei* or *Judenrein*. Heinrich Himmler was the most senior Nazi charged with overall implementation of the Final Solution and therefore overseer of the camps.

Here, the Auschwitz women's orchestra and its male counterparts enter this terrible narrative. Even as the Nazis committed themselves to eradicating all trace of the Jews, a core part of Jewish culture was being preserved at Auschwitz. Music was an integral part of life in almost all Nazi-run camps, although here the music was subverted, no longer allowed to give pleasure but used as an additional method of torture.

While the Auschwitz orchestras included non-Jews, at least half of all the players were Jewish, a delicate balance which the Nazis kept a close eye on. The balance might easily have tipped over in favour of the Jewish members partly as a natural consequence of Jews being by far the largest prisoner group. But it also spoke to the centrality of music for so many Jews of all social classes, wherever they lived, from street performers with little or no formal training to accomplished professional players. Prayers in synagogues had been accompanied by music and chanting since ancient times while klezmer, sometimes referred to as Yiddish without words, was a style of folk music which originated during the Middle Ages among the Jewish people of Eastern Europe, Greece and the Balkans. It was most often played at celebrations such as weddings or bar mitzvahs and also had its own rich tradition which borrowed from Jewish cantorial music,

Hasidic intoning and Yiddish theatre. Music as a reaffirmation of humanity was now being used as an additional tool in the struggle to destroy it.

The Auschwitz orchestras exposed the grotesque contradiction at the heart of the Final Solution – the Nazis' inability to decide whether Jews were to be annihilated because they were the lowest of the low or because they ran the world in some form of evil conspiracy. An orchestra led by a Jew was a visible reminder of this confusion.

In February 1942, a few weeks after the Wannsee Conference, the first transports of Jews deliberately destined for death arrived in Auschwitz I. These victims were immediately gassed on arrival with Zyklon B gas, their bodies later incinerated using the old crematorium in the main camp, a grassy mound over a bunker just beyond the commandant's spacious family house and garden. In March, the killings were moved to nearby Birkenau, where a vastly bigger murder operation was being hurriedly organised.

Initially two farm buildings, a red cottage and a white cottage, standing discreetly behind foliage and trees, were used as disguised gas chambers. After gassing, the corpses were taken out and buried in mass graves. Those prisoners involved in the burials, generally young fit male Jews, were then taken to the infirmary and killed with a phenol injection.[1] A few months later construction began in Birkenau on four large, purpose-built structures to be used for extermination by gas, with associated crematoria. These buildings soon enabled the Nazis to kill on an industrial scale, leaving only ashes behind.

The start of mass transports of male and female Jews to Auschwitz in 1942 created the need for a separate women's camp. On 26 March, the first mass transport of 999 prisoners from the all-female camp at Ravensbrück was tasked with setting up this new women's camp at Birkenau. The Ravensbrück group, who were not

Jewish, included German women classified as asocial or criminal, and a few political prisoners. They were assigned to take charge of the Jewish women who now flooded into Auschwitz, even though Birkenau was not yet ready to receive them.

The same day, 26 March 1942, the first registered mass transport of 997* young Slovak Jewish women set off for Auschwitz, most of them rounded up under threat by the Nazi puppet government from their villages. They had no idea of what lay ahead, except that they were being sent away for some kind of public work service, and that if they did not comply then their parents, who for the time being remained, would suffer.

This initial group were corralled for days at a transit camp in the Slovak town of Poprad as their numbers steadily swelled and were then stuffed into airless cattle cars for the twenty-four-hour train journey to Auschwitz. There were approximately eighty disoriented and bewildered women in each locked carriage, with no toilet, simply a bucket. Two days later another massively overcrowded transport of just under a thousand women arrived from the Slovak capital of Bratislava. From then on, the number of transports carrying women prisoners grew rapidly.

Initially, only young healthy women, up to the age of forty-five, were sent on the early female convoys to Auschwitz because they were intended to work, with no additional selection on arrival for extermination of weak or elderly prisoners. One of the Jewish women on the second Slovakian transport was Helen 'Zippi' Spitzer, almost twenty-four, a courageous and canny survivor who was to create various roles for herself within the camp which ensured she came into contact with the camp hierarchy and later with the women's orchestra set up in Birkenau. Zippi, as she liked

---

* Originally thought to be 999 but two names on the list were duplicated.

to be called,* recalled in a cool, detached way fifty-eight years later, in 2000, her humiliating, brutal ordeal that bitterly cold day in late March 1942 as she entered Auschwitz. The journey itself had been 'not so nice', she said, but 'disembarking went very rough ... unexplainable rough'.[2]

Her group arrived at an open field on the outskirts of the town of Oświęcim where SS guards lined up the exhausted, hungry women and marched them, in rows of five, to the gate of the main camp. They walked through the *Arbeit Macht Frei* arch but Zippi recognised 'Halt' signs and several other warning signs as well as a small white sign with the single word in black *Konzentrationslager* so that 'the moment I entered that gate, I knew where I am'.[3]

The women were forced to strip, shower in ice-cold water, and then have all their hair, including pubic hair, shaved – partly for reasons of hygiene to stop the spread of lice but the procedure, sometimes undertaken by male orderlies, was also degrading. They were disinfected and registered before being roughly tattooed with a number. Auschwitz was the only Nazi camp where prisoners were given these permanent markers on their forearm, a further part of the dehumanising process which reduced all inmates to a mere number.

In her first interview immediately after the war in 1946 Zippi described in emotional terms how she felt as if she and the other women were 'being inspected like cattle. It was going on like a cattle show. They turned us here and there/right and left/ ... [we were] nude ... there was the SS physician Dr Franz Bodmann, that time the Lager physician ... who looked us over.'[4]

---

* The name, derived from her Hebrew name Zipporah, was a clever deception as she was not listed anywhere in the camp under that name. This, she believed, would help her if any of her messages were intercepted by the SS.

When asked if the tattoo hurt, she replied: 'We did not feel pain anymore, because... the removal of hair from the head of a woman... the whole transformation which occurred at that time has hurt much more, so that we did not feel anything anymore. Because we were like... like transformed into stone?'[5]

Zippi was prisoner number 2286, a low figure which set her apart as one of the camp elite, or *prominenten*, the longer she survived. In her various interviews over the years she has never described, as other young Slovak women did, having a hand shoved up her vagina to see if she had brought with her hidden jewels. Those who suffered this violence, many of them virginal teenagers – the initial groups of Slovak women were all unmarried – were so traumatised by the experience that it was forever difficult to put it into words. Several recalled the snow on the ground being spattered with blood, possibly as a result of this treatment or from having no sanitary pads to contain menstrual flows.[6] Zippi was always more comfortable talking about the work that she did in the camp rather than her feelings.

The women were eventually handed the uniforms of newly murdered male Russian POWs, however ill-fitting, blood-encrusted and lice-ridden. No underwear was provided, and only a few women managed to get a pair of shoes which fitted. Shoes were a critical matter of survival for all prisoners who had to walk on muddy, frozen and stony roads. Those with no shoes had to walk barefoot and suffered from cuts which became infected, or chilblains, increasing their risk of selection for gassing. As a result, shoes were a valuable currency, almost more valuable than bread, and were often stolen.

It is not clear how Zippi managed to hang on to the sturdy leather hiking boots with metal clasps in which she arrived, but it is a strong indication of her determination to survive. When asked about this years later she explained: 'because every times

[sic] they were – somebody wanted to take my shoes away, especially with the German women, stopped me constantly, and they wanted to take my shoes off, because they looked so good and heavy. But they were always too small, I had a small foot... and not one of the German women was lucky enough. So I kept those shoes.'[7]

Zippi was assigned to a hard labour, wrecking kommando – a demolition squad where her crew had to demolish buildings to clear space for the new and bigger camp. One day within the first few weeks she suffered a painful back injury when a chimney collapsed on her. Desperate to find a less dangerous assignment, she took the risk of approaching the head prisoner of the women's camp, a German Communist called Eva Wiegel, and asked for a transfer. Speaking good German, Zippi explained to Wiegel that she was professionally qualified as a graphic artist, a rare accomplishment for a woman. A few days later, Zippi was given alternative work indoors.

Zippi's story of survival over three years in Auschwitz makes her an invaluable witness to camp life, highlighting many of the absurdities of the entire system. She often spoke of 'luck' in later interviews. Bizarrely, one aspect of that luck was arriving early enough in the setting up of the camp to witness the chaos and show the female guards she was able to impose some order. She had grown up in a prosperous middle-class Jewish family in Bratislava, and spoke German, Slovak and Hungarian fluently with a smattering of French. Her linguistic fluency helped her in the camp to pick up useful phrases in other languages such as Polish, Yiddish or Russian as well as the essential camp jargon, *Lagersprache*, a kind of German slang that soon predominated.

Music was also part of her basic education. She played the piano and mandolin, which would become an additional route to survival when the women's orchestra was established. Her personality and natural leadership also no doubt helped, but it was her pioneering professional career as a female graphic artist, involving a four-year course with some training in management and bookkeeping, that initially helped her get transferred from the outdoors work kommando.

The Nazis soon ran out of Russian POW uniforms and, with Wiegel's assistance, Zippi was charged with mixing paint from raw materials and painting two vermilion red stripes on the back of prisoners' clothes. 'I got red powder paint and a pot of varnish and brush shoved into my hand. I was ordered to mix the paint. And later prisoners were led before me, and I got the order that a vertical stripe be affixed... They did not want a male painter to come to the women's camp and I was the only woman who had familiarity with paint.'[8]

These garments were sometimes dresses confiscated from the latest convoys rather than the familiar blue-and-grey striped material which was often in short supply. The thick, indelible red stripes meant prisoners could go out to work and still be easily identified regardless of whether they had a uniform.*

Zippi's increasing involvement in the registration process brought her into close contact with the SS-controlled prisoner hierarchy, the Nazi administration and the female guards, who were

---

* Zippi was soon working on other forms of prisoner registration such as printing black numbers which matched the individual's numerical tattoo on small white strips of cloth that the inmate had to sew on herself. Zippi also handed out the various coloured triangles (*winkel*) which would denote that the prisoner was a Jehovah's Witness (purple), a 'criminal' (green), a political prisoner (red) or some other category. Jews were identifiable by a two-coloured, six-pointed star, a yellow *winkel* overlaid by another – both yellow unless the prisoner also fell into another category. A Jewish political prisoner, for example, would be identified with a yellow triangle beneath a red triangle.

sometimes referred to as 'SS women' (incorrectly, as the SS was an all-male organisation). The entire system was overseen by men and even Nazi women in high-ranking positions in the camp were dependent on men for their secondary authority. Zippi was soon seen as an essential cog in the Nazi process of maintaining control by reducing every prisoner to a number.

In August 1942, five months after her arrival, the women prisoners were moved to the still unfinished Birkenau camp. The situation was initially even more chaotic than in the male section of Birkenau, partly because unlike the male Kapos – prisoner functionaries used by the Nazis as a stand-in for the guards to supervise forced labour – who usually had some rudimentary military training, none of the female Kapos had any experience of keeping order. 'They were just ordinary house girls, not professionals. Food had to be distributed and they didn't know how to do that,' Zippi recalled in 2000, although food distribution was usually undertaken not by Kapos but by the more lowly *Blockälteste*.[9]

The primitive, half-finished barracks of Birkenau section B1a could not cope with the constant and ever larger mass transports of women which now began to arrive at Auschwitz. The increasingly overcrowded buildings had no running water or sewage disposal, while the floors were muddy clay. Even a crude attempt at personal hygiene was impossible, with murky water, pit latrines and no toilet paper or soap.

Almost immediately, outbreaks of lice and typhus were reported. Many women died from malnutrition, starvation, physical labour beyond their capacity and the appalling sanitary conditions where mice, rats, worms and lice thrived. The situation rapidly deteriorated out of control, since the mattresses for the women who were transferred to Birkenau were already infested and everyone was suffering with low immunity.[10]

Typhus was spread through the lice that swarmed over prisoners' bodies, clothes and hair. Many prisoners have spoken graphically of how they tried to pick out clumps of the creatures with their hands only to see them return to other parts of the body. In August 1942, in the middle of a typhus outbreak, there was a mass selection when the Nazis rounded up hundreds of prisoners from within the barracks to be gassed to death. But the disease continued to spread and by the autumn, up to 200 women were dying every day, most of them from typhus.

In the autumn of 1942 Zippi herself fell seriously ill with typhus. 'There was one moment when I thought that I will not survive. They were taking people; whole barracks were loaded onto trucks and off to the crematoria. On one occasion I was very sick and had to be hospitalised and the whole barracks was to be gassed. I was selected out as the only person because of my activities and the camp management, they wanted me to live,' Zippi believed. 'I was the one saved out of 10,000 due to my skill . . . I survived; they were miracles those moments.'[11]

According to Zippi, her 'career' in the camp progressed because she spoke good German and used this to develop many contacts. When she was ill that autumn, the fact that she had previously befriended the secretary of the then office overseer, *Rapportführerin* (senior guard) Margot Dreschel (often referred to as Drexler by other prisoners), was enough to make 'the whole hospital hierarchy determined to get me out. The SS wanted me to work.'[12]

Shortly after her recovery she was given increased administrative responsibility for the whole women's camp. 'Somehow by sheer luck,' she insisted later.[13] One of her Slovakian friends was an accountant who had been tasked with establishing a roll-call system, because checking numbers was so crucial for the camp administration. Forcing the prisoners to stand for hours in the pre-dawn cold and wet outside their barracks was extremely difficult because they could not or would not keep still. Some fainted, some moved to other rows and on occasions, the odd prisoner simply dropped dead.

Zippi said she helped to design a system, with forms and a pre-roll call, that made the process more efficient. 'By cutting down the roll call time from four hours to forty minutes you saved lives. People moved indoors rather than stand outside in the cold or rainy weather.'[14] She was proud of this achievement, but arguably exaggerated its beneficial impact, given that almost all the female prisoners who survived Auschwitz and recalled their suffering remembered the horror of enduring interminable roll calls in freezing weather.

Zippi was given a further secretarial job in an office working for the *Haflingsschreibstube*, or prisoner administration, in Birkenau. Her accommodation improved considerably, as she now slept and ate in a small room located directly behind the office. She also managed to acquire soap, towels, toothbrush and toothpaste, unheard of luxuries for ordinary prisoners, because she was expected to look neat and tidy for any interaction with German officialdom.

Her job, along with around thirty other women of various nationalities, was to keep updating the filing system that recorded the personal data of all newcomers who entered the camp and were not sent to be gassed. These 'fortunates' were asked about their previous occupations, information which enabled Zippi and her fellow filing clerks to know which prisoners were skilled in a particular area. Their filing system was crucial when the *Arbeitsdienst* (the Work Registry) lodged a request for a particular type of labour with the *Arbeitseinsatz* (Labour Deployment Department), either for camp assignments or to be dispatched as slave labour for private German companies. 'If they needed tailors or dressmakers, we knew exactly how to provide fifty tailors or 500 road workers,' Zippi explained in a post-war interview in 2000.[15] Occasionally musicians were also noted but in late 1942 there was no useful occupation for them. If given sufficient warning, they would announce themselves with what they thought might be a useful trade such as couturier.

At first, Zippi worked on the administrative organisation of the women's camp with Katya Singer, a fellow Slovak she had befriended on the journey to Auschwitz, and who had also managed to get herself assigned to indoor office duties. 'Katya was in the same cattle car, screaming and crying, on the journey to Auschwitz and I asked her to stop. We all could have cried, and it was no help.'[16]

Katya identified as a Christian although her parents were assimilated Jews. As such, she could not understand how she had been included in the round-up since she had ignored the initial call-up for all young Jewish girls in Bratislava to report to a transit camp. In September 1942, Katya was assigned the position of *Rapportschreiberin*,[17] a high-level camp functionary sometimes translated as a chief operating officer, which entitled her to a maid, a separate small room and wardrobe. This was superior accommodation to Zippi's and exposed Katya to the charge of collaboration then and later because she was working so directly for the Nazi hierarchy.[18]

Working in these administrative jobs was a grey area, which Zippi, while working closely with Katya, managed to navigate far more successfully. Both women were known for saving lives if they could by deploying women to a 'safer' work kommando or by fiddling with the numbers. But the fact that Katya also had a Nazi lover in the camp, a married non-commissioned officer called Gerhard Palitzsch, who was notorious for boasting about carrying out hundreds of killings at Auschwitz's death wall, eventually led to her downfall in 1944. Zippi had always disapproved of the affair. When it was revealed and Katya denounced, Palitzsch was punished for 'Race Defilement' (*Rassenschande*) and sent to fight at the front where he died aged thirty-one.* Katya was sent for extermination to another camp, Stutthof, in 1944, which she survived apparently because the gassing machinery was temporarily malfunctioning.

In a 1991 interview Katya insisted that in 1942 'everything was at a beginning. The prisoners were creating the women's camp and anybody who wanted the job could have become *Rapportschreiberin*.'[19] She described the complicated arrangements and lack of a proper system that confronted them on arrival and maintained that by exploiting the pandemonium she and Zippi were able to create the basic administrative organisation of the women's camp. According to Katya, their work pleased their Nazi superiors and also 'saved many women's lives':[20]

A report was given to the Administrative Office every day by all prisoner administrators or *blokovas* [the Polish word for women prisoners in charge of the blocks for food distribution, roll calls and selections]. The SS office then handed these reports to us from the hospital compound and from all the detached prisoners [those working outside the camp]. We then made lists of how many women were at each site.

I handed Zippi all the records: how many women in the Revier (Infirmary), at the *Stabsgebäude* (Main Office), how many gassed. The numbers had to be precise because if there

---

* Palitzsch was sentenced to several years in prison but was reprieved and instead dismissed from the SS in June 1944 and sent to a penal unit. The exact circumstances of his death are unclear; he is said to have fallen in action on 7 December 1944.

were six thousand women in the camp the numbers of the *Vorappell* (the pre-roll-call) had to be the same. Then the SS *Blockführer* just checked the numbers from the *Vorappell* and those had to coincide with the numbers from the morning *Zahlappell* [the actual roll call].

No numbers were repeated in Auschwitz. The numbers were registered to be running consecutively in the big camp book. When a prisoner died, the number and name were crossed out and we made individual columns for everything in a new book: columns for the sick, the dead, the individual blocks, the number of people in each block who were well, sick, on detachment, *Stabsgebaüde*, agriculture, factories.

With that kind of organisation in the *Lagerbuch* we saved many women's lives. Zippi wrote down numbers that were dead. When there was a selection and they told me the list of numbers I inserted 'dead numbers' instead of live numbers that I wanted to save. If there were five hundred supposed to go to the gas, only a hundred actually went. The rest were dead numbers ... the Nazis wanted only the control list; they did not count the people on the truck. No one ever found out how we had done this.[21]

Every night, either Zippi or Katya had to deposit the information about the women's camp that they had compiled during the day with one of the senior female guards who they said never questioned their figures. Katya and Zippi both risked their own lives by deceptively juggling the numbers, as well as by arranging for some prisoners to have protected inside work rather than be sent on the dangerous outside kommandos, or work units. Katya recalled that 'Zippi kept track of the numbering, together with the tattooing of numbers. If someone visited from the very high ups in the SS, she would show them the model she had made of the camp and her pages and pages of statistics, and they would never come into the camp itself.'[22]

Katya could not explain how the pair were able to get away with this falsification: 'That is how the Germans were,' she simply stated. 'If they got an order they had to follow it. There was the order to count in the morning and in the evening.' She and Zippi took advantage of the system in the best way they could but as Zippi added, 'How can you make sense of the system? You can't.'[23]

By the end of 1942, the two Slovak women now belonged to the camp elite and enjoyed the rare privilege of being able to move relatively freely around the camp. Yet, in contrast to Katya with her Nazi lover, Zippi instinctively grasped that the basic rule of survival was not to be conspicuous. Remarkably she was even allowed to smoke and could go outside the camp for small excursions, but she was extremely careful not to be seen to abuse these privileges. When offered a wristwatch, a prized object signifying a high position in the camp hierarchy which was 'almost a badge of merit',[24] she declined. Nor did she ever wear an identifying armband as did most Kapos and certain kommando leaders to signify a prisoner who worked in the camp administration.

Her work was clearly valuable to the female guards, who struggled to maintain order and could do so only by resorting to brutality; to that extent, Zippi was protected. Her balancing act was to become even more precarious in the months that followed as the female guard hierarchy changed radically in the wake of ever-increasing instability triggered by the sharp, relentless increase in the female prisoner population.

Looking back on this extremely dangerous period for her own survival, Zippi had only scorn for her former friend Katya who, by having an affair, ignored the boundaries. 'She was very stupid. He was a mass murderer. After that our relationship cooled,' Zippi recalled in 2000.[25]

*

In March 1942, when Zippi arrived, the first female guard was also assigned to the female section of the concentration camp at Auschwitz, or FKZ the *Frauenkonzentrationslager* as it was known, to supervise the influx of women prisoners. Johanna Langefeld was a forty-two-year-old former teacher and single mother who had previously worked at the Lichtenburg and Ravensbrück concentration camps for women. Langefeld was transferred to Auschwitz specifically to oversee the projected move of the new female arrivals from Auschwitz I to Birkenau or Auschwitz II. Langefeld had a longstanding working relationship with Heinrich Himmler, who regarded her as reliable and tough, but Auschwitz-Birkenau, while a welcome promotion, proved to be beyond her abilities.

Rudolf Höss, overall commandant of the camp, was disdainful of the female guards, reflecting patriarchal Nazi ideology. He commented later in his 1947 memoirs:

> Frau Langefeld was in no way capable of coping with the situation, yet she refused to accept any instructions given her by the protective custody commander. Hardly a day passed without discrepancies in the prisoner totals. The supervisors ran hither and thither in all this confusion like a lot of flustered hens . . .[26]

After just four months in charge of the women's camp at Auschwitz, it was clear to Höss that Langefeld was struggling to keep control. Höss believed she had been 'spoiled' by better conditions at Ravensbrück. Acting on his own initiative, that summer he tried to put the women's camp under the overall jurisdiction of the male protective custody commander.

When Heinrich Himmler came to inspect Auschwitz on 18 July

1942, Langefeld tried to get him to annul Höss's directive. Since Himmler believed that a women's camp should be commanded by a woman, probably in the hope that this would prevent mixing of the sexes and help maintain order, he decided that for now Langefeld should stay in charge, adding that in the future no SS man should enter the female camp.

It seemed as if Höss had lost the power struggle. However, in late July 1942 Langefeld injured her meniscus, which required a cartilage operation in the Hohenlychen SS Sanatorium near Ravensbrück. During her absence, a new, younger and tougher head female guard was appointed to Auschwitz on 7 October 1942.

Maria Mandl, born in 1912, had already acquired a reputation for remorseless brutality as a guard at Ravensbrück, where the female prisoners nicknamed her 'The Beast'. According to the authoritative Danuta Czech's *Auschwitz Chronicle*, Langefeld's demotion after only six months in charge followed a massacre by their German captors (largely criminals and prostitutes and including some guards) of ninety French Jewish women prisoners on 5 October 1942 at the sub-camp of Budy. Although the sub-camp was not Langefeld's direct responsibility, the savage killings – with prison guards using clubs, hatchets and rifle butts and even throwing some of their victims from the windows in the loft of the building – stoked the deep-seated Nazi fear that order might totally break down in such overcrowded conditions. Langefeld's seemingly weak, irresolute command made such a collapse of authority seem more likely since she was seen by Höss and other senior SS officers at Auschwitz as insufficiently brutal.*

---

* This view was confirmed by Margarete Buber Neumann, who had been Langefeld's prisoner assistant in Ravensbrück, and who believed that Langefeld was dismissed from Auschwitz for excessive sympathy with Polish prisoners.

And it was well known on the prisoner grapevine that Langefeld, while no lover of Jews, had a more humane attitude towards prisoners than Mandl.

Maria Mandl had grown up in the Austrian village of Münzkirchen, the youngest child of a shoemaker and a house-wife. Maria, like most of the local children, left school at fourteen but the Mandl family had just enough money for her to attend a Catholic boarding school for an additional three years. It was here that she learned sewing, secretarial skills, gym, theatre and music. 'She almost certainly learned to play the piano there,'[27] according to her biographer, Susan Eischeid, who believes this is where her love of music began. She left Münzkirchen in her late teens to go to Switzerland, where her married sister lived, and found a job as a cook-housekeeper. Two years later she returned home to look after her sick mother. In the depths of the depres-sion, the best job she could find in Münzkirchen was as a maid in a local inn.

In 1937, aged twenty-five, she was hired by the local post office as postmistress and began a serious romance with a young man from Münzkirchen. Little seems to be known about what went wrong but the relationship ended around the same time that the German army marched into Austria in March 1938 and annexed the country. Mandl was dismissed from her job, probably because the post office played such a vital role in communication that membership of the Nazi party was required, and she was not yet a member. She started looking for her first job as a guard with the Nazi regime's burgeoning concentration camps which offered the chance for better pay and would enable her to break free from living with her parents again.

In 1938 she was hired to work at the Lichtenburg concentration camp in the eastern German province of Saxony, which had just been converted into a women-only prison. Mandl's recruitment was entirely voluntary, and she may even have believed the Nazi propaganda that such camps were places for re-educating dangerous elements in society. At her post-war trial in 1947, Mandl merely said she went to Lichtenburg because the pay was good and she could earn more than if she had enrolled as a nurse, her second career choice.

The Lichtenburg camp was housed in a castle, and it was here that Mandl first manifested the extreme brutality that marked her apart from other female guards. One former prisoner at Lichtenburg, Lina Haag, wrote about how Mandl 'beats us with a dog whip until she can go on no longer'.[28]

In 1939, when Lichtenburg was closed, Mandl was transferred to Ravensbrück, then a new camp 50 miles north of Berlin for women only. Once more, she quickly gained a reputation among the prisoners for her often random acts of violence. Curly hair was one 'offence' which seemed guaranteed to ignite her anger during roll calls. At Ravensbrück she would stride slowly along the rows of prisoners, searching for curls. If she spotted a prisoner with even a wisp of a curl escaping her headscarf, she would regularly single out the miscreant for a savage beating and flogging, ordering her head to be shaved before this was the general rule for all prisoners. The harder she flogged the higher she rose in the ranks. At Ravensbrück Mandl formally became a Nazi party member and in April 1940 she was appointed *Oberaufseherin*, or head overseer, second in command to Langefeld.

In her pre-trial deposition Mandl claimed that she did not lobby to be transferred to Auschwitz-Birkenau, having heard rumours about the appalling living conditions there. She insisted that initially she refused to go to Auschwitz. However, she said that a high-ranking SS officer, Oswald Pohl, advised her that she would be punished if she did not accept.

By her own graphic account, Mandl was aghast when she first

saw Birkenau in October 1942. Sick women were everywhere in the camp, some begging to be allowed to die. Bodies from the recent killings at Budy were still lying on the ramp as what little flesh remained rotted away. Above all, there was the overpowering stench of death mingled with the odour of unwashed bodies, excrement and urine.

Antonina Kozubek, a Polish prisoner who had transferred from Ravensbrück with Mandl, similarly recalled in 1946:

> The conditions were unbearable and I had to shake my head that this was possible, especially since I was used to having a clean camp in Ravensbrück. I did not believe my eyes – terrible conditions! About 7,000 women were cooped up in it, in such a state of exhaustion and apathy that they didn't care about life and showed it, as a result the entire camp was one huge manure pit.
>
> The terrain didn't have sewage and one was walking in boggy ground up to the knees – the soil was clay and one sank into the ground and could barely free oneself, there were no floors in the blocks, so they were wet and muddy and one could sense a catastrophic lack of water. All along the blocks and outside, corpses were lying around.[29]

The non-Jewish Austrian prison doctor Ella Lingens-Reiner, arrested in October 1942 as a result of offering refuge to Jews after the Anschluss, wrote vividly of the 'walking skeletons' she saw in Birkenau when she arrived there four months later 'wrapped in dirty, ragged striped prisoners' clothes'. Reiner, allowed to work as a doctor in the camp, described ditches by the camp street, full of dirt, bowls and food remains, which were also used as a toilet. She also remembered the desperate fight for a tiny amount of water to drink or wash.[30]

The women arrived with pails, mugs and bottles, shouting and jostling each other to get their turn at the water. The result was that none of it reached the latrine ditches, and the sewage system was blocked. From time to time one of the prefects would come and strike at the women with a stick to drive them off. The whole thing was incredibly brutal, yet it was impossible to condemn either the women who were kicking at one another or the 'guardians' of the latrine. It is dreadful to be without water; it is impossible to let people take away all the water while faeces are piling up in the ditches.[31]

At the time of Mandl's transfer to Birkenau, nothing was ready for the guards. Many of them had to live in the upstairs of the *Stabsgebaüde*, a main staff building in Auschwitz I, while work was completed on the large dormitory-style building just outside the perimeter of the new women's camp approximately 3 km away. For some of the younger guards, this was their first time away from home and the support from those who were older created a familial bond between them. Mandl and a few other higher-ranking guards enjoyed their own rooms and more space in separate quarters. But a few months after her arrival at Auschwitz, Mandl procured a private villa nearby where she lived in considerable comfort and was able to receive visits from friends and family. During her trial, witnesses spoke of orgies in Mandl's richly furnished villa, 'orgies which became especially wild after "good" executions, when Mandl would beat up and whip the women'.[32] A good execution here meaning one that was particularly gruesome or bloody in advance of the actual death, since violence, torture and sexual promiscuity appeared to fuel each other.

It was drilled into Mandl and her fellow guards that the only way to instil obedience in the women's camp at Birkenau was through fear and violence. At the same time, as in all Nazi concentration camps, the guards recognised that to keep order it was necessary to build loyalty among the Kapos, the prisoner functionaries who were an essential tool in controlling the ever-growing number of inmates. The relationship between Kapo and *Aufseherin* (the offical term for female guards in Auschwitz) was one of the murkiest aspects of camp life, often depending on an exchange of gifts, mostly stolen from incoming prisoners, or an exchange of privileges, such as being spared outdoor work, in return for keeping order. Occasionally the Kapos were ordered to do the stealing so that if caught the guards would not be punished.[33]

The Auschwitz survivor Primo Levi maintained in *The Drowned and the Saved*, a series of reflections on the extermination camps, that the German insistence on prisoners guarding their own was one of the Nazi's greatest crimes. The Kapos and other prisoner functionaries had no agency of their own, yet it is also true that the system might well have collapsed without prisoners forcing obedience on their fellow inmates in return for favours and privileges.

After the war, some former Kapos at Auschwitz tried to portray individual guards as being less harsh than others. For example, Katya Singer maintained that Margot Dreschel, with whom she forged a good relationship, was honest and had tried to save some Slovakian Jews while most other inmates considered the thin, buck-toothed Dreschel repellent and sadistic as she walked around the camp with her bloodhound, making selections for those to be gassed. In contrast, Katya recalled Mandl as 'beautiful but evil... only interested that everything should run smoothly in the camp and did very little work', which helps explain her dependence on Zippi Spitzer.[34]

When Mandl arrived at Birkenau in October 1942, after Zippi's recovery from typhus, she found that the two Slovak women were, according to Zippi, 'the leading administrative organisation for the whole of the women's camp'.[35] Zippi said that instead of resenting this state of affairs, Mandl welcomed it.

'Mandl respected me from the first,' Zippi insisted. 'She made my life tolerable. Why, I don't know. Perhaps it was because Mandl's boyfriend at the time was in charge of the camp building office and he established my drawing office with wonderful instruments?'[36]

On one occasion Mandl wanted to give a present to SS officer Josef Kramer, a book called *The River Pirates*, and, aware of Zippi's artistic skills, asked her to inscribe the dedication with beautiful calligraphy. Zippi believes the fact that Mandl had chosen a book was significant. She sought to impress with her choice.

'I told her it was a coincidence, but the date [10 November] was my birthday too. So she sent me to the package room and told me to choose any package I wanted, the biggest they had.'

'With her I had good luck. Look it's very hard to understand what really went on in their minds. But with her I had good luck.'[37]

The relationship between Mandl and Spitzer was not unique. In general, the German guards preferred to pick their helpers from among Slovak-Jewish rather than Polish-Jewish women since the former spoke better German while the latter spoke Yiddish. And Dreschel had her favourites too among Jewish prisoners. Even though she was an avid anti-Semite she used mostly Jewish girls in her team of 'runners'. Ella Lingens-Reiner told the story of one of these girls, just recovering from typhus, who was suddenly transferred to her purely Aryan hut on Dreschel's express orders. The next day there was a selection from the very same hut from which the Jewish girl had come. 'In other words, the wardress had hidden the girl from her own selection clearly because she lacked the courage to protect her in the presence of other SS officers.

She wanted to keep her as a runner because she was useful but we had to bear the risk.'[38]

As long as Zippi worked long hours to create apparent order, she found that Mandl largely left her alone. In Zippi's recollection, all that mattered to Mandl was that she should appear to be in control and take the credit.

One of the biggest benefits for all female guards was that they had much more freedom in their time off than they could ever have expected in their home communities at a time of great social conservatism generally restricting women's lives. This liberty was particularly prized by Mandl, who was often seen riding a bicycle around the camp and was once reprimanded for riding a motor-cycle without a licence. In addition, she kept a handsome horse to ride for recreation and often cantered between the barracks, usually at conspicuous times, in a display of power.

Mostly, though, it was her freedom to indulge in relationships with SS men that the prisoners noticed. Her lover for much of her time at Birkenau was the highly educated SS officer Josef Janisch, three years older than Mandl, whose liaison with her gave her added prestige and social standing as well as more authority.

Janisch was a fellow Austrian and a qualified engineer who was a member of the management staff of the SS Central Construction Office in Auschwitz-Birkenau which was involved in establishing the gas chambers and crematoria. On workdays, Mandl and Janisch were often seen riding together outside the gates before the morning roll call or galloping up and down the camp road or back through the paths which led to various killing installations and incineration sites.

On her days off, Mandl often rode around the camp, out of uniform, wearing a white blouse pinned with a red rose from the SS gardens. The prisoners who remembered her riding past described a competent horsewoman with a powerful physical bearing. 'She was very, very straight and self-assured! She would always be marching, it was not just a leisurely walk. Very self-assured. Very proud! She looked always very groomed! She always carried a small whip,' said the Polish political resister Zofia, or Zosia as she was known, Cykowiak.[39]

Despite her commanding presence, especially on her horse, Mandl was mired in various power struggles from the moment she was sent to Auschwitz. Some of these clashes involved fellow female guards – notably Margot Dreschel – but most derived from Rudolf Höss's unshakeable belief that women could not maintain discipline in the camp. After his run-in with Langefeld, Höss introduced several positions of authority in the women's camp, all held by men. From different directions, the ever-watchful Mandl was convinced that the new camp director, report officer and director of employment were all trying to undermine her.

In the spring of 1943, Mandl was not only head supervisor but unofficially also camp commander in the women's camp. She was right to see as her main rival for this post Franz Hössler, a small man with a weak chin, married with three children, who had performed a number of roles since he arrived at Auschwitz in June 1940 and steadily worked his way up. Initially he managed the camp kitchens, but, having risen in the hierarchy, was now busy recruiting non-Jewish female prisoners, with the prospect of better food and care, for a newly opened camp brothel at the Auschwitz I main camp. His zeal for completing this achievement was noted by Höss.

However, as her sense of self-importance grew, Mandl began to refuse to be dominated by any male figure whose authority threatened her own. Her biographer argues that Mandl's resentment of men was possibly due to a feeling that they had let her down in the past, even perhaps the Münzkirchen boy whom she had thought she would marry. Regardless of whether this theory is correct, Mandl's use of extreme brutality to exercise her authority independently of the male SS officers who were imposed on her at Birkenau continued the grim pattern of behaviour she had set at Ravensbrück.

Ella Lingens-Reiner, the non-Jewish prisoner doctor, believed that in general 'the SS women were hitting out not so much from sadism as because they were afraid of not being able to master the situation. They seemed to lash out from a feeling that, though armed, they were in a hopeless minority among innumerable prisoners. Perhaps this was the reason why female S.S. were more addicted to beating than their male colleagues.'[40]

Yet, even surrounded by violent female guards, Mandl stood apart. She kept a short, pliable leather whip tucked in her boots which she used on women prisoners at Birkenau until their blood ran. At the same time, Mandl made some attempt to improve the conditions that confronted her on arrival, if only out of self-interest to safeguard her own position. Antonina Kozubek, one of the Polish inmates, confirmed that Mandl's first actions included connecting the electricity in the barracks so there would be light, placing stoves in some of the barracks for heat, and having a toilet area made from wooden boards installed in the latrine block. Mandl maintained at her trial, when she was fighting for her own life, that she 'tried to get clean clothes and underwear for the women, but the camp laundry could not supply anything, so I organized an unused barrack for a laundry facility with basins and soap'.[41]

In her pre-trial deposition, Mandl also described some steps she said she took within the first month of arriving at Auschwitz to improve conditions such as having 'the walls inside and outside washed and on the outside I had them painted . . . For inside I ordered chalk/whitewash. Beds were cleaned and 600 straw mattresses in awful condition were burnt.' But trying to arrange for internal walls to be torn down was apparently beyond her remit and in response she received a letter from Pohl 'asking why I had acted on my own initiative... and received a severe reprimand'.

Furthermore, Mandl said she asked both Höss and Dr Eduard Wirths, the chief SS doctor, for improvements and a nurse for the hospital block. They suggested she write a letter describing the conditions to another doctor in Oranienburg to request help, which was refused twice due to lack of available nursing personnel and she was ordered to staff it from the camp population. One small success which meant a lot to Zippi and Katya was winning permission for the women prisoners in the offices to wear their hair long, so that they looked presentable when meeting male officers and visiting male guests. Another small but important concession for office workers was permission to wear a bra, an impossible luxury for other prisoners who were allowed no underwear at all.

These extremely modest improvements instigated by Mandl did not mitigate her violence against any prisoner who displeased her. Nor did her 'reforms' have any noticeable bearing on the spiralling death rate from disease and starvation in the Birkenau women's camp, with the population falling from about 12,000 to 5,000 inmates between September and December 1942.

Magda Blau, a Slovak kindergarten teacher who had been on the second transport with Zippi, explained: 'if Auschwitz was hell, Birkenau was... the biggest [thing] that Satan [thinks] can exist... Lice were always crawling all over you and under your skin. Your one dress was in rags with no underwear. Wooden clogs were hard to keep on and if you lost one in the mud that was it... Going to the toilet meant everyone on one plank pulling at each other so people fell in the ditches. If a siren went while you were on the plank you all had to run. But if you fell into the ditch you were taken to the crematorium.'[42] This was because you would have drowned in the urine and faeces. In Magda's view the sadism and brutality of life in Birkenau was so appalling that she perfectly understood why some girls 'run to the electrical um . . . We, we had an electrical fence which was with um electricity. So if you touch it, you been dead. But some girls, they said, "I'd rather that. I can't take it anymore. And I can't see any end to it." '43

Staying alive in Auschwitz-Birkenau had become desperately hard and marathon roll calls, supervised by Mandl and other female guards sometimes lasting many hours, often turned into a form of savage selection. On Saturday, 6 February 1943, a bitterly cold day, Mandl initiated a roll call of the Birkenau women's camp which started at 3 a.m. and was not over until 5 p.m. The women, dressed only in flimsy rags, stood to attention as best they could the entire day. But more than 2,000 prisoners died as a result. Those who survived never forgot how the weakest among them were so stiff and frozen by the end that they could not move. They were simply pulled aside and gassed.

Needing workers, by the spring of 1943 the SS had abandoned incoming selections of male and female non-Jewish prisoners, while selections were still applied to weak, sick or other Jews throughout the operation of the camp. What did not change was Mandl's terrifyingly unpredictable, sadistic rule. The only constant was her need to demonstrate her power over the women prisoners and her own authority in relation to the male officers with whom she was meant to be working 'alongside'.

According to Zippi, early in 1943 Mandl began to see a way she could gain further influence for herself in the camp while satisfying her pleasure in music. She decided that the time had come for the women, like the male prisoners, to have their own orchestra.

Making good music for the SS

For Mandl the orchestra was a personal prestige project which she believed would give her cultural gravitas as well as increased authority in front of male Nazi leaders. To this end, she used every means at her disposal to make the orchestra function well, even if that meant working alongside a Jewish prisoner. Zippi's view of why Mandl's reliance on her was accepted by the male hierarchy was straightforward: 'Because if women could do a job in the camp it released men for war,' she commented in a 1983 interview.[1]

Like all Nazis, Mandl was steeped in an ideology which used music as a powerful tool to sway the masses, from huge rallies to smaller marches and parades. From the moment the first camps were established in 1933, guards routinely ordered detainees to sing while marching or even during punishment exercises. Forcing prisoners to sing unfamiliar songs or popular SS tunes was a means of further humiliating them. If they sang too loudly or too softly, they might be beaten. In some camps music from radio broadcasts or record players was blasted over specially installed loudspeakers, while in others marching music was played especially loudly during executions to drown out the screams from the condemned prisoners. At Buchenwald, opened in 1937, loudspeakers broadcast nightly concerts from German radio to deprive prisoners of sleep.

The development of musical ensembles in the camps was ultimately a decision of the commandant. He decided whether these orchestras and bands should include only imprisoned professional musicians or also admit amateur players, and whether only non-Jews should be allowed to perform.

The first of the official orchestras were set up in the camps of Duerrgoy, Oranienburg and Sonnenburg as soon as Hitler came to power in 1933. When a new generation of larger concentration camps was established in 1936, they all had their own orchestras, as did the larger sub-camps and death camps. Auschwitz I had several ensembles, including a brass band with around 120 members and a symphony orchestra with around eighty male musicians, of whom about half had been professional players. At the end of 1942, the already high standard of this large, entirely non-Jewish orchestra, which played four times a day, was boosted

The men's orchestra playing in Auschwitz 1 in 1941, just by the Arbeit Macht Frei *gate as the prisoners marched to work*

when an entire professional radio orchestra was arrested and sent to Auschwitz.

This orchestra was riven with feuds and friction. It was led by a Polish conductor called Franciszek Nierychło, known by his German equivalent Franz, a political prisoner who in the 1930s had lived in Krakow, where he worked at the post office and directed the post office orchestra. Arrested in 1940, he was eventually released in May 1944. Nierychło was unpopular, according to historian Dr Jacek Lachendro in his study of all the camp orchestras at Auschwitz: 'Most of the former prisoners, especially those employed in the kitchen, assessed him negatively. They emphasised above all his violent behaviour to fellow prisoners (beatings, throwing insults) as well as servility towards the SS men.' However, some orchestra members recognised that it was only their musical performances under Nierychło which kept them alive. They refrained from criticising Nierychło and justified his brutality as the result of his 'inability to do otherwise in the presence of the SS men'.[2]

These musicians were not excused other work duties, while being required to play marches as their fellow prisoners went out to work and back in columns of five abreast, with Nazi guards jeering and making ominous shouts all the while of '*Zu Funfe*' (In Fives). The orchestra also had to provide occasional entertainment for SS men, more or less on demand. Mostly these special requests occurred at Sunday concerts attended by prisoners who stood at a distance to listen behind SS officers who relaxed on chairs and applauded pieces that pleased them. Sunday performances included salon music, camp anthems, popular songs from films and operetta medleys.

One Polish prisoner, Wojciech Kawecki, recalled in his memoir listening to 'sounds from a Verdi opera, a Wagner march, an Offenbach melody and a Schubert serenade. The orchestra plays them beautifully.'³ Sometimes new compositions and original arrangements were created, such as Mieczyslaw Krzynski and Henryk Krol's '*Arbeitslagermarsch*' (the Concentration Camp Labour March).

It was such jaunty marching tunes that pointed up most sharply the Nazis' abuse of music as a form of torture, forcing some prisoners to play, others to listen, against a backdrop of death and suffering. Labourers were often kicked by 'Esmen' (SS men) – the colloquial camp term – if they failed to keep time while marching, especially tough on the return to the camp after hours of back-breaking labour with no food. Often, the returning marchers had to carry the corpses of men who had died or been killed during the day and it was impossible to stay in step as they tried to bear this terrible burden. 'We hated those musicians,' one former inmate recalled. 'We couldn't keep our clogs on. It was 20 below zero . . . death was magnified by the orchestra.'⁴

'Suddenly my ears filled with music – they were playing "Violette",' recalled Janina Janiszewska, a Polish female prisoner who remembered watching from the women's camp one day as the men returned:

When I went to the window, I witnessed a sight that made my heart ache. Along the camp street walked, or rather staggered, a procession of living corpses. Around that column scurried prisoners with heavy rods, striking the others for marching too slowly. Every clump of men carried their dead comrades on provisional litters [stretchers] made of poles. It was a woeful sight. The contorted faces and open eyes of the corpses expressed the agony that had preceded their passing . . . Throughout the whole processions, marching music played.⁵

Despite the contempt from other prisoners, there were always more musicians, or would-be musicians, than places for them in camp orchestras. In August 1942, a few months after Birkenau became operational, another male orchestra was established there, boosted by the success of the first. This orchestra, originally formed of sixteen Polish musicians transferred from the Auschwitz I orchestra, was set up on the wishes of Johann Schwarzhuber, a former printer and experienced camp officer given the military rank of SS *Obersturmführer*, approximately equivalent to lieutenant colonel, whose principal job was to oversee selections for the gassing of thousands of people. Like the main Auschwitz I orchestra, the new ensemble was intended to play marches as the men went in and out of work from Birkenau, as well as provide occasional entertainment for the SS.

The Birkenau male orchestra's first conductors were Jan Zaborski and Franz Kopka, both Polish non-Jewish prisoners. Yet following Zaborski's death in November 1942, after some jockeying for position, the role of leader fell to the Polish-Jewish violinist and composer Szymon Laks, a graduate of Warsaw Conservatory, who had been arrested in 1941 while studying in France. Before he took charge, Laks had been mostly employed as the orchestra's music copyist and sometimes had to write out tunes from memory. As its conductor, he remained clear-eyed about how any orchestra in Auschwitz inevitably inflicted pain on those who had to listen and severe difficulties for performers trying to create real music. Laks wrote that when he effectively became conductor at the end of 1942, although Kopka was still officially described as *Kappellmeister*, he was 'appalled at the frightful sour notes from some of the wind instruments... and the only fortunate thing is that they are drowned out by the powerful pounding of the big drum and simultaneous smashing of the brass cymbals'.[6]

49

Laks believed that 'music was simply one of the parts of camp life and that it stupefied the newcomer in the same way as did everything else he encountered in his first days in the camp and to which he gradually became habituated in time – up to the moment of complete acclimatisation and callousness... Music kept up the "spirit" (or rather the body) of only... the musicians, who did not have to go out to hard labour and could eat a little better.'[7]

Finding enough time to rehearse was difficult when the orchestra was set up in August 1942, because the male players were not excused hard labour. They were expected to play, go out to work, return slightly earlier than their colleagues, and then play again. Slowly Laks won some privileges, including more rehearsal time, thus decreasing the hours of physical labour for his musicians. Meanwhile, the relentless arrival of European Jews to Auschwitz dramatically improved the standard of the Birkenau male orchestra. Laks drafted some high-calibre Jewish performers into his rapidly growing ensemble, including a few who specialised in jazz, a forbidden but much-admired genre of music for some Nazis.

Setting up an orchestra also gained additional impetus from the forced seizure of musical instruments, often of a wonderful quality, when unsuspecting Jews who thought they were being 'resettled' were stripped of their most precious family possessions on arrival at Auschwitz. Laks wrote of a 'dazzling sight'; how the orchestra now had at its disposal

all sorts of brass and woodwind instruments everything polished to a bright shine. I distinguished in turn a huge tuba helicon, a trombone, a few trumpets, a brass tenor and alto horns, saxophones, clarinets, two flutes and one piccolo. Leaning against the wall in one of the corners was an impressive double bass with a bow stuck under the strings, in another a bass drum with cymbals and a snare drum with all of the percussion paraphernalia. On a wide, solid shelf specifically designed for this purpose, were a few accordions and violins in cases. One of them somewhat bigger than the others, probably contained a viola. I failed to see a violoncello.[8]

Although Laks added that he had seen a second, somewhat smaller shelf filled with music scores and a pile of blank paper, suitable sheet music for marches and copying paper with musical staves remained in constant short supply, with only just enough music on which to build a limited repertoire.

The success of the men's orchestra, smaller than the big symphony orchestra in Auschwitz I and known as the *Lagerkapelle* (or camp chamber ensemble) under Laks's direction, was likely a major source of inspiration for Maria Mandl's idea to develop a women's orchestra. The Laks orchestra played in the men's sector of Birkenau, known as B1b, and Mandl proposed that the women's orchestra should be housed in a separate but nearby section known as B1a, which would similarly play marches for the female prisoners going out to work.

'I had to organise the orchestra under Mandl,' Zippi Spitzer said in an interview in 2000, adding that 'she noticed I'm an artist and a musician'.[9]

Zippi's comments are an interesting indication of the degree to which she had ingratiated herself with Mandl. She had a sure instinct of how best to survive the Nazi extermination system, deploying every aspect of her varied background and wide-ranging abilities to make herself indispensable to Mandl, who had the power of life and death over all the women prisoners. 'Even she did not understand the system,' Zippi said of Mandl. 'She wanted results. If she asked for 18 or 20 diagrams for Berlin she couldn't care less when I did it, how I did it, as long as it was done.'

Once, when Zippi was ill with stomach cramps, she needed to lie on her bunk bed until they passed, a serious infringement of camp rules. Mandl found her there, but, instead of punishing Zippi, the normally brutal guard simply touched her gently on the forehead in a motherly way and allowed her to remain. 'She knew I did my job and delivered and worked during the night sometimes. So I could have the day free,' Zippi explained in the same interview. 'Some kommandos were protected ... I didn't investigate how I knew it. I just did.'[10]

As soon as Mandl discussed her orchestra project, Zippi realised that her claim to be a 'musician', even though she could only play the mandolin to a basic level, would create further dependence. And in this way the ring of mutual manipulation tightened.

However, establishing an all-female orchestra was bound to be complicated, especially since the decision was not up to Mandl alone. First, she had to clear the project with a senior male SS camp official. In early 1943 she approached Paul Müller, camp director and number two to the commandant, who, fortunately for her, saw there were advantages as it simplified counting the rows of prisoners marching to work and made the imposition of faux military discipline easier. He agreed to help her with the paperwork that was necessary to propose the project to Höss.*

Zippi's role in helping Mandl set up the women's orchestra was in fact rather more ambiguous than she made it sound. Although Zippi explained that she had already been 'very creative' in the camp drawing office and so now grabbed 'the chance to talk about music and artistic things', she nonetheless said that Mandl had initially turned to Katya for help with this venture and it was

---

* Müller remained in post until August 1943 when Franz Hössler was appointed new camp commander in the women's camp (see chapter 3).

Katya who then approached Zippi. 'The camp hierarchy wanted Katya, because she was the top administrative inmate at this time, to go with them to Auschwitz I and make contact with the men there partly to get instruments and partly to discuss procedures . . . But Katya did not understand music so she suggested I go in her place. So that was the beginning.'[11]

Katya did not speak about the origins of the orchestra in her one known interview but spoke highly of Zippi as her assistant. 'Zippi never did anything harmful to anyone. She was always straightforward with me.' In an earlier interview in 1983, Zippi described the origins of the orchestra slightly differently, omitting Katya's initial role.

'[Mandl] was coming to our camp office and started to discuss how to go about it . . . we promised her we'd get professional musicians from the card index and if not we'd make enquiries.' Zippi was clearly keen to be involved: 'I wanted the contact with the men,' she said, claiming later that she thought they would be a useful source of information for any resistance activities. She thus asked for permission to be included in the group that went to the men's camp in Auschwitz I 'to see how they did it'.[12]

Zippi provided a slightly different version in 1982 of how the women's orchestra began. 'We wanted to see how the men functioned,' she said. 'I had a dual role working with and reporting to Katya Singer on the negotiations with the men's orchestra. They agreed to supply us with violins and all the necessary instruments in abundance. They had their own and there were thousands of instruments from all over Europe from deportees . . . even the sheet music they brought with them was used by the camp orchestras . . . after four weeks the orchestra had a barracks. It was Block 12.'[13]

In early 1943, while these preliminary discussions were continuing, a specially convened block leaders' meeting in Birkenau announced the plan to start another orchestra, this time for female-only players. Hanna Szyller (later Palarczyk), deputy block elder in Block 12, attended the meeting and was in no doubt that the idea for an all-female orchestra originated from Mandl. Female block elders, the slightly privileged prisoners whose job was largely to maintain discipline and distribute food, were now instructed to seek out prisoners who could play instruments.

Among the first to volunteer immediately when she heard about the creation of the new orchestra was Zofia Czajkowska, a thirty-six-year-old Polish music teacher, who had arrived on 27 April 1942 from her hometown of Tarnów on the first Polish women's transport to Auschwitz. Zofia had been tortured in prison before deportation, and then spent a year at the camp assigned to the most exhausting physical labour. By early 1943 she was in a weak physical and mental state and saw the orchestra as possibly the only means of escaping from her plight.

Although she lacked formal training as a conductor, and had no repertoire at her disposal, Czajkowska was given the job after being recommended by a former pupil of hers in the camp, Stanislawa Starostka, known as Stenia.[14] She had been a choir leader at the prestigious National School of Commerce in Tarnów and, as a result, had committed to memory several well-known Polish folk tunes which she now relied on. By this tenuous route, the underqualified Zofia thus became the Birkenau women's orchestra's original organiser and leader. She was officially called Kapo as well as conductor and sometimes also Pani Zofia, 'Pani' being a mark of respect in Polish to an older or married woman, since she was considerably older than the rest of the orchestra. Possibly to bolster her position, Zofia allowed a rumour to circulate that she was related to the great composer Tchaikovsky. It is not clear whether Mandl really believed the rumour or whether it suited her to pretend she did. Czajkowska also insisted on having her friend Stefania Baruch, a fellow Pole known as Pani Founia who had come with her on the same 1942 transport and played guitar and mandolin, join her in the early enterprise. Having this much older friend (Founia was born in 1891) to share the burden of setting up the new kommando, finding recruits as well as preparing the repertoire, organising rehearsals and conducting the marches, was crucial.

According to post-war testimony from the political prisoner 'Zosia' Cykowiak,[15] when the call first went out for qualified candidates camp authorities stipulated 'above all Aryan females'. There is no corresponding document to back that up. Although Zosia, who played the violin to high school standard, became one of the orchestra's first members, she was initially deeply reluctant to join the girls' band, as it was called, on the strength of five years of violin playing at school. She was in a fragile emotional state, and initially refused to audition. When the camp recruitment office ordered her to attend, she deliberately played badly, hoping to fail. In response, Czajkowska gave Zosia a hard slap 'for not volunteering for something when any normal person would give their right eye to be here' and told Zosia she was to be in the orchestra regardless of her wishes.[16]

Zosia had good reason to be so emotionally fragile. Her story is emblematic of many of the Christian Poles in Auschwitz who had been imprisoned and often tortured before they arrived in the camp on account of their anti-Nazi activities. Yet that did not make their interaction with Jews any easier. Before the war Zosia had been a girl scout and had joined the underground resistance movement as soon as the Germans invaded in September 1939. She was arrested in Poznań during a round-up after one of her group cracked under interrogation. Some of them were shot after a savage cross examination while Zosia was severely tortured and left with permanently impaired hearing and loss of sight in one eye. She was imprisoned in the western Polish town of Bydgoszcz and transported to Auschwitz in April 1943.

Zosia remained depressed throughout her time in the orchestra. At times she managed to mask her condition but there were days when she fell into a state of numbness and near total apathy, which made her unable to eat anything, and therefore become even weaker. She sometimes found it impossible to play for the Nazis while her fellow prisoners paraded past exhausted and sick. Ultimately the constant witnessing of Nazi brutalities became too much for her to comprehend and she frequently had to be rescued by her fellow Poles, in particular Jadwiga Zatorska, known as Wisia.

Wisia's story was similar to Zosia's. Born in 1916, Wisia was older by seven years. She had been taught by her uncle to play the violin and was a kindergarten teacher in Krakow before the war. In September 1939 she became a courier for the Home Army and was arrested in May 1942 for illegally crossing the border between the Nazi-run General Government of western Poland and the Third Reich. Wisia was tortured during interrogation before being transported to Auschwitz in February 1943, where her three brothers had been sent before her. She was made to work in one of the worst kommandos in Birkenau, forced to dig drainage ditches, dredge out fishponds and demolish houses.

The latter assignment was the most dangerous work of all, but for Wisia, dredging the ponds was even worse. She had to stand with the other girls in waist-deep cold water, chopping reeds and removing mulch, returning to camp every evening in freezing wet and dirty clothes. Wisia believed she was lucky to catch typhus in 1943 and be sent to the Revier, as the sick bay was called, because here she met another Polish political prisoner, Maria Swiderska, who was working as a prisoner clerk in the admissions office.

Swiderska's job was to list all female admissions to the camp in the prisoner register. She immediately sent Wisia to join the newly formed women's band.[17]

In the orchestra, Zosia and Wisia soon became the close friends and supporters of a third Polish woman, Helena Dunicz, the talented violinist in the ill-fated Beethoven quartet who was to the orchestra in October 1943. Helena, born in 1915, recognised Wisia's special qualities, her 'readiness to help, her ease at making decisions and her concerns for those who had broken down under the oppression of concentration camp conditions'.[18]

Danka, or Danuta, Kollak, born in 1918, was another Pole in this first group of players. Danka came from Warsaw where she had worked in the resistance. 'Someone in Warsaw simply betrayed her because of jealousy, a woman who fell in love with her husband,' according to camp gossip. 'She betrayed her.'[19] Danka's role in the orchestra was crucial. Before the war, she had been studying to be a professional pianist but, given that the orchestra had no piano, she agreed to play the drums and cymbals which set the marching tempo for the band. Danka was strong and well-built but carrying heavy brass cymbals around the camp took a toll on her already depleted energy.

Two other Polish women were among the early musicians. Marysia Mos, born in 1916, came from the city of Będzin in southern Poland. She was able to play the guitar but was employed by Czajkowska as a copyist. Czajkowska had discovered Marysia by accident after noticing Marysia's long blonde hair, a rarity in Auschwitz. She asked Marysia how long she had been in the camp. 'I told her I had been there for nine or ten months,' Marysia recalled in her post-war testimony. 'She asked me if I knew and could write musical notation. I answered that I did because in school we all learned how to read music. Czajkowska invited me to the block set apart for the future orchestra, gave me paper and pencil and had me rewrite notes for specific instruments, the violin and mandolin. The first music was the march from Schubert's *Rosamunde*. Then came little songs which Czajkowska had written down from memory and I copied them.'[20]

Irena Lagowska, a violinist who shared a music stand with Wisia, was on the fringes of this first Polish group. Born in 1908, she was always referred to as Pani Irena because she was some twenty years older than most of the other women. She kept largely to herself, rather apart from the younger Polish women who formed such a supportive bond.

While Czajkowska was conductor, the only language spoken was Polish and although the musical standard was weak, the solidarity was strong. Zippi believed Czajkowska was an excellent negotiator, necessary in those early days, who worked hard to get the group underway. She arranged access to instruments and the small amount of music that was available, working with prisoner representatives of the men's orchestra as well as camp officials.

It was here that Zippi's access to paper was especially important because the new orchestra had no music of its own. They had to make copies of any music they borrowed from the men, a laborious process which involved ruling lines on blank pages and inserting staves before a single note could be written. As Laks explained, a key problem for his own orchestra was that they had no music apart from a few continually repeated marches:

Our commander, *Hauptsturmführer* Johann Schwarzhuber who, as it turned out, was a great music lover, constantly insisted on expanding the repertoire both of marches and light music. Time and again another *Esman* – the commander's emissary – brought us the bare melody of a new march or some popular piece that not only had to be harmonised but orchestrated for a larger group and then transcribed for individual players. This was tedious and demanding work and had to be done under all the usual camp pressures plus this additional one.[21]

From time to time, prisoners arrived in the camp with favourite pieces of music in their possession which were discovered lying about the camp. But these scores tended to be classical works and not marches.

The non-Jewish violinist Zosia Cykowiak was clear, looking back, that 'the camp authorities' had stipulated Jews were to be excluded in setting up the women's orchestra. It is likely that this was Mandl's original intention, an experience with which Szymon Laks was familiar for his orchestral group. Yet within a few weeks, by early May 1943 Jewish musicians were readily included, possibly because of the low number of non-Jewish females in the camp who knew how to play well enough. At the same time, day after day, trains were disgorging onto the ramp thousands of Jews from all over Europe, many of whom were gifted musicians.

The first iteration of the orchestra numbered approximately fifteen women, rising to twenty by the end of June 1943. The band had a narrow range of instrumentalists but there were always more than enough mandolin players as this was such a popular instrument in Europe during the 1930s and considered suitable for a young woman to learn, along with the piano, the violin and singing. Developed in Italy in the mid-eighteenth century, the classical mandolin looks like a guitar but has the same tuning as a violin, with eight rather than four strings. It is easier to play because it is plucked rather than bowed. The tremolo technique on a mandolin can produce very soft or powerful sounds by simply plucking the strings with a pick. However, the note tends to fade quite quickly, which was not helpful for an outdoors band.

By contrast, there were few cellists competent or otherwise, and throughout the life of the women's orchestra there were never any dedicated brass instrumentalists. Mandl was displeased about the dominance of strings in 'her' orchestra, with only a small woodwind and percussion section. According to Hanna Palarczyk, the block's assistant, 'it took a long time to explain... to Mandl that... women's orchestras are usually not brass bands... and that this is a chamber or lounge orchestra. In any case one that consists of violins, cellos, and other instruments but not trumpets. But at least there were cymbals... to beat time.'[22]

Czajkowska tried to make the best of the players at her disposal, with the band gradually strengthened by the admission from May 1943 of the first Jews into the orchestra. Hilde or Hildegard Grünbaum, who died on 28 February 2024, had the dubious distinction of being the first Jewish member, having arrived in Auschwitz on 20 April 1943. An only child born in Berlin in 1923, Hilde came from a middle-class background and went to a Christian elementary school in Berlin followed by a Jewish high school once Nazi restrictions on Jewish children's education came into force. Her parents had insisted their daughter have a broad musical education, and Hilde had learned the violin and taken music theory lessons with a private music teacher, as well as playing in various school and youth orchestras and taking singing lessons at her synagogue.

Hilde's friends and her parents' friends were all Jewish and while they were not Orthodox, they were all members of a more progressive, or Masorti congregation who were also early adopters of Zionism, the idea that there should be a Jewish homeland established in British-mandated Palestine. One of Hilde's aunts had emigrated to Palestine in 1925 but Hilde's father, who owned a textile shop in Berlin, believed like many German Jews at the time that the Nazi horror could not last in a cultured country such as his. When he was proved wrong, Hilde's parents discussed sending her to Italy to attend university there. They also encouraged her to study English so that the family would be better equipped if they managed to emigrate to America or Britain.

Hilde remembered many conversations which revolved increasingly around how to emigrate. Yet her parents failed to act. Her father had been born in the southern Polish city of Będzin where there had been a Jewish settlement since the thirteenth century. In October 1938, before he got around to selling his shop, he was expelled back to Poland from Germany along with all Jewish-Polish nationals. A frightening period followed for Hilde and her mother, left alone in Berlin. Hilde sometimes went to synagogue on her own on Saturdays, simply to keep in touch with other Jewish friends and hear the latest news.

Worse was to come. On 9 November 1938, Kristallnacht, the pogrom known as 'Night of Broken Glass', unleashed Nazi violence on Jewish properties and businesses. Synagogues across Germany were set on fire during the most terrifying night so far of Hilde and her mother's lives. The November terror, or pogrom, was sanctioned by Hitler and orchestrated by Goebbels, with the major perpetrators the black-booted SS and brown-shirted SA thugs. Yet for Jewish children and adolescents like Hilde the most shocking sight was seeing the supposedly idealistic Hitler Youth, sometimes boys they had once known, now bawling songs about Jewish blood spurting from their knives while flaunting their swastikas and party badges.

Hilde and her mother had already been forced by the Nazis to move from their home to a much smaller apartment in a predominantly Jewish area of Berlin. This meant that on 9 November, they witnessed at first-hand the destruction of Hilde's father's shop. Still in shock, Hilde's mother sold what remained of the contents and visited a man who she had heard could smuggle Jews into

Belgium. She was betrayed and never returned. Showing immense courage for a fifteen-year-old, Hilde went to the same address where she discovered that the Gestapo had been tipped off about the smuggler and arrested her mother and another woman who was there at the same time. The Gestapo now searched the apartment where Hilde was living on her own. The police did not find the small amount of money that her mother had hidden and was all that Hilde had to live on, apart from an equally small reserve of family money in the bank. Soon both sources of cash were exhausted.

Hilde frantically tried to register for 'Aliyah', the process by which Jews were helped to escape and make a new life in Palestine. Several Zionist organisations where she had connections offered to organise a permit to get her to England and from there, she hoped, onward to Palestine. But she was desperately torn after she discovered the prison where her mother was being held. Despite her mother's pleading, Hilde felt she could not now leave Germany, so she spent her dwindling cash learning to speak better English. Just before war broke out in September 1939, she received a permit through the Maccabi Youth Movement which would have allowed her to emigrate to Palestine, but following her mother's arrest, Hilde decided to stay in Germany. Instead of a place on the Kindertransport, a British rescue effort to evacuate almost 10,000 predominantly Jewish children from Nazi Germany and other recently annexed countries in the Greater German Reich to Britain, she made weekly visits to her mother who had been sentenced to two years in a Berlin prison, while also hiring a lawyer in a futile attempt to secure her release.

These months were agonising for Hilde. By September 1940 she had no money left and was forced to move away to the village of Neuendorf in the countryside, an hour and a half south of Berlin, where she lived with a Zionist youth group called Hakhshara that prepared young people to work on the land prior to settlement in Palestine. For a year, she continued to return to Berlin once a week to visit her mother.

But by September 1941, all Hakhshara operations were wound up and Jewish children older than twelve were required by the German government to undertake some kind of forced labour, often deeply unpleasant, such as cleaning toilets or weeding cemeteries, prior to deportation to the concentration camps. Hilde worked in a cemetery by day but at night, during an enforced curfew, she and her friends from the Hakhshara settlement could at least read, study and listen to music.

Life was now extremely precarious, with the Gestapo never far away, waiting to pounce. In early 1942, the Jewish director of her group was asked to provide fifty people to be sent on a transport east. When he refused, the Gestapo took them anyway, choosing those without German citizenship. Hilde was among them as the daughter of a Polish Jew and was now sent to Frankfurt an der Oder.[23]

She and her former Hakhshara group were aware of the significance of deportations because many had received postcards with cryptic warning messages from friends who had direct experience of what happened to deported Jews. Hilde was able to remain in Germany for several more months only because the growing labour shortage meant she was required once again to work on the land. Meanwhile her mother had been released from prison in early 1942, now in a much-weakened condition. Hilde found a temporary hiding place for her mother, but not for long. At the end of 1942, Susanna Grünbaum was deported to Ravensbrück and Hilde never saw her again.

And then finally Hilde was ordered to Berlin. In April 1943, aged nineteen, she was deported onwards in a foul-smelling, over-crowded cattle car to Auschwitz in transport number 37 with a thousand other Jews, men and women. More than half (543) were gassed on arrival. Hilde, young and strong, was with a few of the friends she had made at Neuendorf. She always remembered the ferocious barking of the German shepherd dogs as they arrived and were taken away for shaving and tattooing.

After a brief period in quarantine, Hilde joined her first kommando, which was assigned to haul rocks, one of the toughest jobs. Hilde and her Hakhshara friends were physically strong from all their previous outdoor work, but she realised she needed to be emotionally strong as well. Her optimism and deep-rooted belief in Zionism were both reinforced by the discovery of friends in the camp who helped her cope. Hilde's natural leadership qualities also came to the fore – perhaps the result of being an only child forced onto her own resources when her mother was arrested. Several of the younger girls, missing their mothers, remembered how she looked out for them.

Shortly after joining the rock-hauling kommando, Hilde heard the call for musicians and immediately raised her hand. She auditioned and Czajkowska said she would like to take her on to play the violin, recorder and percussion, making her the first Jewish member of the orchestra. Just before accepting, Hilde consulted Esther Loewy and Sylvia Wagenberg, two younger girls who had travelled to Auschwitz in the same transport with her and were now in the same kommando. She did not want to leave them.

Esther was born in 1924 in Saarlouis, a town in southwest Germany then under French control as a result of the punitive terms imposed on the Weimar Republic by the Treaty of Versailles. She was one of the four children of Rudolf Loewy, a teacher and cantor in the local synagogue who had met his wife Margarethe as teenagers in Berlin when Rudolf had taught her the piano. After their marriage, Margarethe continued to play and sing at various concerts.

Esther Loewy, a musical teenager who survived
Auschwitz by learning to play the accordion

In 1936 Germany took over the Saarland and subjected the region's Jewish population to Nazi race laws. Life for the Loewys became worryingly restricted. Esther's two older siblings, a brother and sister, managed to emigrate while her sister Ruth had escaped to Switzerland – or so the Loewys thought. But Esther and her parents were stuck. Kristallnacht on 9 November 1938 was a wake-up call for the Loewy family, who like so many other German Jews were not especially political. Esther's parents be-latedly began trying to organise their youngest daughter's emigra-tion to Palestine, sending her to the same Zionist training camp at Neuendorf run by Hakhshara where Hilde had fled, even though Zionism had not been a particular goal in her family before this.

In December 1942 Esther was undertaking forced labour in the countryside at Neuendorf when she heard about the tragic fate of her sister Ruth. Like many other fleeing Jews, Ruth had managed to reach Switzerland, a country officially neutral but which enforced strict immigration policies and so she was deported back to Germany and murdered in a concentration camp.[24]* Her parents had also been deported and shot in Kaunas, Lithuania, a tragedy she only discovered after the war. Like Hilde, she managed to remain for a few more months but in early April 1943 Esther was sent to Berlin prior to deportation. On 19 April 1943 she too was shoved into an airless cattle truck and deported to Auschwitz.

Esther remembered arriving on the ramp, being separated from the men and the elderly and sent to the washhouse, always referred to as the 'sauna'. She was shouted at and shaved until only stubble on her head remained, showered and tattooed and expected to dry herself without a towel. In 1995, when she eventually felt able to talk about this ordeal for the Museum of Auschwitz archive, her memory of the entire process, including having to undress in front of SS men, was clear and unemotional. 'I became number 41948,' she said.

Hilde knew from working in the same kommando as Esther, now eighteen, and Sylvia, aged just fifteen but whose petite frame made her look even younger, that the two girls had some basic musical talents. She urged them to audition for the orchestra.

Esther had a rounded musical education, playing the piano as her main instrument and also the recorder, as well as being a good singer. By coincidence, Esther's uncle had been Hilde's

---

* The controversial Swiss immigration policy meant that between 10,000 and 24,000 civilian Jewish refugees were refused entry and deported to concentration camps and murdered, a policy that has been criticised by Holocaust historians.

music teacher and had directed many choirs in Berlin schools before the war. Other Jewish children remembered Herr Loewy as a man who taught them to love music.

'We heard about Mozart, Beethoven, Schubert, Schumann, Brahms and many other composers. We sang songs for choirs... including the final chorus from Beethoven's 9th Symphony,' one of his former pupils, Inge Franken, recalled in 2003.[25]

Sylvia could play the recorder and flute and had also been taught in Berlin by Esther's uncle. 'The one teacher who was unforgettable to me was Herr Loewy, whom we called *Stifte* (meaning pencil) because he was such a tiny man,' she recalled in a 2003 interview shortly before her death.[26] 'He taught us bible studies but his real specialty was music. He was a fantastic music teacher. From him I learned the notes and how to play the flute. That saved my life in Auschwitz but unfortunately not his.'[27] According to Hilde, the two teenagers, pressed by her, agreed to give the new band a try. After a brief audition, Czajkowska accepted all three of them into the orchestra.

Sylvia elaborated on Hilde's account of how events unfolded. Sylvia said that Hilde offered to audition for the orchestra as their representative and check it out for the other two girls. 'If it was good, we would follow her, and if not – at least only one of us would suffer. And so it was. She joined the orchestra, and after a very short time, they came and took me and my sister.'[28]

Esther in turn had her own memory of how she joined the orchestra. In her account, after the cold shower in the 'sauna' she was taken to her barracks and expected to share a blanket-less hard bunk bed with approximately eight to ten other women. Four weeks of rock-hauling followed until one day, when Esther knew her body could not take more of this heavy work, Czajkowska walked into the barracks asking who was the musical one. Czajkowska explained that she had heard that one of the girls regularly sang in order to win extra bread rations as a reward from the block elder, the woman who divided the bread portions and kept order. Now she wanted her for the orchestra she was trying to set up.

'She asked me what instrument I played and I said piano but as they did not have one of these, she said to me if you can play the accordion I will take you,' Esther recalled in her 1995 interview for the Auschwitz Museum. She said 'yes', despite never having even held an accordion. 'But I thought "How hard could it be? Either she will take me or she won't."'[29]

'So she asked me if I knew how to play a popular hit song of the day – *Du hast Gluck bei den Frauen, Bel Ami* (You're lucky with women, my friend).' The song had been popularised in the 1939 German film *Bel Ami*, based on a novel by the nineteenth-century French writer Guy de Maupassant about an unscrupulous social climber whose success came from his conquests with women. 'I knew it by heart as it was very popular so I had no problem with the right hand, which was like a piano keyboard,' Esther recalled. 'But the left-hand buttons were harder. It was only thanks to my musical ear that I managed.'

The song was a favourite of the SS in all the camps, with the Esmen often demanding that it was played as a way of mocking the deplorable physical state of most Jewish prisoners. Grotesquely, this and similar tunes were also sometimes played as background music to accompany punishments and executions as recorded in several camps. On 30 July 1942, after his failed escape from Mauthausen, prisoner Hans Bonarewitz was accompanied to his execution by the song *Komm zurück*, an adaptation of *J'attendrai* by Dino Olivieri played by camp musicians, while at Neuengamme a small wind ensemble, forced to play by the gallows where a man was hanging, was vividly drawn by prisoner Hans Peter Sorensen.[30]

However, although almost all the women forced to play in Birkenau remember the experience as a form of violence, none specifically recalls being ordered to play deliberately at executions. As Szymon Laks wrote, 'it was said after the war that in the German concentration camps the hanging of runaway prisoners took place to the sounds of music. As far as Birkenau is concerned, I must categorically deny this.'[31]

Although Hilde, Esther and Sylvia were all accepted by Czajkowska, Sylvia was now concerned for her elder sister, Carla, who had been transported with her to Auschwitz but who initially did not want to join the orchestra. Until this moment, Sylvia and Carla Wagenberg had not been especially close. Their parents had divorced in the 1930s when their father had managed to emigrate to Palestine while their mother had stayed in Germany but struggled to look after the children alone especially once she became ill. In 1939 Sylvia, aged eleven, was sent by her mother, believing she would be safer there, to a Jewish children's home in Berlin. Carla, then fifteen, was dispatched to the Zionist settlement in Neuendorf to get agricultural training in preparation for her hoped-for emigration to Palestine. In 2003, Sylvia recalled how completely alone she had felt in the home. Once she arrived at Auschwitz, music became a lifeline for Sylvia which she desperately wanted to extend to Carla.

Carla's initial reluctance to audition for the recorder may have been due to sisterly resentment or concern that her school-level playing might not be good enough. Fortunately, a Slovak friend called Piri persuaded Carla at least to try and she was taken on as a recorder player, the fourth Jewish member of the orchestra after Sylvia, Esther and Hilde. This small group of German Jewish girls within the orchestra stayed close thanks to many shared life experiences but they did not at first live together in a separate orchestra block.

*

A day or so after the four German girls – Hilde, Esther and the Wagenberg sisters – arrived, a family of Greek Jews was also deposited on the station ramp at Auschwitz after a hideous and much longer journey. Lili Assael, thirty-three, newly married to Samuel Hasid in whose popular band she played piano, and her sixteen-year-old sister Yvette had been arrested by the Germans in their native Thessaloniki (Salonika) in northern Greece in February 1943. Lili, Yvette (whose birth name was Bonita) and their aunt were among a group of 2,800 Jews who were deported in transport number 13, which left Salonika in the early hours of 22 April and finally arrived in Auschwitz on 28 April. This journey alone might have killed them.

The Assaels were part of an unusual Jewish community in Salonika with roots in pre-Inquisition Spain which had preserved Sephardic customs such as the medieval Judaeo-Spanish language known as Ladino. The family had once been comfortably off and the children had grown up in an attractive house at 62 King George Street, overlooking the ocean. David Assael, their father, ran a successful tobacconist's shop and small-scale currency trading venture – a profitable business in this cosmopolitan city where Jews had lived largely untroubled for centuries alongside Greeks, Turks and other nationalities and religions.

However, in 1938 David suffered a business reversal which made life tough for the family. Their parents had insisted that Lili, Yvette and their older brother Michael, known as Michel, who followed them to Auschwitz, all learned to play the piano as children. Michel, eight years older than Yvette, was twenty when his father ran into business problems. He went to work in a nightclub playing the piano to help the family finances. Lili became a well-regarded piano teacher in Salonika, as well as playing professionally in Sam Hasid's band.

'My father was very religious,' Yvette recalled in 1995. 'He went every day to synagogue and on Saturdays he took me with him. But the family was not defined by being Jewish. We spoke Spanish at home, although we learned some Greek, and I was sent to a French school, the Alliance Israélite Universelle (AIU) and later an American school until the Nazis closed down all schools for Jews.'

Yet it was Yvette's musical ability that really mattered to her survival when she eventually arrived at Auschwitz with Lili. In the early days of the war, despite not having much money, Yvette's mother Doudoun bought a piano for the family, even though she did not play herself. Yvette was first taught on it by Lili. 'She used to rap me over the knuckles when I made mistakes,' Yvette recalled. 'Then my brother tried. And I'd cry.'[32]

In the end, Lili and Michel gave up trying to teach Yvette the piano, saying she was not good enough. As a much younger child, Yvette was especially close to her devoted mother Doudoun, who now spent two years teaching Yvette the accordion and trying to persuade her to learn the double bass. Doudoun even bought a double bass but Yvette was too small to handle the instrument and it remained largely unplayed.

'I told her I would only learn it if I could play the drums first and I did for six months,' said Yvette in the same 1995 interview. Her father made her practise for two hours every day.[33] 'He said "one day you'll thank me for it", although of course he could never have imagined how.'

On 8 April 1941 the invading German army occupied Salonika. The Assaels soon lost their home along with their piano, which was requisitioned. The city's Jewish population of around 50,000 people were subjected to 'Jewish laws' restricting their movements and work occupations, while Salonika's historic Jewish cemetery, dating back to the fifteenth century, was desecrated and destroyed. In February 1943, Jews were forced to move into ghettos, facilitating the German extermination plans. 'Suddenly we had to wear yellow stars and share a house in the ghetto at the end of town where the trains went from,' Yvette remembered.[34]

There were two of these ghettos, or transit camps, all surrounded by barbed wire. From February onwards, Jewish capital was confiscated, the municipal archive destroyed by fire and finally the Jews of Salonika were dispatched onto cattle trains for the long journeys east. The Assaels had been moved into the largest ghetto, named after the Jewish philanthropist Baron de Hirsch, who had created a Jewish quarter in the western part of Salonika to help Jews made homeless by the great fire of 1917. Conveniently for the Nazis, the ghetto was directly opposite the central railway station. In March 1943, the deportations to Auschwitz began, with Lili and Yvette deported in April. They were pushed onto the cattle trains with eighty people per wagon – men, women, the elderly, the sick and children – for the week-long journey to Poland. The captives had to survive with only the food they were able to take with them – mostly dried figs and raisins. The only toilet in each carriage was a bucket, which soon overflowed with urine and excrement. Another bucket contained water, which rapidly ran out, while the only ventilation came from a small strip covered by wire mesh.

It was almost midnight when they finally arrived at their unknown destination on 28 April. They were immediately surrounded by dogs barking, floodlights trained on them, a sensation of freezing cold air and angry shouts of '*Raus Raus*' ('Get out, get out') as they were forced out and their luggage taken.

Yvette felt even more desperate because she had opted to travel with her older sister and aunt, rather than her parents. Misled by the Germans, she had thought she was being offered a chance to travel and see the world, which she had always longed for. 'I didn't

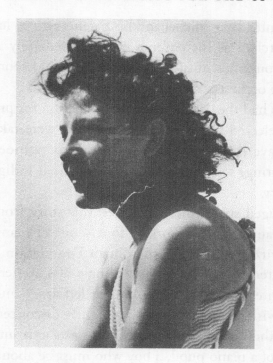

Yvette Assael, here post-war, was part of a musical family of Greek Jews from Salonika, and one of the youngest in the orchestra

want to leave my mother,' she recalled. 'I loved her so much. But I said I would meet her again here. She was crying... we thought we were going to work in Germany. I was so young...'

On their arrival in Auschwitz, the family were immediately separated; Yvette and her older sister in one group, her grey-haired aunt in another. 'I ran back to be with my aunt,' Yvette remembered. 'She was my mother's sister. But my sister saw this and realised what was happening. She grabbed me. But I ran back to my aunt again. Of course, Lili understood the reality and was very strict. She loved me and saved my life. She was my mother and my teacher but there were times when I hated her.'[35]

Two months later Michel and his parents arrived in Auschwitz. Michel watched as his parents were immediately taken to be gassed. Through his musical contacts, he would soon be playing in the male orchestra.

The girls had the usual Auschwitz induction for prisoners who were not selected for extermination. They were taken into the camp to have their hair shaved, their arms tattooed and were given ill-fitting, scratchy clothes. At this final indignity, Yvette began to cry.

Yvette, aged sixty-nine, recounted this story from her living room in Plainview, New York in 1995 – one of many interviews by Auschwitz survivors for the Shoah Foundation. Her *almost* cheery matter-of-factness as she willingly lifts up her cardigan to show the interviewer the tattoo on her left arm – number 43293 with its Jewish triangle* above – is slightly disconcerting. But at this point the interview suddenly stops as she is interrupted by the arrival of a piano pupil, a boy who must be about the age she was at the time of the events she is remembering.[36]

A period in the quarantine block followed, and then a terrible day carrying bricks and boulders to and from the camp four times. Yvette was a delicate child and knew that more days in that kommando would kill her. On her arrival, she had told the camp registration office that she played the piano and accordion. It was crazy, she thought at the time, how could such things matter in a place like this? But a few days later a camp function-ary came and called out two numbers – hers and Lili's. Yvette quickly checked the tattoo on her left arm and realised that they had both been summoned to an audition with the bandleader Czajkowska.

---

* Triangles as part of the tattoo were not compulsory. Most prisoners had numbers only.

'She gave me an accordion and told me to play a tune, which I managed by heart. Then she gave it to my sister who was very smart as she didn't know how to play the accordion, only the piano. So she played it with one hand, telling Czajkowska that was the way to do it. And she too was taken on.'[37]

Despite being in the orchestra, the Greek sisters struggled to cope with the horror and bleakness of Auschwitz. Used to Salonika's warm climate, they suffered especially from the extreme cold and felt isolated because they did not understand the camp language. In addition, Lili's husband, Sam Hasid, had been killed on arrival at Auschwitz in April along with the Assael parents and so Lili, a young widow, was required to be a mother to Yvette. Both sisters resented the relationship that had been forced on them. Yvette often felt and behaved like the child she still was. At first, she petulantly refused to eat the camp soup, complaining to Lili that it tasted of glue. Eventually she learned it was that or nothing other than two slices of bread in the evening and occasionally a slug of liverwurst.

The roles were reversed somewhat in the orchestra, at least initially, because Yvette had to teach Lili how to play accordion chords with her left hand. The talented Lili picked it up rapidly. 'But playing classical music on the accordion was not that easy and my sister never learned to play by heart so although both of us were playing accordion in the orchestra, I was put up front for the marches,' Yvette remembered. Even though Lili was a more accomplished, classically trained musician, she 'sometimes just walked behind'. But that did not last and it was soon Lili in front.[38] Czajkowska may have turned a blind eye because she had grasped from the audition that Lili was a 'proper' musician who might be useful in other ways.

*

During the early days of the orchestra, the players simply practised without performing. Rehearsals lasted from morning roll call
until evening roll call, with a short lunch break. According to the
violinist Zofia (Zosia) Cykowiak, it was not until June 1943 that
they were good enough to play in the hospital block as well as
perform marches for the departing and returning women's work
kommandos. She explained in her 1982 testimony: 'The playing
area was located at the entrance gate to the Birkenau women's
camp near Block 25, the death block, opposite the hospital blocks
located across the road of the B1a camp . . .' Everyone knew Block
25 because it was used as a holding area, with no food and water
given, until it was full to overflowing with the half-crazed occupants screaming for help and then every occupant was killed.

But as the numbers in the camp constantly increased, agreeing
on living quarters for the orchestra women posed a problem and
the Nazis kept shifting them around.

'Soon however the band was moved to a wooden barrack
numbered 12 (in the autumn 1944 the barracks were re-numbered
and it became 7) and it was in this barracks, which also housed
a separate room for the parcel service, that a rehearsal room and
second room for living quarters was created.'[39]

The growing band had sufficient scope for two accordions,
but three pushed the whole ensemble out of kilter. One of the
accordionists, Esther Loewy, fell ill with typhus in June, soon
after she joined the orchestra. She recovered after three weeks only
to find when she returned from the hospital, still very weak, that
her place had been taken by Lili. Czajkowska then gave Esther a
place playing the flute, but she fell ill a second time within weeks,
this time with whooping cough, and could not play at all. That
ought to have spelled the end of Esther's career in the orchestra,
but even then Czajkowska arranged for her to take guitar lessons
and she survived.

'I feel that Czajkowska was a very good woman [and] that she helped whenever she could as can be seen in my case,' Esther recalled in 1995. 'A thousand times she could have said: "You're out of the orchestra." But she did not do so. She wanted to find a way of saving my life.'[40] 'I have only the highest regard for Czajkowska,' Esther continued. 'She had no ambition beyond making good music for the SS and I admired her for that.'[41] Soon afterwards, in September, Esther left Auschwitz for Ravensbrück voluntarily, having been told that those with at least one non-Jewish grandparent like her would be looked after by the Red Cross. Anything seemed better than Auschwitz.

Meanwhile, Hilde developed a painful abscess from her ears through her neck a few months after joining the orchestra. The abscess was impossible to treat in the camp and so bad that Hilde could not hold a violin. But Czajkowska did not get rid of her either; instead she reassigned Hilde to write sheets of copy music. Like Esther, she was saved by Czajkowska.

Czajkowska, who had been at Auschwitz for over a year, was also remembered by some for her short temper and occasional hysterical outbursts. She 'was very nervous and frequently shrieking', according to Zosia. But she could also be motherly towards some of the youngest players in the orchestra, 'accepting and coaching girls who hardly knew how to hold their instruments'.[42] Above all, Czajkowska clearly had the drive and discipline to establish the orchestra as a viable performing band in its first year. Those who knew her at this time considered she was fair and, unlike some of the other block leaders, she did not take a cut from each ration of bread that passed through her hands but shared it equally. According to the son of one of the musicians, researching the story of his mother in 1998, he learned that: 'She also ensures that the *Stubendienst* [the block orderly who brings the rations] distributes the soup evenly by making them stir the mixture – very important! – so that each of the girls gets her share of the few scraps of meat and potatoes which would otherwise remain at the bottom of the bucket.'[43] In addition, she helped the youngest girls like Yvette, whom she called Yvetka, learn about life:

> When Yvette, during breaks from rehearsals, sits outside on what passes for grass, she is increasingly joined by another woman who takes a great interest in her, which Yvette thinks is kind until one day Yvette receives a fiery letter from her which she doesn't understand. She goes to see Czajkowska, who reads the letter and bursts out laughing recommending to a stunned Yvetka that she shouldn't go and sit on the grass for a while.[44]

The older woman was trying to protect the innocent girl from the predatory demands of a desperate prisoner.

Looking back on their time in the orchestra, Yvette and her sister Lili both saw Czajkowska positively as a teacher doing her best with no experience of conducting. Yvette remarked that Czajkowska 'could be very nice but she was also weird... sometimes she'd just go off in the middle of a rehearsal and eat something'.[45] At other times she gave Yvette extra food to eat, such as an apple or a piece of bread.

Lili, strong-willed, outspoken and a professional musician in her early thirties, had a better-informed perspective on Czajkowska. She respected her for trying so hard to be a competent conductor but could see as well how much Czajkowska relied on her. Like the rest of the players, Lili knew that Czajkowska had been assigned a role that was well beyond her limited musical abilities.

3

Something beautiful to listen to

By the early summer of 1943 Czajkowska had almost twenty girls who were part of her performing troupe, plus two copyists. But they lacked cohesion, had a limited repertoire and an imbalance of instruments: four mandolins, five violins, three flutes, two guitars, two accordions and a clash of cymbals. They were almost entirely non-professional, with those who had some professional experience carrying the weaker players.

One outstanding addition at this time was Helga Schiessel, born in 1907, a percussionist with an impressive mastery of a professional drum kit who had arrived in Auschwitz in April 1942 on the first transport of Polish women with Zofia Czajkowska, the one a political Jew the other a political Pole. Helga had been a popular professional drummer and jazz singer at a nightclub in Munich who had been denounced in 1942 for passing as an Aryan in a mixed marriage and sent to Dachau, where she had been tortured. Shy and withdrawn, Helga did not join the orchestra until August 1943. Czajkowska was extremely happy to have discovered such a talented and important new member.

Three Belgian Jewish girls also joined the orchestra in the summer of 1943. Elsa Miller, twenty, was 'gentle, good and serene. Even in Birkenau'.[1] She had red hair, a milky white complexion and was slightly plump when she arrived in April 1943. Elsa had been a promising violin student and, shortly after her arrival, while waiting in the quarantine block, heard a call for musicians and asked to audition. She was accepted but had to wait another month before she could join.

A few weeks later Elsa noticed a fellow Belgian among the latest transport of women queuing for the humiliating shaving and tattooing process. Hélène Wiernik, known as Itta, just sixteen, was howling and crying as prisoner functionaries cut off her long, thick curly hair. 'I was petrified,' Hélène recalled in 1997.[2]

Hélène had played the violin since the age of eight, when her father, a cabinet maker, had made her a miniature instrument. She lived for her violin. At the time of her arrest in June 1943 she

*Hélène, or Itta, Wiernik, the talented Belgian violinist
who cried when her beautiful thick hair was shaved off*

was an outstanding student at the Saint Gilles music academy in Brussels, in grave danger since the German invasion in 1940 because she was Polish by birth. 'When my professor saw I wore a yellow star [required by Jews in occupied Belgium after October 1942] she was upset and wanted to save me,' Hélène recalled. 'She wanted me to go into a convent.'

Hélène's parents, feeling especially at risk since they were Yiddish not French speakers, went into hiding early in 1943 shortly after deportations began, leaving the then fifteen-year-old Hélène in charge of her younger brother, Léon, eleven, which meant this was not an option. Fortunately, another solution was found. A non-Jewish boy agreed to marry her that year in what was known in French as *mariage blanc*. 'He was about twenty... it was a gesture... he did it to help,' Hélène explained. 'He was a comrade not a lover.'[3]

After this, Hélène stopped wearing the star and became a mother to Léon, who lived with her, hardly venturing out. They were denounced and arrested by pro-German Belgian civilians, even though Hélène's new young husband tried to push them away, screaming 'She's my wife.' Hélène and Léon were taken to a transit camp in the north Belgian city of Mechelen, known as Malines in French, where Léon fell ill with blistering boils spread by lice and was hospitalised. Hélène last saw her brother on a hospital train being taken to Auschwitz where he was gassed on arrival. She kept this terrible image in her head throughout her own captivity, wondering how she would ever tell her parents should she and they survive.

Hélène had plenty to cry about that day in Birkenau, for in addition to having her head shaved, she also missed her violin. 'It was the one thing I knew how to do,' she recalled.[4] Trying to console the new arrival, Elsa Miller brought Hélène water and told her that if she was asked when she registered 'What can you do?' she should say that she was a *couturière*. Rumours had quickly spread that having a useful job was the route to survival and there was a need for dressmaking skills to satisfy the requirements of the female guards. But Hélène was spared from inventing a talent she did not possess because other women on her convoy had already passed on the news that she was a violinist. Czajkowska wasted no time in seeking her out.

Initially Hélène refused to go with Czajkowska. 'I will not play for the Germans,' she said. Elsa told her sharply to 'Shush' for as Hélène realised later, 'Elsa knew that an angel had come to take me by the hand'.[5]

'Czajkowska led me to the music barracks . . . I was in despair. Everyone was dying. I had no shoes and no hair. She gave me a violin. I played the Chaconne of Bach.'

Hélène said later she knew that technically she was not capable of playing this monumental piece, considered not only one of the most challenging masterpieces in the baroque repertoire but sometimes said to express the entire range of the most intense human emotions. As she played, 'my tears flooding the instrument', it was clear that this teenager understood all too well the themes of struggle, grief and pain embedded in the music and her response to them was proof that she was more than qualified to join the orchestra.

'I cried on that violin,' Hélène recalled of her audition. 'Frau Croner and her sister cried too and the others cried with me. I did not realise that my life depended on the audition that day.'[6]

'It was Elsa Miller who saved my life,' she commented in 1997.[7]

Before joining the orchestra, Hélène had to remain in the quarantine block for a while and walk each day to the block being used for rehearsals. As soon as she realised her good fortune,

Hélène encouraged another Belgian, Fanny Kornblum, to audition. Hélène had met Fanny, born in 1926, at the Mechelen transit camp where she too was about to be transported to Auschwitz with her mother and grandmother. Fanny could sing and play the mandolin, and while she was not remotely as accomplished a musician as Hélène, her mother Frieda could see that the orchestra was a potential lifeline from observing Hélène go to another block each day. She begged Hélène to see if she could possibly find a place in the orchestra for Fanny. So Hélène asked Czajkowska, who agreed to audition Fanny, and she too was accepted as a mandolin player and later violinist.

'We were now three Belgian girls and we stayed together during our entire captivity,'[8] said Hélène, who would become the orchestra's concertmaster. As a trio, Fanny Kornblum, Elsa Miller and Hélène Wiernik formed one of the strongest friendship groups within the orchestra. 'That was an enormous thing for me,' Hélène remembered. 'Without the help and support of each other we wouldn't have made it.'[9]

Playing in the orchestra was never an easy option, but it was preferable to being sent out on tough demolition work while the camp was still being built as orchestra women were almost from the start exempt from other kommandos. Their day often started at 4 a.m. with roll call, followed by carrying the heavy stools, instruments and music stands to the gate, playing for marches and then practising for several hours until they went back to play marches for the returning workers. Yvette Assael remembered sometimes seeing women on these other kommandos dragging as many as three dead bodies with them on their return to camp. She did not want to be one of them and, even when she was part of the orchestra, found watching this daily suffering from a few metres away almost unbearable.

For it was here at the camp gate that most of the interaction between musicians and marchers took place. As the Austrian prisoner Mali Fritz who arrived in 1943 commented:

> The return march into the death camp is arduous, we can lift our legs only with difficulty and are too tired to say anything. Always this sense that I am carrying on my shoulders layers of muck and dust and above all the ashes of those who are no longer marching ... as we march into the camp, this madhouse music really tries to play in time but why? Our ghostly column must look as if it has come crawling out from the bowels of the earth. And left and left and left two three ... damned rhythm of fear.[10]

It was several months before the players in the music kommando had a dedicated practice block. At first they remained in their own barracks to sleep and came together for rehearsals while the ordinary prisoners in their barracks went on brutal work assignments outside the camp. Women prisoners in Birkenau at this time mostly lived in unconverted wooden horse stables, now expected to house over a thousand prisoners. Each barrack was equipped with twenty-eight three-storeyed bunk beds. The boards frequently did not fit and shifted in every direction. One to a bunk would have been a squash but by 1943, after the first wave of women had arrived at Auschwitz, each of them was used to sleep up to fifteen prisoners.

Prisoners slept on torn and paltry straw mattresses, usually sharing one ragged, lice-ridden blanket between three. According to the Jewish doctor prisoner Lucie Adelsberger, who arrived in Auschwitz in May 1943, the sleeping arrangements were perhaps a little more bearable on the top tier simply because the more agile patients were able to climb up there. On the other hand, rain frequently leaked through the inadequate roof, soaking their blankets. 'Underneath, where the seriously sick who no longer had the strength to sit up or crawl out of bed to attend to their business were berthed, was a mire of faeces and urine drenched blankets,' Lucie recalled in 1956.[11]

It is not clear exactly when the orchestra was considered by Mandl a large enough ensemble to merit its own barracks for sleeping and practising, as well as being excused all other work. At the beginning some Kapos occasionally tried to send some players outside to work in between rehearsals, which led to absences during practice. It soon became evident that the musicians could not be turned into a cohesive unit that was good enough to perform until they lived and practised together in a single block. The players were eventually moved to Block 12, close to where the new railway line leading to the crematoria was being built, but none of them could later remember the precise date.

According to Cykowiak the orchestra initially rehearsed in a small room in Block 4 where its members later slept. However, Auschwitz scholar Jacek Lachendro states this information appears to be inaccurate because barracks 4 burned down at the end of March or beginning of April 1943, before the prisoners could have been sent there. Esther Loewy, who at various times played accordion, flute and guitar, recalls that first rehearsals took place in a room in a different barracks from the one where they slept and that the instruments were also kept there. But she did not give the number of this barracks. The Polish banjo player Bozena Kaczynska, who was only in the orchestra from June to July 1943, stated that the rehearsals took place in a room in a barracks she referred to as the 'remiza', which was a volunteer fire company hall and sometimes a storage shed. Bozena, who hated the airless room, added that it was not the same barracks as where she slept. Lastly Maria Mos, the Polish copyist and mandolin player known as Marysia in the block who had the early number of 6111, spoke of having her interview with Czajkowska in the 'block set apart for the future orchestra, [SHE] gave me pencil and paper and had me write notes for specific instruments'.[12] But this barracks, in Maria's memory, was not yet the same place where the orchestra slept.

The most interesting aspect of these different accounts is that they illustrate the challenge of remembering accurately details when the most pressing concern facing all of the women was staying alive from one day to the next. Nobody was writing a diary; barrack or block numbers were changed by the Nazis; groups of women were moved around depending on incoming transports and the camp's current ability to gas whole populations. Timekeeping was often a matter of recognising the seasons or awareness of religious holidays from incoming transports.

The conductor of the male orchestra, Szymon Laks, told a revealing story about how impossible it was to remember accurately in Auschwitz. He was convinced that his friend Zuk had died while both were prisoners, but then he met Zuk after the war.

At this point our recollections differ. After so many years what is strange about that? As far as I can remember, soon after he returned to Birkenau, Zuk came down with typhoid fever and was taken to the infirmary. After a few weeks, news reached me of his death. In the first letters I received from him after we had re-established contact, he said that he had returned to the orchestra and had played in it until March 1943 when he was transferred to the Gross-Rosen camp. And so he wrote to me: 'I took my leave of the orchestra and I remember my march out of Birkenau when you looked at me sadly from the podium of the *lager kapelle* and this picture has remained forever in my memory.' So it was I who was in error.[13]

According to the musicologist Gabriele Knapp, who wrote one of the earliest accounts of the *Frauenorchester* in 1996 after interviewing seven of the then twenty surviving members of the orchestra, 'the women's first performance took place at the camp entrance in June 1943'. Cykowiak also identified this playing area as 'located at the entrance gate to the Birkenau women's camp near Block 25 . . . the death block'. She added: 'the band began performing at the end of June 1943 in the hospital blocks'. Other prisoners also recalled the orchestra performing for the patients in the grounds of the camp hospital at this time, because the weather was warm.

When they played marches, the musicians had to arrive at their positions at the entrance of camp early, in order to set up before the other kommandos went off to work. At the end of the day they also stayed late until the last returning kommandos passed through the gates. The musicians were not yet released from musical duty when it rained. At this stage, they could only play a very small number of pieces such as the *Radetzky March* by Johann Strauss Sr and Schubert's *Marche Militaire*. Under Czajkowska's direction, the players simply repeated this tiny repertoire over and over, sometimes playing for several hours as the rows of women prisoners tried their best to keep in time while marching past.

Preparing to play for an audience was demanding for this untested young ensemble and some musicians struggled to cope with the indoor rehearsals. As Esther commented, they were a group of exhausted, half-starved young people who had never played together and were required to perform under the eyes of potential Nazi killers who were watching out for mistakes. 'We were amateurs,' Esther recalled. 'First, the parts had to be written out, everything for the whole orchestra, and it was necessary to know which part the violins were to play and so on. All of this took a long time.'[14]

The banjo player Bozena Kaczynska recalled that aside from exhaustion and hunger, what bothered her most during rehearsals was the lack of fresh air. After several days of practice, she volunteered to join a labour detail working outdoors, thinking this would be preferable. However, the block elder recognised her and gave her a thorough beating for disobeying orders. She returned briefly to orchestra rehearsals but then caught typhus and was admitted to the camp hospital. After recovering she never went back to the orchestra. As a non-Jew, and therefore not normally subject to selection for gassing, Bozena survived the war.*

Gradually the orchestra grew in size, for the hardships of rehearsing and playing under relentless pressure were seen by the steady stream of prisoners who auditioned for Czajkowska as as a better option than slavery in the outdoor work kommandos. According to Knapp, by the end of July 1943 the numbers stood at twelve Jewish and fifteen non-Jewish players. The total headcount fluctuated, mostly because illness, especially typhus, repeatedly depleted the ranks. This was one reason why the orchestra in these early months struggled to reach a decent standard. The band was 'foundering', Zippi recalled, adding that the sound they produced initially sounded like *Katzenmusik* (cat music).¹⁵ 'We tried hard, but we were like monkeys on an organ grinder,' she said, including herself in the group.

And then, in August 1943, rumours began circulating of a virtuoso violin player being in the camp.

*

* Plenty of non-Jews, in particular several thousand Soviet POWs, several thousand Roma as well as some Poles and sick prisoners in the infirmary, were also selected for gassing. Prisoners of other nationalities also died during the period from mid-1941 to spring 1943 when selection took place in the camp, usually in the blocks for the sick.

Alma Rosé, born in 1906, was one of Europe's most talented and notable musicians, descended from German musical royalty and the niece of Gustav Mahler. Alma's mother, Justine, was Gustav Mahler's sister who named her daughter after Mahler's wife, Alma Schindler. Her father was Arnold Rosé, concertmaster of the Vienna Philharmonic and State Opera orchestras and founder of the Rosé string quartet, which had premiered several chamber works by Brahms. Meanwhile Alma's uncle Eduard Rosé, the cellist in Arnold's original quartet, was married to another of Mahler's sisters.

Alma's family were deeply assimilated, having changed their name from Rosenblum to Rosé and converted from Judaism to Christianity. Alma had probably never entered a synagogue because her father and mother were fiercely secular. Nevertheless, she was unquestionably Jewish by any Nazi definition.

Alma made her debut as a violinist on 16 December 1926 at Vienna's *Musikverein*, playing Bach's D minor Double Concerto

Alma Rosé at the wheel of her white Aero convertible,
a gift from her husband in the early 1930s

accompanied by her father. In 1930 she married the Czech celebrity violinist Váša Přihoda and went to live with him in Prague. They were a glamorous couple who toured together in the early 1930s, attracting regular coverage in popular women's magazines, with photo shoots showing them both wearing smart clothes and driving flashy cars. But the marriage soon deteriorated, mostly because of their competing ambitions as concert soloists.

Alma's own career was undoubtedly hindered by the entrenched sexism and anti-Semitism of the day. According to the musicologist Michael Haas, she 'recognised that she would never be able to enter into direct competition with her husband and decided to strike out on her own. The decision was daring as it represented a departure from serious music.'[16]

In 1932 Alma founded an exclusively female orchestra, *Die Wiener Walzermädeln* (the Vienna Waltzing Girls), which successfully toured Europe at a time when female orchestral players and especially conductors were rare. The orchestra was not a vehicle

Alma and her orchestra, the Vienna Waltzing Girls, playing in Berlin in 1933

where Alma could shine as a soloist because they mostly played Strauss waltzes. Meanwhile, Alma and Váša were divorced in 1936.

By 1938 the Rosé family faced difficulties on several fronts. Following the Anschluss with Germany in March 1938, Arnold Rosé – now in in his seventies – was forced to retire from his orchestral positions because of the new Nazi laws. He faced an old age with a reduced pension and very little savings and without Alma's mother Justine, who was in failing health and died in August 1938. Alma was now left alone to look after Arnold; her only brother Alfred and his wife had fled Vienna and emigrated to the United States in September, just a month after their mother died. For the next few months Alma was frantically making plans to get to London with her father and then-lover, a young blond Austrian called Heini Salzer who was neither musical nor Jewish and eight years her junior. Heini was the rich son of a successful Viennese businessman whom she hoped to be able to marry in England 'as there was no English law that would prevent her marrying a Gentile and Roman Catholic such as Heini'.[7]*

The final days before she left in March 1939 were a torment as she queued for many hours to get valid travel documents and made secret plans to take a plane from Hamburg to London with Heini, hoping her father could follow swiftly. But it was an agonising further six weeks before he too managed to get out. By the time he had paid a year's tax and other financial demands made on Jews who wanted to emigrate from the Nazis, he had no money left. Heini and Alma found a small flat in Maida Vale, northwest London, and took a room close by for her father.

As an Austrian, Heini could not find work in London and so, under pressure from his friends and family, left London at the

---

* According to this friend Alma had recently been received into the Roman Catholic Church.

end of June to return to Vienna where he soon married another woman. Alma felt abandoned, alone and acutely conscious of her responsibility for her father's wellbeing. At the end of 1939, after the outbreak of war, she returned to continental Europe, believing she could perform in neutral Holland and earn more money than she could in London to send back to her impoverished seventy-six-year-old father now dependent on her there.

With hindsight it is easy to criticise Alma for her naivety in not getting out of Europe sooner or for being disorganised. In May 1940, she failed to get an extension on her British visa, barring her from re-entry only a week before Nazi troops occupied the Netherlands. Perhaps she believed that either her fame, her Czech passport or friends of her famous uncle might save her. Instead, she was forced into hiding in the Netherlands, moving for the next two years from one hiding place to the next. In March 1942, realising she needed more protection, Alma entered into a sham marriage with a Catholic medical student from Utrecht, Konstant August van Leeuwen Boomkamp, brother of a well-known Dutch cellist, in order to obtain false papers with a Dutch name. The pair never lived together and the Nazis, on the lookout for Jews making this sort of arrangement, prowled around making frequent random arrests. In a panic, Alma decided to try and escape via occupied Belgium to Switzerland. She only made it as far as Dijon in eastern France, where she was betrayed.

Alma was first sent to Drancy in the northeast suburbs of Paris, where a French-run transit camp based in an unfinished housing block with no windows was used as a massive holding pen for arrested Jews destined for Auschwitz. As a friend wrote to her brother after the war to explain, '[Alma] had a dreadful fear of having to go underground and felt she didn't possess the necessary temperament to live with strange people who might be quite incompatible, or indeed, be left alone in a single room.'[18]

After six months in Drancy, on 18 July 1943, Alma Rosé, along with a thousand others, travelled in a foul-smelling, packed cattle car on a three-day journey to Auschwitz-Birkenau. She was part of Convoy 57, which left from Paris's Bobigny station at 9 a.m. This transport was full of children who were told they were going to *Pitchipoi* – an invented name intended to cheer them up – while the adults, most of whom had spent the night sleeping on the floor ready for departure, tried to believe they were going to work for the *boches*.[19]

One of Alma's fellow passengers, Henry Bulawko, left a vivid account of the appalling journey the deportees endured.[20]

> Only once, at Cologne I think, we were allowed out of the wagon for some minutes. It happened that some prisoners risked all in an attempt to escape at one stop . . . they set fire to their car, gambling on someone opening the door to attend to the fire. But they paid for it. When the fire attracted attention, a German policeman put his head up to the tiny, barbed wire-covered opening and ordered the leader of the car of deportees: 'Put out the fire or you'll burn everybody in there.' He disappeared. He was not pleased. My outwitted companions quickly extinguished the fire.

Alma survived the first selection at Auschwitz when she was pushed out of the train onto the ramp. She registered under the name of van Leeuwen Boomkamp, occupation *geigenspieler* (violin player), and was put through the usual humiliating procedures of shaving and showering. After being tattooed with the number 50381, given a coarse, striped prisoner uniform, she was sent directly to the medical experimentation unit housed in Block 10 of Auschwitz I with a group of women of childbearing age.

This two-storey brick building with closed windows was

the only women's block in the main camp or *Stammlager* and overlooked Block 11, the execution yard with its blood-spattered back wall. The block was run by the gynaecologist Dr Carl Clauberg, who was conducting pseudoscientific experiments with female sterilisation. Senior Nazis, including Heinrich Himmler, believed that the only way to fully exterminate the Jewish race was to ensure that all Jewish women were sterilised. To this end, Clauberg and his assistants subjected young Jewish women to extreme radiation, surgical removal of their ovaries, and other painful procedures such as injecting formaldehyde preparations into uteruses without anaesthetic. Clauberg had promised Himmler that one doctor with ten assistants should be able to sterilise as many as several thousand Jews in one day. The operations were conducted with such callous ineptitude that women who survived were often so weak and damaged that they died in Birkenau after their discharge.*

At first Alma, with no hair and a strange name, was not recognised by anyone in the experimentation unit. By coincidence, one of the prisoner nurses in the block was a twenty-two-year-old Dutch woman called Ima van Esso, a flautist from a musical family, who realised Alma's true identity once she struck up a conversation with her. Ima remembered an occasion when she was a child and Alma had played at her parents' home.

'I was so shocked to see Alma in Block 10 so totally changed from the last time in Holland, yet still looking fresh and charming, that I had to tell everybody, even the *Blockälteste* [block elder] Magda Hellinger,' Ima recalled in 1983. 'This was such unusual

---

* Clauberg was arrested by Soviet authorities in 1945 and was tried and sentenced to twenty-five years' imprisonment for his crimes related to sterilisation. He was released in 1955 as part of a German-Soviet repatriation agreement but rearrested by German police. He died before his trial began in 1957.

news to Magda that she listened... although at first she didn't know of whom I was speaking. The name Rosé did not set off a reaction immediately but, when I mentioned Váša Přihoda, she paid attention. In central Europe at the time Přihoda was held in the same esteem as Yehudi Menuhin today.'[21]

Magda Hellinger was one of the early Slovak Jewish prisoners, a former kindergarten teacher who was then in charge of the experimentation block. She was not especially knowledgeable about music, but with great presence of mind arranged for a verbal message to be sent quickly to the administration office, where it reached Katya Singer. 'We have Alma Rosé here, the wife of Váša Přihoda.'

Back in the experimentation block, Alma, believing she was going to be killed, made a final request as a condemned person: she asked for a violin. Magda ensured this request was immediately dispatched to Zippi in person. Zippi made sure that Alma was given a good one.

Magda never claimed to have saved Alma. Nonetheless, it is clear that without her actions Alma might indeed have been killed in Dr Clauberg's pseudo-medical torture chamber. Magda always insisted that her role in the camp was to try and help as many escape the gas chamber as possible. 'And I tried to help them; well, because either you try your best or you don't care. But I cared.'[22] Years later she expanded on that.

'Very few can understand what it was like to be a prisoner at Auschwitz-Birkenau – really only those who were there. Fewer still can understand what it was like to be forced into the role of "prisoner functionary" within the concentration camp,' Magda explained in 2003 aged eighty-seven. 'To find yourself in a position in which, if you were brave and clever, you might be able to save a few lives... while being powerless to prevent the ongoing slaughter of most of those around you. To live with the constant awareness that, at any moment, you could lose your own life to a bored or disgruntled guard who perceived that you were being too kind to a fellow prisoner, when all you were doing was trying to be humane.'[23] And so, 'violin in hand, Alma waited eagerly for 6 o'clock when the two female SS wardens left the barrack locking the door from outside. Inmates were placed as door watchers to spread the alarm if anyone came near the building. When all was quiet, Alma began to play,' is how Magda described the occasion to Richard Newman in 1983.[24]

'Beauty had been a long-forgotten dream in Block 10 until that night,' recalled Ima van Esso, who also witnessed this scene. 'Nobody there could have dreamed of such beauty as her playing at that moment.'[25]

According to Magda, Alma played for several more nights after this first performance in the experimental block, with the events turning into impromptu cabaret-style shows.

'In the evening when all the SS doctors and SS *blockführer-innen* left, we planned that the women should come down the stairs one by one in a kind of fashion parade in the gowns they had received. Imagine the show – a small woman in a big gown, a large woman in a small one. It was a comedy – a tragicomedy. Laughter on the sad faces.'[26]

A Polish actress prisoner, Mila Potasinski, took charge of the cabaret and volunteered to sing. Alma played Spanish-American tunes on her violin as Mila taught the women how to dance. In Ima's recollection, 'the chance to hold someone close, to dance and end it with a kiss – often meaningful – helped the women realise they were alive in the Auschwitz dominion of death'.[27]

Rumours of the performances soon circulated among Nazi officers, some of whom began to attend, including Maria Mandl. As soon as Mandl heard Alma play she knew she had to transfer her immediately to Birkenau, believing correctly that only Alma could transform the rag-tag band into a proper women's orchestra, fit to compare with Lak's male orchestra. She was excited by the prospect as she could see that 'her' orchestra was struggling to perform at a comparable level to the men's. With Alma, they could outperform them, and it could not have come at a better time. In August 1943 Camp Commandant Höss appointed Franz Hössler as camp director in the women's camp knowing well that this arrangement would cause friction as the position was previously filled unofficially by Mandl. Although Höss issued a notice at the same time stating that Mandl was still the top supervisor while suggesting rather optimistically that 'she and Hössler work together in agreement with one another', their relationship was fraught because Mandl would not submit to Hössler's direction.

Yvette recalled the moment in August 1943 when Alma was transferred to Birkenau.

> I shall never forget the day the SS brought Alma to the music block. She was placed at the third desk of the violins and she seemed to have difficulty seeing the notes. That day she was merely introduced by the SS as a new member of the orchestra. The next day the SS told the girls in the music block who Alma was and that she was going to play something for them. She played I think Monti's 'Czardas' [her signature tune]. We immediately realised she was really something. Then they announced that she was the new leader.[28]*

Young Sylvia Wagenberg, the German Jewish recorder player, was shocked by the sudden shift in command from Zofia

---

* A *czardas* is a traditional Hungarian folk dance which starts slowly and gets faster and faster, often to showcase the technical virtuosity of a violinist. Vittorio Monti's *Czardas* was written in 1904.

Czajkowska to Alma Rosé. 'One day the SS arrived at the music block and told us they had discovered a musician conductor, Alma Rosé. She turned the orchestra upside down on its head... we played from morning to night.'[29]

The most urgent requirement for Alma when she took charge was how to deal with Czajkowska. The Polish teacher was in a sufficiently strong position to have prevented her relationship with Alma working. Yet once it became clear to Czajkowska that she would only cease to be conductor and would continue to be the orchestra block 'elder' with the principal task of translating Alma's directions into Polish, she understood that this would strengthen the orchestra and still protect her from being ejected from the band. 'Instead of sulking and making Alma's work more difficult, Czajkowska proved to be a great help,' Zippi said.[30]

But Zippi recognised that it was 'an emotional crisis for Zofia, who was showing signs of so much stress that she was given to violent outbursts of temper... It could have been a tragedy for her. But she and Alma were such fine ladies.'[31] It was Zippi's belief that Czajkowska also accepted that having Alma in charge offered a better chance of survival for them all.

In August 1943, when she became the conductor, Alma had been on the run for almost two years, followed by six months of near-starvation in the grim, unhygienic Drancy internment camp, three days on a crowded, airless cattle train, and finally a terrifying spell in an experimental block expecting to lose her life on a makeshift operating table as a human guinea pig. Now she suddenly found herself as Kapo of the music kommando, in charge of a barrack as well as an orchestra.

A Jewish Kapo in Auschwitz was rare and some Poles in the camp felt that Alma had somehow usurped Czajkowska's position, a dangerous situation which was enough to give vent to ever simmering Polish anti-Semitism, as Laks too had found. To strengthen Alma's position, Mandl had her classification changed from 'Dutch Jew' to *Mischling* (or part-Jew) and her registration officially changed back to her maiden name of Rosé.[32] But the rest Alma had to do herself, searching for inner resources from deep inside her.

On a practical level, Alma knew immediately that the orchestra was not remotely up to scratch as a performing unit. Although the average age of the musicians was nineteen, with the youngest fourteen and Alma herself among the oldest at thirty-six, there were also the two Croner sisters, Helena aged fifty-eight and her younger sister Charlotte (Lola) aged fifty-six. Yet they called themselves 'the girls in the band',[33] a phrase that sounds jarring to modern ears.

'No conductor in the world ever faced a more formidable task,' said Zippi. 'Alma was charged with making something out of sheer rock.'

How did she do it?

Alma immediately started making musical and technical demands on her girls, which represented a seismic shift away from Czajkowska's makeshift regime. In imposing her will, Alma had only one circumstance in her favour – the fact that she and the players all lived in one block, Block 12, where there were approximately sixty women at any one time, the number swelled by those who kept order in the block but still far less than the typical quota of around one thousand prisoners per block. Each member of the orchestra had a small bunk bed to themselves with their own rough sheets and blanket, a pillow and thin mattress. They could use toilets and washrooms normally reserved for German prisoners almost when they needed, so did not risk soiling their beds, and were also able to take regular showers. Some musicians recall these as daily, others as twice a week or more. There was even heating to protect the instruments, most of which were now kept in the barracks. These were huge, potentially lifesaving privileges compared to the squalor faced by other prisoners. The improvement in hygiene alone enabled the women to feel a restoration of humanity and with that came a corresponding sense of solidarity and sisterhood.

According to Hélène Wiernik, 'it was Alma who got us all the privileges'.[34]

The barracks was divided into the dormitory room, the adjacent rehearsal room and two tiny, separate rooms for Alma and the newly demoted Czajkowska, with just enough space for a bed, chair and table. The dormitory room also had shelves to hold precious mugs, bowls and food parcels for those eligible to receive them – mostly Polish non-Jews. Three prisoner functionaries, who were not members of the orchestra but given the title of *Stubendienst*, kept the place tidy, administered discipline, and brought and distributed food from the camp kitchens.

Most of the time the musicians still wore camp uniform – stripes if these were available – except when they played on Sundays and holidays, when they were given white blouses and pleated navy blue skirts with blue scarves on their heads. They were now allowed to grow their hair, one of the most humanising of all orchestra privileges, because Mandl felt it was important to look attractive as well as play well. For summer concerts the girls wore navy blue dresses with white polka dots, a uniform which made them visible to other prisoners some of whom believed that, if they enjoyed such obvious privileges, they must be doing Nazi bidding in some form.

'It was grotesque,' commented Kitty Hart, a Polish teenager sent to Birkenau with her mother in April 1943. 'Alma Rosé made up to the authorities in order to keep her privileges and above all so that she might continue living for music, no matter how inadequately played on the odd selection of instruments which made up the orchestra,' she wrote in 1981.[35]

'There must have been jealousy,' Hélène admitted, 'but you can't imagine if you weren't there. It wasn't my fault I was there.'[36]

Perhaps the single factor that made the most dramatic difference to the musicians' self-respect was being allowed the use of underwear. They were given more than one set so that they could surreptitiously wash it themselves. Stanislawa Gogolowska, a Polish prisoner who was not in the orchestra, described what happened to her friend, 'Halinka', presumably violinist Helena Dunicz as Halinka was the name Alma used for her to avoid confusion. 'She changed beyond all recognition,' Stanislawa recalled in her memoir in 1973.

> She is [sic] clean and neatly dressed like all prisoners in the orchestra... is well rested and smiles a lot. She says that the block she lives in is completely different from ours, that it's clean there, that there are beds with little pillows stuffed with straw and clean blankets and everything is covered with white bedlinen, and they don't go out for roll call at all.[37]

According to Hélène, Alma was 'formidable' as she single-mindedly won these privileges and comforts for the orchestra during her first months in charge. 'But the most amazing thing was how she made something beautiful to listen to.'[38]

The orchestra was able to use part of the barracks for rehearsals, which under Alma usually lasted for about eight hours, in addition to the daily performances. This was a dramatic demand by Alma, given that a professional orchestra with conservatory-trained musicians might typically rehearse for around three to four hours per day. Alma's regime was especially hard for the younger, teenage players, some of whom had never played in any kind of orchestra before.

The musicians' day started early, often at about 3.30 a.m. for the first roll call, albeit now held inside the barracks. The players then collected and tuned their instruments from the adjacent rehearsal room so they were ready to play outside during the 5.30 a.m. march to work by the other female prisoners. It was tough under Alma but not nearly as tough as hauling rocks or dragging the corpses of fellow prisoners back to the camp at the end of the day.

While she was improving conditions for the orchestra, Alma also eagerly sought out musicians who could improve its quality from among the thousands of women offloaded every week in the autumn and winter of 1943–44 from the transports arriving at Auschwitz. Alma left no diary nor letters and no other record has been found of how she negotiated with the camp administration to obtain these newcomers. She knew from her desperate spell in the experimentation block that survival for a Jewish woman at Auschwitz was perilous at best. She was now in a position to save others as well as herself by immersing herself in her beloved music.

Those orchestra members who observed their new conductor in action all agreed that Alma was demanding, but never asked more from her musicians than she was prepared to give herself.

'Alma was very proud!' according to one of the violinists. 'She would stand up to the SS . . . Alma behaved with dignity, her posture always straight up, never smiled to them, always related seriously to them never with servility.'[39] First, they needed better instruments if they were going to reach her required standard. 'Alma picked the best instruments among those brought to the camp by people arriving in transports,' Sylvia Wagenberg recalled.[40] These violins, accordions, mandolins and other instruments were piled up with a mass of other confiscated possessions in warehouses collectively called 'Kanada', the name derived from the notion of a country full of riches. Alma had a high-quality, relatively valuable violin for her exclusive use, although it was nothing like the precious instrument she had left behind in Holland. She kept the violin in a special, purpose-built cabinet in the rehearsal room which was built for her by camp carpenters.

Yvette Assael recalled that once Alma had obtained better instruments there was always 'someone going to Berlin', to get new strings or other accoutrements when the players needed them. And as autumn turned to winter, Alma also won her girls a reprieve from outdoors playing in frost and rain by demonstrating to the Nazi authorities how rapidly instruments deteriorate in these conditions. Nonetheless, the girls were still expected to play in the cold and wind and some of them devised a special type of glove that offered some protection for their fingers.[41]

From the outset, Alma insisted on acquiring her own music for her players rather than relying on hand-outs from the men's orchestra. All her scores, piano parts, sheet music and other aids such as music stands were now supplied directly by the camp authorities. Sylvia said that Alma would take 'the basic piano score which she then orchestrated'.

Alma soon released some of the non-Jewish women from the orchestra, knowing they did not face the same danger of selection for gassing as the Jewish girls. 'Alma always saw to it that the women removed from the orchestra were placed in a "good Kommando",' said the Polish violinist Helena Dunicz.[42] Musical considerations determined which of these non-Jewish players she fired. Her main priority, though, was creating the best possible orchestral sound, which necessitated replacing some of the mandolins with violins, regardless of the player's ethnic or religious classification. Irene Walaszczyk, a Polish mandolin player, was kept on as a room elder, as was Founia Baruch, the schoolteacher who had helped start the orchestra with Czajkowska and who suffered from a type of facial paralysis with a lopsided mouth. Henryka Brzozowska, a violinist and fierce Polish patriot, decided of her own accord that Alma's arrival was the time to leave.

Alma made other changes once she had been able to assess the calibre of the remaining musicians. She demoted some of the less capable Jewish girls such as the Belgian violinist Elsa Miller, whom she moved down to third desk, while she promoted Hélène Wiernik, the star violin student from the Brussels conservatoire, to concertmaster, effectively her second in command. She was trying to save as many lives as she had the power to. Alma's predecessor had done the same only with disastrous consequences. She brought in her friend, Danka Kollakowa, to play cymbals in the orchestra replacing a young Greek schoolchild, Lillian Menasche, who was let go, fell ill and was killed in the gas chambers. Without the protection of the orchestra, sixteen-year-old Lillian did not stand a chance. As she scribbled in a note she managed to get to her father, a member of the men's orchestra in the camp with whom she had been deported from Salonika: 'My sweet Papa, I fear I shall never see you again. I fear I shall never see my mother again. Send me your blessings.'

A few days later her father, Dr Albert Menasche, was playing as usual in the men's orchestra when truckloads of starving, desperate girls were driven past them on their way to be murdered. He learned the following day that his own daughter was among the 2,500 killed that October day.[43]

Alma was engaged in a delicate balancing act. The anecdotal evidence suggests that some young Jewish girls taken on at this time were acutely aware that their musical talents were almost negligible. Yet even as she set about raising the orchestra's standard, Alma seems to have been intent on saving as many young Jewish women as possible. To this end, she needed to expand the size of the orchestra from about twenty to just over forty in order to comply with the Nazis' insistence that Jews did not 'swamp' Christians in the playing ranks.

The elementary school in Będzin boasted a large number of mandolin players including Rachela Zelmanowicz, third row, second on left, and Regina Kupferberg, bottom row, sitting extreme left

Rachela Zelmanowicz, born in 1921 in Będzin, Poland, was one of these lucky ones. The well-educated daughter of an accountant, she was twenty-one when she and her father were deported to Auschwitz on 3 August 1943. Her mother was already dead while her older brother, who had served in the Polish army and then joined the resistance, had been deported to Auschwitz two days before her. Rachela travelled to Auschwitz with her brother's fiancée, Ruszka Rembiszewska, who was already living with Rachela because her own parents had been deported and killed. Looking back, Rachela always maintained that she owed her life to Ruszka.

'She was this kind of person who can make a decision,' Rachela recalled in 1984. 'Such people always know what to decide . . . she said when we arrived by train to Auschwitz: "Now walk upright . . . show them that you have strength."'

At exactly this moment, the women saw Rachela's fifty-three-year-old father being led away in a different direction to be gassed. They watched powerless, not knowing precisely what was happening but having a clear premonition that he had been selected for extermination, having heard all the rumours about gas chambers.

'A few days later – we were in Block 15 after the shaving and the tattooing procedures,' Rachela continued. Newly tattooed as prisoner number 52816, 'it did not take a lot of time until someone came and asked "who can play any instrument?"'.

> So she [Ruszka] told me: 'You can play!'
> I said: 'Are you crazy? I am here in Auschwitz! I was playing the mandolin in elementary school, that's what I know.'
> 'Never mind, you have nothing to lose! Maybe you will meet your brother; maybe you will meet your father. First get out of here. Maybe you will take me later. Maybe you can bring some food . . . One of us should be out!'
> She was truly my good angel.

At the audition Rachela could not at first sight read the music put in front of her but was helped by a Greek violinist, a kind and gentle girl called Julie Stroumsa. Alma Rosé instructed Julie to start playing, to give the new girl the tune, and, as soon as she had played it, Rachela was able to copy.

Rachela Zelmanowicz Olewski showing her tattoo
from Auschwitz in post-war Israel

'I have a good ear for music. I caught the rhythm immediately and played thereafter. Julie simply helped me stay in the orchestra.'[44]

Rachela recalled that soon after joining in August 1943 there were approximately forty players who spoke many languages, all living together in one block. She knew she was lucky to have been accepted by Alma, and now she had an additional stroke of good fortune because she discovered she had a connection with Hilde Grünbaum, the violinist from Berlin whose Polish-Jewish father David Grünbaum had been deported back to Będzin before the war. Rachela's family had befriended David, who by coincidence had moved into a second-floor apartment in Będzin directly above their own apartment. Rachela had become like a daughter to David, who read to her all the letters he received from Hilde describing her activities in the Hakhshara youth movement. Rachela, too, had been active in a similar Zionist training group.

Hilde was overjoyed to hear news of her father from Rachela:

When I arrived to [sic] the orchestra and she heard that I brought regards from her father she immediately gave me a glass of milk. I didn't know how she got that milk, but she gave me a glass of milk. I cannot tell you how much this glass of milk was worth in those days. Until today [Hilde] tells me: 'You with that story about the glass of milk! As long as I am alive, I will never forget it.'

Such small friendship groups within the bigger orchestral group were critical to survival. Once she had met Hilde, Rachela felt that although she had lost everything from her previous life at least she had a place in the growing orchestra, as safe as anyone Jewish could possibly be in Auschwitz. Her friend Ruszka was not so lucky. She joined a sewing group, so at least avoided the heaviest work, but she caught typhus and died. 'One day she was standing next to me and talking and at the same time she was dripping diarrhoea, so they took her to the Revier and I saw her no more,' said Rachela.[45]

Regina Kupferberg, also known as Rivka, born in November 1922, was another arrival from Będzin who had been 'processed' in the local soccer stadium with around 30,000 other Jews and then taken to the town's beautiful art deco railway station en route to Auschwitz. She arrived on the early 1 August transport with her younger sister, Rachela's older brother and many other friends and family. Initially, Regina did not apply to the orchestra because she was sure her mandolin playing would not be good enough.

She finally agreed to audition when pressed by her friends and was not surprised when Alma rejected her.

However, a few days later she heard, via Hilde, that Alma wanted her to go back. According to Regina, Alma had said to her 'there is something in your eyes. My heart doesn't allow me to let you go.'[46] Sivanne, Regina's granddaughter, heard the story many times as she was growing up. But perhaps it was nothing to do with the eyes and Hilde played more of a role than she admitted to Regina in trying to get one more Jewish girl into the group. Alma seems to have decided that she would save Regina and that was it.

So Alma asked if she could write musical notation and when she passed that test told her what she planned to do. 'Officially we will tell the SS you are a note taker but unofficially you are my maid.' Regina always said that Alma was very modest in her demands but also very difficult because everything had to be perfect. When the orchestra girls left to play Regina stayed behind with some of the non-Jewish Polish women to chop wood for the fire. They called her Cinderella.[47]

Like Cinderella, she found these were difficult times for a young girl doubly alone in an already hostile environment.

Some applicants who failed their audition could not be found other roles, even if they already had friends in the orchestra. Eighteen-year-old Violette Silberstein had been arrested in Lille along with both parents on 31 July 1943 as they returned from watching a film. Although Violette was French, she was deported via Belgium and arrived in Auschwitz in early August. She watched as her father and mother, Anton and Rosalia, were loaded onto a truck with other Jews who were deemed unfit to work. They were forty-three and forty. She never saw them again.

When she asked during the tattoo process what had happened, she was told with a gesture by a fellow prisoner who pointed to the plume of smoke from the nearby gas chambers. She instantly regretted that she had not climbed into the truck with her mother and nursed a fury for the rest of her life about her aunt's Italian lover who she was convinced had betrayed the family.

Violette decided to try for the orchestra after six weeks in the quarantine block with eight or nine women sharing a bunk and many dying from despair or disease. She had started to play when she was seven because her mother had thought it might 'come in useful' and her father, a tailor and textile merchant, had paid for lessons by making jackets for her violin teacher. However, she had not played at all since the start of the war and now, overwhelmed by grief for her parents, Violette was reticent about applying for an audition with Alma. Like everyone, she had heard the orchestra play during their morning outing and had watched Hélène Wiernik and Fanny Kornblum, whom she had met in the Belgian transit camp of Mechelen a few weeks before, going to and fro each day to rehearse and play and starting to look more presentable. Finally, Violette summoned up her dwindling courage to give the audition a go.

Bravely, she tried to play Massenet's *Meditation from Thaïs* which she had once learned. Without practice the piece was too hard and she was rejected by Czajkowska, who was still the conductor. A few weeks later, Hélène told Violette that there was a new conductor and that she absolutely had to audition one more time. Summoning up her courage again, she played a catchy gypsy-style tune from an operetta by Hungarian composer Emmerich Kalman called *Countess Maritza* that was not too technically difficult. Violette asked Alma for permission to have half an hour to warm up her fingers by playing scales, hoping that this ritual would convince the others that she was a serious musician. After she finished Alma commented of the piece: 'This isn't famous.' Violette was devastated, assuming she had been rejected again. Instead, Alma said to her: 'Never mind. I'll take you on a trial basis. Maybe it'll improve. You'll have another audition in eight days.'

In this way Alma offered Violette, in whom she had seen a spark of musical desire, if not musical aptitude, a chance to live. Her conditional acceptance in the orchestra was a lifeline, for she passed her second audition. Later, Alma would save her again.

4

You will be saved

Once Alma had shown the Nazis what an orchestra under her direction was capable of, she was addressed by officials, including Maria Mandl, as 'Frau Alma'. This was an unprecedented form of respectful address to a Jewish woman at Auschwitz. Other prisoners in the camp described the near reverence that Mandl, who was six years younger, displayed towards Alma as 'incredible, unbelievable'. A measure of respect even filtered through to the musicians who soon became aware that they were no longer struck at random by female overseers or by SS men, as happened to ordinary prisoners.

The biggest privilege of all was soon revealed: Jewish women in the orchestra who were ill in the Revier were not selected for subsequent gassing. Most of the musicians succumbed to typhus at one time or another and yet almost all were nurtured back to health. According to Rachela Zelmanowicz, the first time one of the musicians was sick with typhus the summer after Alma arrived and sent to the gas chambers 'Alma made a scandal about this! She ran to everyone and said: "Listen you are destroying the orchestra! If there is typhus in the camp and each time you will take one of the girls then" . . . So, an order was issued that it is forbidden to touch the members of the orchestra.'[1]

Dying from typhus was not always preventable. Survival, even with so-called privileges, remained a matter of luck, fate and, most of all, of mutual assistance.

Violette Silberstein was already ill when she was conditionally accepted into the orchestra and was not yet living in the orchestra block. This meant she had to walk there and back. On her first day in September 1943, finding her shoes had been stolen, she had to make the journey barefoot walking on icy mud. When she arrived, Czajkowska, now in charge of keeping the block tidy and no longer playing, immediately ordered her to wash her muddy feet in a tub of cold water used by the musicians specifically to wash mud from their shoes. Violette went through the motions willingly at first but then, suddenly overcome with despair at everything she had lost and the horrors she had seen at the camp, could not stop crying. Soon Alma, together with the orchestra who had been playing at the gate for the departing workers, returned and asked what the matter was. Responding gently, Alma took Violette to the clothing warehouse and had her kitted out with warm clothes, shoes, woollen socks and the musicians' uniform. It was a start. But Violette still could not put aside the pain of her parents' death as well as the pain, now getting worse, in her arm from an infection in her finger. Someone in the camp had advised her that, in the absence of medicine, urinating on it would help. But that made it worse and now Violette was fighting a high fever, a painful inflammation on her arm and the beginning of a deep depression as she felt completely isolated and questioned the purpose of continuing the struggle to live. Then, ten days after being accepted into the orchestra, she caught typhus as well.

Violette spent six weeks in the Revier, at times almost comatose that first autumn. The abscess on her arm was incised but there were no proper bandages to keep the wound clean and rats scurried around in profusion occasionally gnawing at the flesh of a comatose patient. Violette herself was barely able to eat anything. At this early stage in Alma's time as conductor, Jewish orchestra members who fell ill were still vulnerable to selection for the gas chambers. On 3 September a hundred women were selected from within Birkenau and gassed the same day. The following day a convoy of one thousand male and female prisoners arrived from Drancy of whom 762 were gassed on arrival. Somehow, Violette passed the first selection when the Nazi doctors toured the infirmary to see who was too ill to waste time trying to cure them, and a second inspection when she managed to stand, keep her head straight and pull in her abdominal muscles, trying to look strong. Just when she thought she was sinking so low that her depression was dangerously close to taking over, a desire to live kicked in. As she lay ill, Violette reflected on what she would need to do in future.

'She realised that she had to fight like never before; not just anyhow, though and certainly not by trampling anyone in her path,' wrote the son of a fellow camp violinist who interviewed Violette in 1995. She told him how she realised she 'must block out her imagination at all costs in order to distance herself as much as possible from the virtual certainty of her death'.[2]

Weak and thin, she returned to the orchestra on 4 November 1943 – a date she never forgot as it was the wedding anniversary of her murdered parents – determined to survive. For a while Alma assigned her a new role, carrying the stools and music stands to the playing area – *Nach Vorne*, as it was called, because it was near the front of the camp. But these were heavy and Violette was still weak, limping and breathless and unable to keep up with the others. When Franz Hössler, camp commandant, asked Alma who was the girl who looked like a *Musselman* – camp jargon for one so thin and ill they were about to die* – Alma shot back in Violette's defence that she was 'one of my best violinists', thus saving her life for the second time.

'In which case you'd better build her up a bit, put her on the diet for three months,' Hössler replied.[3]

'The diet' was a phrase used to explain extra rations; an extra litre of soup, sweet oatmeal porridge and white bread. Violette believed that the exchange between Alma and Hössler not only gave her crucial additional food but helped cement her position in the orchestra, as from this moment on the inmates who had witnessed the conversation 'showed her their concern'[4] and accepted Violette into their group. Being fully integrated into the orchestra saved her as much as the extra food because she was still frail and afflicted with a severe kidney infection after her bout of typhus. She also suffered from a raging thirst, like many who had barely recovered when they were sent away from the infirmary with little possibility of finding water to slake their thirst.

One night, in desperation, she slipped out of the music block and urinated in the snow. The following morning when block elder Czajkowska saw the mark in the snow she knew it must be from Violette, the one still suffering the after-effects of typhus, too weak to control her bladder. So she gave the invalid a beating. After this incident, Alma took her back into the orchestra itself and placed her in the third desk of violins, where her role was mostly simply to join in on the downbeats and make sure she stuck to the beat. She knew that being here behind better players was not an excuse to slack, for Alma was just as demanding and strict with those at the back of the orchestra and did not allow any wrong notes.

---

* The origin of this description is not clear. According to some explanations it arose because these people were often lying prostrate as if praying.

During the winter of 1943, twenty-two-year-old Rachela Zelmanowicz, the mandolin player from Będzin, was also in the infirmary sick with typhus and certain she was going to die. 'It was very cold and snowing. But I felt so good about the cold wind ... I was so hot because of the fever.'[5]

> We were lying without cover, without clothes, naked and I remember I lay next to another woman and we warmed each other's body ... and when I woke up in the morning, I slept next to a corpse ... and you know it made no impression on me. We were so ... I think that we had a feeling that this is not important: today comes our end and if not today, then tomorrow. It was totally hopeless. Then [Dr Josef] Mengele passed next to me and asked, 'What's with this one?' so they said: 'This is from the Kapelle [the orchestra]' and he continued on his way. He left me alone.[6]

When the hospital decided that Rachela had recovered sufficiently to be discharged, Czajkowska, in her role as block elder, was summoned to take her back to the orchestra. Rachela was so weak that she could not walk unaided and as it was still cold and wet, the ground underfoot was icy.

> I asked her to give me a hand. She didn't want to give me a hand ... I crawled on all fours all the way to the block ... When I arrived at the block she looked at me with disrespect ... so Rivka [Regina Kupferberg, the blue-eyed girl from Będzin who worked as Alma's maid] said, 'Rachela you need now to begin eating.' Slowly, slowly not too much at once, every quarter of an hour she put something in my mouth and this is how slowly my energy returned. We were a group. I mean we were a group based on youth movements.[7]

It is not entirely clear why the older Polish woman treated several of the young Jewish girls with such barely suppressed contempt. Czajkowska, the former teacher, had spent months being brutally tortured in Tarnów prison before being sent to Auschwitz and life in the camp, where violence was the norm, brought out the worst of many in authority. Such behaviour fed into the many stories of Polish failure to understand the particular fear for Jews and made the smaller friendship groups, mostly based on language, even more important for the Jewish players.

Illness constantly stalked the orchestra girls in spite of the small improvements in living standards. Within a week or so of Alma taking over, the elder one of the pair of unmarried German Jewish sisters from Berlin, Helena Croner, a much-needed conservatory-trained violinist aged fifty-eight, succumbed to typhus. She was not 'selected' but died in the infirmary in August 1943 having played in the orchestra for just a matter of weeks.*

Helena and her younger sister Charlotte had arrived in the camp four months earlier, on 29 June, severely weakened having hidden in Berlin together for much of the previous year following the deportation of their mother to Theresienstadt, until they were denounced by informers. Tragically little is known about this pair, who did not form part of any of the sub-groups, probably owing to their age and superior talent. It is not clear how they managed, given their ages, to avoid being gassed immediately on entry to the camp but it was possibly a result of their political status as Jews arrested in hiding, as opposed to those Jews who had reported to the Nazi authorities when they received their

---

* Hitherto this player has always been listed as a cellist called Maria Kroner. Thanks to research by Holocaust historian Bruce Colegrove, it is clear she was Helena, an accomplished violinist who was in fact the elder of the two talented Croner sisters.

deportation notices and who would not be classified as political prisoners, a bizarre anomaly of Nazi procedure that delayed
inevitable gassing especially if there was paperwork involved.
More likely it was because Czajkowska had put out the word that
she needed good musicians and these two were extremely good.
Helena's loss was a terrible blow to her younger sister Charlotte
aged fifty-six (born in 1887), who was often referred to by the
other musicians as Tante Croner, because of her age and her
kind and motherly attitude towards the younger girls, whom
she sometimes helped to make their beds properly. Sometimes
she was called Lola, possibly as a mark of affection. Lola was an
experienced flautist, classically trained with symphony orchestra
experience, who had worked as a private music teacher in Berlin
and was often the butt of jokes in the orchestra for her habit
of nodding off during rehearsals, despite Alma's strictness, and
needing to be poked awake to make her entry on time. She was
now both the oldest member of the orchestra and one of the
quietest, courageously continuing to play without fussing after
the loss of her sister with whom she had lived her entire life, the
last few months in underground conditions of severe deprivation.
But Charlotte Croner, like the other players, had taken to heart
Alma's often-repeated reminder when they played badly that only
the orchestra could keep them alive, and that their privileges
depended on an improvement in playing standards.[8]

As soon as she took over, Alma expanded the orchestra with
violinists, accordion players, guitarists and also vocalists. Among
the latter was Dorys Wilamowska, born in 1910, a German Jew
and classically trained coloratura soprano with a rare ability to
reach particularly high notes and trills. She had studied music,
singing and piano in the Leipzig Conservatorium and became an
exceptional performer. Dora, as she was known, moved to Berlin

around 1930 but after Hitler came to power in 1933, soon found that the opportunities for Jewish musicians to perform were increasingly limited. In 1933 more than 8,000 Jewish musicians and actors in Berlin alone had left Germany of their own accord or been fired from their positions with German orchestras.

Dora joined the *Jüdische Kulturbund* (the Cultural Federation of German Jews), a controversial organisation established by Jews in 1933 in response to the worries of this pool of unemployed Jewish artists. The idea for a specifically Jewish cultural organisation suited the Nazis who used it as a vehicle to show the world that Germany's Jews were not being mistreated while at the same time removing them from mainstream German culture. The *Jüdische Kulturbund* had to be staffed and funded entirely by Jews, only the Jewish press was allowed to review its events and only Jewish members could attend just two events per month. In this way, the Nazis could keep track of the activities of artistic Jews. Although the *Jüdische Kulturbund* enabled some 70,000 artists to eke out a living for a while, Zionists did not support the organisation, believing that as many Jews as possible should leave Germany while they could. Other German Jews believed it was a form of ghettoisation which isolated them from wider German culture.

For Dora, the *Jüdische Kulturbund* provided her only route to continue performing, albeit in front of solely Jewish audiences. For five years, between 1936 and 1941, she regularly toured Germany, performing a wide variety of operatic roles in Hamburg, Leipzig, Berlin and other cities to high acclaim. In 1937 she sang the role of Tatiana in Tchaikovsky's *Eugene Onegin*, which brought her an array of glittering reviews praising her 'magnificent appearance... and her gorgeous voice that gained in differentiation enormously and exceeded the strength of the orchestra effortlessly'.[9]

During this time, Dora developed a relationship with a writer in the *Kulturbund*, Curt Franz Loewy, whom, according to a nephew, she had hoped to marry. However, in 1941 the Nazis abolished the organisation, abruptly ending Dora's singing career, and she was sent to work in a Siemens factory in Berlin as a slave labourer. In September 1943 she was deported to Auschwitz. Dora, already weak after almost two years of long shifts and forced labour at Siemens, never recovered her strength. She fell ill from typhus and was sent to the Revier in November 1943 at the height of a typhus epidemic in the camp when patients were dying every day from lack of medicine or were being selected for gassing. Yet one day that month, when a German official was visiting the camp, she was dragged out of bed because of her extraordinary voice and forced to perform in front of him.

'She did not have enough strength even to stand on her feet and she sang a song by [the Spanish romantic composer Pablo] Sarasate and it was a heartbreaking song,' recalled Rachela, who never forgot Dora's voice but could not name the Gestapo VIP.[10] Dora died, aged thirty-three, days after this final act of forced labour.

Her outstanding talent could not be replicated but Lotte Lebedova, a Czech Jewish singer who was born in Vienna in 1908 and joined in August 1943, and Ewa Stojowska, a beautiful Polish actress and singer who was born in Galicia also in 1908 and came on board in November, did their best. Ewa also worked as a copyist, along with a fellow Pole, Kazimiera Malys, and in addition became the orchestra's librarian, responsible for keeping copies of the various arrangements of the music they played. Ewa's most valuable contribution to the orchestra, however, may have been her deep compassion, which enabled her to bridge the divide between the non-Jewish Polish performers and the other Jewish musicians. Ewa had worked for the Polish underground from 1941 onwards, carrying weapons and documents and hiding several Jews who had managed to get out of the ghetto in her Warsaw apartment. Betrayed by an informer, she was arrested on 17 May 1943, severely tortured in Pawiak prison in Warsaw and deported to Auschwitz. Unlike some of the other Polish women, she made friends easily among the Jewish musicians. As a singer, Ewa was in awe of Alma's creative treatments of operatic tunes and her ability to coach her female singers in ranges traditionally covered by male voices, even though it demanded considerable work for those like Ewa herself who were tasked with the copying and transcribing.

Two French Jewish violinists, Hélène Rounder, born in 1922, and Fanny Rubak, born in 1907, were on the same transport from Drancy to Auschwitz in July 1943. Hélène and Fanny were soon invited to join the orchestra and were both given the epithet 'little' before their names to distinguish them from other players with the same name. Alma was now able to establish a fourth violin section.

Hélène Rounder, the third Hélène (there would have been four if Helena Croner had survived), was an art student at university in Paris and a long-time leader among Communist youth groups who had been constantly active in a resistance group when she was picked up, aged eighteen, in November 1940 for distributing anti-German literature. She endured a short prison term in Paris's La Roquette jail, and as soon as she was released, began distributing anti-collaborationist information again. In June 1942, she was rearrested and this time sent to Fresnes and then to the Nazis' notorious Fort de Romainville internment and transit camp in the northeast Paris suburbs. From there she was sent to Drancy and Auschwitz. She was just twenty-one years old.

'Little' Fanny Rubak, so called to avoid confusion with Fanny Kornblum, the Belgian mandolin player pushed to apply by her mother, had been working as a cinema violinist in Paris and was picked up after being denounced by a neighbour for not wearing the compulsory yellow star.

In September, soon after taking over, Alma decided she could use another accordion player in addition to Lili Assael from Salonika, with whom she had an uneasy relationship. Also, Esther Loewy, the pianist from Saarlouis who had taught herself the accordion, was forced to give up while she was so ill, first with typhus then with whooping cough, during the summer and autumn of 1943. Places in the orchestra were now talked about in the camp as something so highly prized, a kommando where you had a chance to survive, that auditions were oversubscribed. When news spread around the camp that Alma was looking for a new accordionist, around 150 women in Birkenau claimed that they could play the instrument, a 'long list' which Alma narrowed down to a shortlist of just three.

From these, with great difficulty, she chose a pretty Dutch woman with a fair complexion and a big smile, Flora Jacobs. Just nineteen the previous June, Flora had arrived at the camp on 9 September 1943.

Flora came from a musical background; her father, who owned a textile shop in Amsterdam, had been a member of the Amsterdam Philharmonic who played the trumpet and double bass and had once performed with Alma as soloist. After paying for several years of piano lessons for his daughter, he insisted in 1939 that she undertook training on the accordion, learning popular songs. But Flora had only spent six months learning the instrument before the Nazis invaded the Netherlands in May 1940 and started rounding up Jews for deportation. Flora and her family, now issued with identity cards stamped with a 'J', could not go out beyond the Jewish quarter. In the winter of 1942–3 Flora bought herself a forged card which enabled her to go on the run, staying at various different addresses with an invented

Flora Jacobs, the Dutch accordionist

story. Using this card, she sought refuge with a Dutch woman who had two German soldiers also billeted on her who wanted to take Flora on a dinner date. Thinking quickly, Flora pretended that she had a fiancé serving with the SS at the front. 'But the ground got too hot under my feet there.'[11] She returned home to her parents but in February 1943 they were all arrested and taken to Westerbork, the Dutch holding camp where approximately 100,000 Dutch Jews, gypsies and political prisoners passed through, most on their way to be killed at Auschwitz and other extermination camps.

While at Westerbork Flora agreed with little enthusiasm – 'our characters did not match'[12] – to marry a German Jew, Emmanuel van Praag, because, according to Flora, he believed, in desperation, that perhaps if she married him he would stand a better chance of remaining in the Netherlands and not being transported. Marriage to a Dutch woman did not in fact help him as they were all taken to Auschwitz. Her new husband and mother were gassed on arrival, while her father was killed six months later. She did not then know the fate of her only sister, Beppie, who had gone into hiding but was subsequently taken to Sobibor and killed.

Flora stayed in the quarantine block for almost two months after her arrival. 'I had all the sicknesses you can think of, typhus and what not,' she recalled in a 1983 interview.[13] 'I could have lived only four or five more days... other inmates told me I would die or be the victim of the next selection if I didn't do something.'

At that point Franz Hössler, by now a keen advocate of the orchestra having seen the success Alma was making of it, came into the block asking who played music.

'I said I played piano. He said no, no piano.' Later Flora said that 'even if I was a doctor, I'd have said I was a musician'.[14]

But another girl went over to Hössler, having extracted from Flora that she could in fact play the accordion. Flora, despite feeling weak, hungry and underqualified, desperately wanted to survive so she agreed to go off to an audition in her uncomfortable stripey dress. While she knew she was not a good player, she hoped her general musicality would help.

Learning that she had won a place in the fabled Block 12, years later Flora said she understood this was her 'doorway to life'. But at the same time, she felt sorry for Alma having to make such a hard choice, especially as she had played 'fabulously out of tune' and those Alma sent away were probably doomed to die.

When she took on Flora, Alma agreed to give her extra help and training on the accordion, explaining that she had a special love and respect for the Dutch people who had looked after her so well before her final attempt to flee.[15]

From time to time, Maria Mandl came to discuss with Alma how the recruitment process was going. As she attempted to find competent musicians to fill gaps in the playing ranks, Alma became increasingly concerned that her Nazi bosses would not allow the orchestra to be top heavy with Jews. So she was grateful to have found in early October 1943 a non-Jewish violinist of the calibre of Helena Dunicz. Helena, born in 1915, was an experienced musician who loved teaching and playing for pleasure. She had played in the Lwów Youth Symphony in 1934, had passed her exams in violin and music theory at the Polish Musical Society Conservatory in 1939, had a degree in pedagogy from the Jan Kazimierz University and was building a reputation as a private violin teacher in Lwów when she was seized with her mother in January 1943. She was a serious-minded Catholic girl who had grown up in a middle-class household where her two brothers and mother regularly played family quartets. When war broke out one brother immediately left Poland to pursue his chemistry studies in England, a dangerous journey that involved crossing icy rivers wading up to his neck; another had joined the Polish resistance while her father was in hospital dying of cancer in June 1940. This left Helena and her mother Maria alone in the family apartment with various lodgers billeted on them.

In June 1941 the situation in Lwów, a city with some 200,000 Jewish inhabitants at the time, changed dramatically when Nazi occupiers replaced the Soviets, and it became Lemberg. They were all in grave danger and Helena recalled how one of the little Jewish boys to whom she had given violin lessons at the time of the Soviets now came knocking at her door asking her to conceal his valuable violin. She never knew what happened either to the violin or the boy and his family.

Mother and daughter were arrested at dawn one freezing cold morning in January 1943 by German Gestapo officers who burst into their apartment after receiving a tip-off. Apparently, Helena and Maria had been implicated in their lodger's activity in the Lwów underground. They were taken away to be interrogated by the SS and forbidden from talking to each other on the way. Before the interrogation began the pair were ordered to strip naked. Helena recalled in the memoir she published in 2014: 'it completely paralyzed Mama and me to have to stand naked in the presence of men. This unimaginably embarrassing situation left us feeling even more humiliated, defenceless and dumbfounded.'[16]

For Helena, this was the deepest and most overwhelming feeling of abasement and shame that she had ever experienced. Her love for and inability to protect her mother became the leitmotif of her life from then on. After nine months in Lacki, the local Polish prison, mixing with Jews, Ukrainians and other Poles, plagued by head lice, hunger and boredom, they were finally transported on 30 September 1943 by cattle car into the unknown. Helena and her mother, already in extremely poor health before the seventy-two-hour hellish journey, tried to stay together when they finally arrived at Auschwitz.

They were marched into a barrack, locked in for another night with nothing to eat or drink and scrabbled around for a dirty blanket and space on a plank of wood or what passed as a bunk bed. At dawn another day of harassment and humiliation began with the complete shaving of their heads, as well as all body hair, a shower in water that was alternately scalding hot or freezing cold, further nudity as male prisoners swabbed their private parts, followed by a long wait to be given the camp rags that were described as clothing. After this they were tattooed and realised, like so many prisoners, that in this single act their humanity had been removed. At this precise moment Helena was told by the Polish woman registering her in the camp about an all-women orchestra, information she found 'electrifying'.[17] From the depths of desperation, she wondered if she 'might have a chance' to survive. She remembered learning at school how banished musicians were always a little better off in Siberian exile.

But what about her mother?

'We'll come up with something,' responded the prisoner registering her, a Pole called Maria Swiderska who was a friend of another Pole, Wisia (Jadwiga) Zatorska, the former kindergarten teacher she had got to know during their time together in the women's military training organisation pre-war.

In her memoir, Helena wrote in unsparing detail about conditions in Block 25, the death block where she and her mother had been sent to begin their enforced quarantine and which most did not survive for more than twenty-four hours. For a few months this most appalling of prison barracks was also used as a holding pen for new arrivals and the sick. SS *Unterscharführer* Adolf Taube was in charge and if, occasionally, anyone tried to escape he would ensure they were beaten to death. The two Dunicz women could neither wash nor visit a latrine other than in public and then only when allowed. Like all the prisoners, they had no paper nor towels, and sleep was almost impossible on an overcrowded and broken wooden bunk that was placed on a damp cement block with no mattress and only a louse-ridden grey blanket. They felt dirty and repulsive and certain that they could not survive this hell. Not many did.

And yet, when, after just three days, her number was read out calling her for an audition – Swiderska had forwarded her name – even though she was mentally and physically exhausted, feeling debased, and desperately concerned for her mother, Helena's instinct for survival took over. She realised later how strange it was that this thought was dominant, since being in such a hellish place precluded her from thinking clearly.

'At the time, however, I was not conscious of the infernal ends served by the making of music in a German concentration camp. I did not know that we would be forced to play against a background of flames and black smoke billowing from the crematorium chimneys.'[18]

She was taken to Block 12 for an audition where 'to my great amazement, I was brought before Alma Rosé. I recognised her at once. Before the war I had attended a concert in Lwów where she and her husband Váša had given a masterful performance of the Bach Double Violin Concerto. Her playing made a great impression on me as did her career and her exceptional beauty. Now, her dark hair growing back was speckled with grey.'

Alma handed Helena a violin, placed a score on the music stand, 'and I began playing, an examination for my life'. Despite feeling intimidated and weak, and conscious that she had not played for months, Helena easily performed well enough for Alma to immediately accept her into the orchestra. From then on she would mostly be known as Halina, to differentiate her from the other two Hélènes in the orchestra.

Separated from her beloved mother, Helena's success was bittersweet. When she was allowed a week or so later to move permanently to Block 12, she could not bring herself to say goodbye to her mother. Both were too emaciated and emotional. Helena had arrived as a rehearsal was already underway, and Alma wasted no time in motioning her to sit in the first desk alongside the Belgian concertmaster Hélène Wiernik, eleven years younger than her. Helena thus replaced Wisia, who had been the second violinist up until now.

Wisia did not make a fuss about her demotion. On the contrary, Wisia 'took me under her wing', recalled Helena, as a fellow non-Jewish Pole with seniority from the length of time she had been at Auschwitz. Helena and Wisia, together with Zosia Cykowiak, the former Polish resistance member, formed a tight-knit Polish friendship group who sustained each other. A devout Catholic, Helena Dunicz acquired a reputation as a peacemaker and thoughtful consoler who occasionally tried to bridge the Polish-Jewish divide. She later regretted she had not done more.

Another addition to the orchestra in the summer of 1943 was Margot Anzenbacherová. Born in 1915, Margot was an active Communist, poet and linguist who had been arrested with her husband Karel in Pilsen, Bohemia in 1942 for distributing anti-Nazi leaflets. She endured torture in a number of prisons before arriving in June 1943 at Auschwitz, where she was registered as a political Jew number 46155. Her numbered triangle meant she would not normally be subject to gassing, despite being Jewish, but was no guarantee if her health failed.

A native Czech speaker, Margot was also a gifted linguist, fluent in German and English with some knowledge of other languages too. She had worked as a language teacher in Pilsen and her linguistic fluency helped her survive in the camp and to straddle the various groups in the orchestra. As a child, she had had early violin lessons and played the guitar. But she never imagined that her modest musical talents would be enough to save her life; and so, once she was given her flimsy clothes, including wooden shoes and trousers held up with string, she submitted to being assigned to an outdoor kommando.

She described her work in a 1979 written account. 'One stood all day in water,' Margot recalled. 'When my foot was injured I was ordered... to get pails and bale out the latrines into carts and pull them away. It was hell.'[19]

'A saving grace was that I was allowed to give out the food.

Because I gave big portions the food did not go around. For this the barrack worker hit me on the head. Then I got jaundice. I stopped eating the little I received. Then I was sent to the *strafkommando* [the punishment detail].' For many this signalled the end and Margot feared that she might never emerge from the camp alive.

Margot told how her luck changed. She watched one day as an SS dog was eating a piece of bread and tried to speak gently to him.

I said to him: 'Do you know that I am not angry with you? You are doing what you are trained for... give me a piece of bread.' He didn't give it to me but watched my every movement as I sat down in front of him. I reached out my hand talking to him quietly and slowly. Finally, I patted him on the head. The SS was watching me. One of them pulled out his revolver. I thought this was my end. Then the dog was ordered to go. The SS man shot the dog. He ignored me.

Unable to make sense of what she had just witnessed, the episode made Margot, who was in constantly worsening health, so miserable that her friends told her she must at least try out for the orchestra. Alma agreed to audition her as a violinist, and although Margot did not play well, Alma said she could have an eight-day trial in the music block. Margot's hands were by now so badly damaged from hard labour that she could barely hold the violin she was given from the music store. She was sure she would fail her probationary period and was sitting alone during a rest break one day, rueing her fate, when she spotted a guitar. After tuning it, Margot started to play quietly.

'Alma emerged and said "that sounds nice. You know notes and something of music and you know languages..." she accepted me into the orchestra.'[20] And so, two months after arriving at Auschwitz, Margot was given a role in the orchestra playing guitar as well as working at the copy table and composing poetry to be sung. 'When we played Dvořák it seemed Alma was looking at me and in another world. She must have thought the music had a special significance for me and for her and her former husband Váša – when he practised and she would accompany him on the piano or playing with her father.'[21]

Margot became one of the few musicians who was relatively close to Alma, possibly because of her Czech background or because she was useful as an interpreter. Across the orchestra, her mellow personality and linguistic abilities made Margot one of the most popular members. She gave English lessons to some of the musicians, including Helena, even if these had to be fitted into a few minutes before afternoon rehearsals. Helena recalled that she took notes on whatever scraps of paper she could find – usually wrapping paper from parcels or in the margins of letters. All the while, Margot was struggling with a haunting guilt about her job in the orchestra, and only just managing to hold off an emotional breakdown.

'The reaction of most prisoners forced to listen to light music was negative,' according to Margot speaking in 1999.[22] 'They thought it was cynical in such a tragic situation, as I did before joining the orchestra. It was annoying being forced to march to the music. One day we had to play in front of a block and we played Hungarian pieces and a woman screamed that we should be ashamed of playing Hungarian music. HER music, that she had listened to when she was free and now she was a prisoner.'[23]

Margot finished her account by saying that what kept her going was the determination to survive 'so I can bear witness' but admitted that she still, fifty years later, had nightmares she was back in Auschwitz playing with the orchestra.[24]

In late 1943, Alma heard about the arrival of a teenage German Jewish cellist, a potentially vital piece of good fortune for the orchestra, which had no bass instruments at all. Anita Lasker was sent to Auschwitz under unusual circumstances which bizarrely saved her from being instantly gassed. She arrived as a criminal not a Jew, a piece of Nazi bureaucracy which she never forgot. In July 1941 Anita had celebrated her sixteenth birthday in her hometown of Breslau, then part of Germany, now Wroclaw in Poland. Despite the war, Anita recalled that she was given presents including an art history book, soap and a pair of socks. 'In the afternoon we played quartets.'[25]

The youngest of three daughters, Anita was born in 1925 into an assimilated middle-class Jewish family. Her father Alfons was a lawyer, while her mother Edith was a fine amateur violinist and all three girls played an instrument.

' "Culture" was a very important part of our lives,' Anita recalled in 2015.

> We read the classics every Saturday afternoon, a great deal of chamber music was played in our home and we were brought up speaking French. In fact, there was a rule in our house that on Sundays French only had to be spoken. My father maintained that people have as many souls as they have languages. Life seemed normal and it was inconceivable that it should not continue to be so.[26]

From an early age, it was clear that Anita was an extremely talented cellist. However, her cello lessons ended when she was twelve, because there were no Jewish cello teachers left in Breslau and it had become too dangerous for an 'Aryan' cellist to teach a Jewish child. With some difficulties, her parents got permission for Anita to leave school and go to Berlin, where she had a small amount of private tuition in school subjects and music lessons with one of the few remaining Jewish cello teachers in the German capital. Leo Rostal, blacklisted at the time, was grateful for the income, but he was not Pablo Casals, the teacher Anita dreamed of.

It is possible that this extraordinarily courageous decision to send a child to live alone in 1938 in a strange city ultimately helped save Anita's life, making her wise and resilient beyond her years. 'I enjoyed my cello lessons very much and had a good friend in my teacher. I learned a lot from him, smoking included,' Anita remembered.[27] Yet while she was in Berlin, the world situation deteriorated dramatically for Jews. Rostal did not suffer personally from the terrifying destruction of Kristallnacht in November 1938. Nonetheless, he decided he had to leave Germany and managed to emigrate to America.

So Anita returned home, where she found her distraught parents now unable to emigrate, having left it too late. They were desperately pinning all hopes on Marianne, their eldest daughter who had managed to get out just in time, in June 1939, weeks before war was declared. Marianne had trained as a carpenter, considered a useful skill in Palestine where she hoped to make her home, but instead found herself stranded in London for the duration of the war. Her mother wrote begging her to 'do everything in your power to help us'.[28]

They soon gave up hoping for their own emigration but painfully concentrated all their efforts on trying to help their younger daughters, now fifteen and thirteen, and wrote a series of frantic letters to Marianne.

'If only there was a little hope for Anita and Renate ... it would be so wonderful if Anita could get her longed-for tuition with Casals,' Edith wrote the following month.[29]

Reading these letters today, filed in London's Imperial War

Museum, provides a sharp reminder of the desperation faced by so many German Jewish families in 1939. Renate was on the cusp of leaving Breslau to live with the family of a British clergyman, the Fishers, found thanks to Marianne's connections, and there were vague plans for Anita to go to Paris which came to nothing. Anita's father wrote a letter to the Reverend Fisher on 12 August 1939, explaining that since his daughter would not be able to bring any money with her, his wife would make the necessary school uniform dress in advance in Germany. But it was tragically all too late. War broke out in Germany on 1 September 1939.

Life became immediately more precarious with the introduction of ration cards – stamped with a J for Jews – the moment war was declared and with shopping hours for Jews restricted too. Even then, Anita's father did not give up hope of emigrating and 'we were buoyed up by these false hopes for a considerable time... right up to April or May 1940', Anita wrote.[30] But once direct communication with England had ceased it was clearly impossible to expect Marianne could extricate either of her sisters from Germany.

Meanwhile Anita continued with lessons in harmony and played occasional quartets with her mother and other Jewish musicians even after the Laskers had been forced to move out of the family home and lodge uncomfortably with relatives. And for a few months in 1940 she was able to return to some form of schooling, trying hard to catch up, having missed the last two years of formal education. In April 1941 she wrote to Marianne that she had recently given four concerts – 'twice I even had to play an encore'. But there would be no more of these as her school was now closed down.

In 1941, once compulsory war work for Jewish children was introduced, Renate was given a job working at a rubbish tip sorting dead rats from empty tin cans. She was then transferred to a paper factory, considered a useful occupation for unskilled children, and within a few months sixteen-year-old Anita joined her there.

As she wrote to Marianne: 'I'm sticking labels on about 5000 rolls daily, working in two shifts, 6–2 and 2–10 and have a journey of approximately one hour. Renate is working in a different department: napkins.' The long hours they had to work and the distance they had to travel meant that it was almost impossible for Renate and Anita to get to any food shops during the hours permitted for Jews.

On 9 April 1942, while they were both working at the factory, their parents were deported. Anita and Renate wanted to go too when the letter arrived demanding that Alfons and Edith present themselves at the assembly point, prior to deportation, even though the girls' names were not on the list.

'Where we are going you get there soon enough,' Anita's father said resignedly. And then he told her that he was counting on her.

'All is now over and done with,' Anita wrote drily to her older sister in England.[31] 'I am aware of the fact that on the night of 8–9th April I took on responsibility not only for the rent and the gas but for something much bigger. Especially because Renate was asleep at the time and I was alone. Do you fully understand? That night was decisive for me although I only became conscious of its real significance much later.'[32]

The two younger sisters were now entirely alone. As they were still minors with no one to care for them, the tiny remnant of the Jewish community in Breslau decided that they should be moved to an orphanage and continue their compulsory work at the paper factory from there. The factory workforce now included a large number of French prisoners of war and in their desperation, the Lasker girls could not fail to be aware of clandestine activities – which involved forging identity papers – being carried out. Old beyond their years, the girls decided to forge their own travel papers. 'We took the decision that we would attempt to make a run for it ourselves and try and reach the unoccupied zone of France,' Anita remembered. 'It was a desperate step and, needless to say, it did not succeed.'[33]

As they were about to board a train at the main station in Breslau, which would, they hoped, have taken them out of Germany and into the unoccupied zone of France, they were arrested by the Gestapo and taken to the local prison.

It was late at night by the time they arrived at the jail. 'Luckily for us, the Gestapo showed their total incompetence once again because they did not instruct the prison staff to put us in separate cells. That meant that we had all night to plan how we would handle the Gestapo interrogation we were expecting the next morning.'[34]

The girls realised, after several days in a tiny cell with two other female prisoners and just one bucket between them, how miserably unhappy and frightened they were. Days passed into weeks with nothing more than half an hour a day for exercise. Yet gradually they became accustomed to their situation and the uncertainty of not knowing what was to happen to them next.

Writing in 1996, Anita said that 'it never ceases to amaze me that the human species is capable of adjusting to almost anything. Even when you are locked into a small, stinking cell suffering hunger and acute discomfort, a sort of routine emerges which you can start to live by. Your horizon merely contracts. Although I thought at first I could never survive prison life, in fact I stood it extremely well. What is more to the point, later on, when I became a concentration camp dweller, I was to look back on my time in prison as I would today on a very enjoyable holiday.'[35] While awaiting trial, the girls were given work painting toy soldiers. Anita and Renate enjoyed the visits from Miss Neubert, the woman who brought them supplies to work on as well as a glimpse of ordinary life and great moral support. At the bottom of Miss Neubert's basket Anita sometimes found bread and once even a cake.

In June 1943, after almost a year in prison, the sisters were finally brought to trial, charged on three counts: forgery, aiding the enemy and attempted escape. They were calm for they knew they could not possibly be acquitted, as nineteen-year-old Renate commented to Anita at the time. The best they could hope for was further delay before being sent to a camp. They had no illusions as to the outcome for Jews on the transports because prisoners sent back from Auschwitz to Breslau prison for further interrogation confirmed rumours of the gas chambers.

Looking back, Anita now believes that a former colleague of her father must have intervened to ensure they could stay in prison and await trial. 'Every day NOT spent in a concentration camp was a day gained. Prison is not the most wonderful place to be, but nobody murders you there,' Anita wrote laconically in her memoirs.[36]

The trial was a farce and the girls were both sentenced to a further period of protective custody, only now they were separated. Renate was sent to Jauer penitentiary in lower Silesia while Anita spent almost five more months alone in Breslau prison until she was summoned to sign a document declaring she was going to Auschwitz 'voluntarily'. She was given civilian clothes and duly awaited transportation.

Anita's arrival at the camp was unlike that of other deported prisoners as she was sent in a train which was fitted out with a locked police cell. She arrived late at night and remembered – as everyone did – the black figures in capes, dogs barking and a great deal of shouting. The critical difference from the Jewish transports was that there was no selection at the station. She was with a handful of other prisoners who were all the subject of court cases and had to serve prison sentences. 'That classified us as . . . prisoners with a file. This status meant that we could not be sent straight to the gas chamber, allegedly so that we could be available in case we received a summons to reappear in court. Clearly it was better then to arrive in Auschwitz as a convicted criminal than as an innocent citizen.'

At dawn the next day, a cold December morning, she was treated to the usual traumatic indignities. Anita was stripped, shaved and tattooed with the number 69388. She realised she had been deprived not just of her clothes 'but of every vestige of human dignity and become indistinguishable from everyone around me'.[37]

During registration in the sauna delousing block, the prisoner who was processing her bombarded her with questions. First the girl asked for Anita's shoes, which she said would be taken from her in any case. Seeing she had no choice, and not imagining how fortuitous the gift would be, Anita handed them over. As she did so she told the girl that she played the cello, 'a superfluous piece of information under the circumstances'.[38]

The girl's response was immediate and unexpected. 'That is fantastic,' she said. 'You will be saved.' She told Anita to wait where she was. Still naked but grasping a toothbrush, Anita worried she might be standing in a gas chamber about to be killed. Instead, she was greeted by a well-dressed, handsome woman in a camel hair coat with a headscarf.

'I had no idea who she could be. Was she a guard or a prisoner? She was so well dressed that I was absolutely baffled. She introduced herself as Alma Rosé and said she was simply delighted that I was a cellist and asked me where I came from and who I had studied with and so on. The whole thing was like a dream.'

'Again she too said: "you will be saved." But she said I could not come immediately. I would have to have an audition and until that time I had to return to the quarantine block.' Anita recalled that 'very fortunately' her wait was quickly over. In early December 1943 the energetic Franz Hössler came in person to call for 'the cellist' to attend her audition.

Being known as 'the cellist' rather than a number was key to restoring Anita's sense of her humanity and that her life was still worth living. 'I had not melted away into the grey mass of name-less indistinguishable people.'[39] For her audition she played both the slow movement of the Boccherini Concerto and then, with the orchestra, Schubert's *Marche Militaire*, a piece that was well within her grasp and which she quickly came to detest. She had not played at all for around two years, but she understood there was no real danger of her not passing the audition because Alma and the other players were so desperate for a bass instrument. The day after, she moved into the music block and started to make friends, trying her best to answer all their myriad questions about the outside world.

One more factor played a role in Anita's ability to focus on staying alive with a shred of self-respect: her sister Renate. She had given up hope of ever seeing Renate again after she was taken from the prison at Breslau. However, almost a week after Anita's arrival at Auschwitz the sisters were reunited in the strangest of ways.

On her arrival in the camp with a group of prisoners from Jauer penitentiary, Renate had noticed that the girl registering her was in possession of some very distinctive pigskin shoes, dyed black with red laces. Since she was not wearing them, she was probably hoping to barter them. Renate, convinced she recognised them, asked where they came from. The girl said that they had belonged to someone who had only recently arrived in the

camp who was a musician. Renate knew immediately this must
be Anita, who on seeing how the girl processing her coveted
the shoes, and figuring she was going to lose them anyway, had
willingly handed them over. Given the vast size of Birkenau and
the numbers coming through the whole time, this coincidence
was 'truly a miracle', as Anita wrote later. 'The same girl came
running into the block and asked me to come immediately to the
Reception Block with her. She said: "I think your sister is here."
I raced over and there she was. It was incredible.'[40] Renate was
in extremely poor health and deteriorated rapidly once she had
to go into the quarantine block. Although being together once
again gave the girls an added incentive to live for each other,
Anita could see that her sister was unlikely to survive if she stayed
there much longer.

> Renate became a total wreck in no time at all. It was horrify-
> ing. Her appearance and general state were so bad that she
> was not allowed to enter our block. So she came and stood
> outside and waited for me to give her some soup or whatever
> else I could give her. She developed huge festering sores on
> her legs which would not heal caused by a lack of vitamins.
> And then she caught typhus.
> There were times when I hoped she might quietly die so
> that her misery would be brought to an end. It was awful
> watching her sinking.[41]

Renate was moved to the Revier where somehow she survived
typhus, only to emerge looking worse than before. Then Anita
had an extremely risky idea. She saw Maria Mandl and asked
if her sister could become a *Läuferin*, a messenger. She staked
everything on the fact that, as the much-needed cellist in Mandl's

Anita Lasker aged about thirteen in Berlin where she
was studying the cello with Leo Rostal

beloved orchestra, she was irreplaceable and therefore she would
not be punished for daring to ask.

She was correct in her assessment. Mandl listened to her
politely, asked which block she was in and, shortly afterwards,
Renate was duly appointed an official messenger, which meant
slightly improved rations and better housing.

According to Richard Newman, Anita did something else to
ensure her sister's survival: she 'organised' medicine for Renate
with the help of a man called Henry Meyer who came from
Breslau like the Laskers and was now in Auschwitz. Meyer, along
with Michel Assael – the musical brother of Lili and Yvette –
was part of a work kommando whose job was to push a wagon

around the camp collecting and delivering. They also played in the men's orchestra, and so were able to ensure that the medicine was delivered to Renate via Anita and the music block, even though the men were forbidden from entering the women's camp. Renate slowly recovered and survived.

5

The orchestra means life

The orchestra under Alma quickly became more international with Polish, German, Austrian, Ukrainian, Russian, French, Belgian, Greek, Czech and Dutch members. Despite her attempts at recruiting players of a higher standard, there were never more than about five or six 'true' musicians. As Anita Lasker saw it, the only prerequisite for being part of this extraordinary troupe was 'that you had some more or less remote idea how to hold or play an instrument. Any excuse was good enough to attempt to rescue as many people as possible and bring them to this relative haven. Some people who could not really play at all were taken in.' This broad range of ability meant that Alma had to drill some of the weaker players daily, almost note by note, and to arrange pieces so that the stronger players dominated; her determination to make this an orchestra of quality never wavered. The work was demanding, especially for Alma, who threw herself into the enterprise, usually working long into the night – a rare 'privilege' for which she also needed special permission as it required her light to remain on.

This wide musical divide between the players was not the only challenge. There were many smaller friendship groups, usually formed around a shared language, within the one larger orchestral unit. Alma gave her musical instructions in German, which most players somehow managed to interpret. But the most painful divide and the hardest to bridge was always that between the Jews of various nationalities and the Polish non-Jews. The simple fact that Jews and non-Jews were living together in one dedicated block – the only such block inside Auschwitz – made the viability of the orchestra astonishing.

Anti-Semitism in pre-war Poland was a deeply rooted part of mainstream culture, combining both religious and political origins. Among Catholics there were still those who saw Jews as the Christ killers and at the same time a growing number of Polish nationalists who saw the large and vibrant Jewish community, swollen to 3.4 million on the eve of war, as an existential threat. Poland, as the country with the largest concentration of Jews in Europe, became fertile ground for right-wing Polish nationalist groups such as the *Endecja* movement, who were both openly anti-Semitic as well as anti-Nazi. This apparently confusing attitude was reflected by some of the Christian musicians in the women's orchestra who had been arrested for their work saving Jews, yet nonetheless, when forced to live alongside them, believed that when misunderstandings arose over food or jokes it was because of 'the attitude of the Jews'.[2] This age-old prejudice against Jews was reinforced by brutal Nazi attitudes to Jews, for example when there was a selection from inside the camp and those condemned were sent to Block 25, the so-called death block, to starve until their time for gassing, Nazi guards explained: 'They were killing Jews because they said that the Jews were responsible, that they caused the war.'[3] Dr Lingens-Reiner later testified that in the infirmary non-Jews criticised doctors for giving precious medication to Jewish patients who were 'going to die anyway'.[4]

Hilde Grünbaum, the German violinist who worked as a copyist, described additional strains even between the Jewish musicians due to religious, cultural or linguistic difficulties. The most extreme example was the way the Greek Jews, who did not speak German or Yiddish but the archaic Ladino, similar to but not at all the same as Spanish, felt cut off from the Ashkenazi Jews. 'There were atheists, Communists, devout persons and Zionists among us. The Russians wanted to go back to Russia, the Poles wished for an ever-independent Poland. Everyone lived with her own world view and was convinced she was right.'[5]

Non-Jewish Polish teacher Eugenia Marchiewicz, not in the orchestra, recalled 'Jews from the Warsaw ghetto hated Alma because she was an assimilated Jew and because she was like a German Jew, who they said was more German than Jew',[6] her status as Kapo inevitably making her appear to some as part of the German infrastructure although she was in fact Austrian. Alma's ability to keep these and other simmering tensions under control for performances makes her achievement even more remarkable. When it was a matter connected with the orchestra and the music they played she could be a stern disciplinarian who forbade any emotional response to the constant murder and suffering they witnessed. Yet it was also noted by several musicians that she hated arguments so would retreat to her cubicle room rather than confront a dispute head on.

'She had lots of migraines,' Hélène Wiernik remembered. 'I wondered if she had a tumour. She had her own room, well a "*chambrette*", and often had to go and lie down there if she was unwell. We were really frightened as to how the orchestra would manage without her.'[7]

Much of the ill feeling in Block 12 revolved around food parcels, which the Polish women shared among themselves. They had a separate corner of the dormitory with their own table, which the Russians and Ukrainians also used. The Jews were not allowed to receive parcels, even if they had anyone left at home to send them provisions, so it was especially painful to watch and smell these extras being enjoyed by their fellow musicians. 'The sight and smell of unattainable food did not enhance friendly relations. I remember only two Poles who ever spoke to us,' said Anita.[8] One of them was the singer Ewa Stojowska, and the other was the percussionist Danka Kollakowa.

This attitude arose partly from the belief among the Poles that the Jews had contacts with women prisoners working in the various Auschwitz warehouses, collectively called Kanada, from where they could obtain extra food. By December 1943 Kanada was an area of the camp near the crematorium which comprised thirty wooden buildings used for sorting through the stolen and abandoned possessions of those arriving at the camp. Most items of any use or value were sent back to Germany, but that still left plenty in the warehouses. Working in Kanada was a prized job for the thousand or so women prisoners who could theoretically steal objects for bartering, especially food. But it was a risky enterprise and by no means a source of regular additional nourishment.

Helena Dunicz was emphatic, even as late as 2014 when she wrote her memoirs, that the barrier between Jews and Poles in the orchestra resulted from the behaviour of the Jews.

> They had close contacts with the prisoners working in Kanada, the majority of whom were Jewish. From them they could obtain better clothing, undergarments and even cosmetics thanks to which through the barter system they could 'organise' additional food for themselves – bread, potatoes, carrots, onions and so on. Having no contacts in Kanada I had to make something like hairpins for myself out of metal E strings when my hair grew back and started getting in my eyes...

we could hardly fail to note the luxury goods from Kanada that the Jewish women had and additionally the behaviour of some of them struck us as somewhat haughty and aloof.[9]

Helena's feelings about Jewish behaviour reveal deeply rooted prejudice on all sides. However badly she may have wanted to build bridges, she did not succeed. She was well aware of the tensions between Polish Christians and Jews but insisted that its foundation was not anti-Semitism, 'rather it was the brutal strength of hunger that in the German camp defeated the ideal of universal solidarity, humanity and empathy'.[10]

Anita commented 'There was an assumption on the part of the Jews that they [the Poles] were all anti-Semitic. I found out later the terrible stories of their suffering.' She elaborated in an interview with me at her home in 2023: 'Why should you share with people you can barely speak to? I understand it. It was a matter of survival.'[11] Almost fifty years after the war Anita and Helena began exchanging letters. Only then did the two women recognise how much more they had in common than divided them. Both came from upper middle-class families where playing music was prized. But living in such an unnatural hell perverted normal responses and made it easier for prejudice to flourish. Helena regretted she had not done more in the camp to remove barriers but insisted she had been timid from birth 'and horrified in the camp'.[12]

Helena saw herself as a quiet intellectual who had failed to live up to her own high expectations but, like most Auschwitz survivors, also maintained it was impossible for anyone who was not there to make sense of what went on in the camp. 'It is connected with great stresses and with the feeling that the inter-locutors don't understand and don't enquire sufficiently deeply our pronouncements. My German or English is not rich enough to express all my thoughts and feelings and, after all, I don't want to exhibit my deepest experiences.'[13]

Also writing to Anita in the early 1990s, the Polish violinist 'Zosia' Cykowiak said how she looked forward to 'an occasion when they could meet to talk frankly and explain the misunder-standings which in that time could have [taken] place because of language barriers. I think it could allow us now, from the perspective of [decades] to find much in common in the way of living through that painful experience which Auschwitz has been for us.'[14]

Inevitably with such a diverse mixture of women, there were often heated discussions about what was happening elsewhere in the camp and what, if anything, were their own responsibilities in these circumstances. Like all Jewish prisoners at Auschwitz, the Jewish orchestra players also worried about their own relatives who had most likely been gassed on arrival.

Occasionally the women discussed the future and what they would do if they survived. The Zionist group focused on what was happening in the rest of Europe and where, if they survived, they hoped to live. Hilde Grünbaum, the German violinist who had stayed behind in Germany to support her mother in prison and turned down a chance to get to Palestine pre-war, was the leader of this group. She did her best to organise a weekly celebra-tion of the Sabbath initially for the girls from the Hakhshara, the Zionist pioneering agricultural training programme, now in Auschwitz. But the group also included Rachela, the mandolin player, and Regina, Alma's factotum, both from Będzin, as well as the Wagenberg sisters, Carla and Sylvia, both recorder players from Germany.

During these gatherings Hilde read excerpts from books she had managed to obtain in the camp, either German literature including *Faust* or Rilke poems or quotes from *Ethics of the*

Fathers, a book of Jewish wise sayings and advice on behaviour and relationships. Hilde also wrote down prayers in a small calendar given to her by her friend Anneliese Borinski. Four years older than Hilde, Anneliese, another German Jewish girl from Berlin, had been a counsellor at the Hakhshara farm in Ahrensdorf. The girls were deported to Auschwitz together and Anneliese managed to get a job in the camp laundry and then in a sewing room, where she survived partly by sewing dolls for the camp's female SS staff. Hilde, who had access to paper as a copyist in the orchestra, gave Anneliese a small notebook in which she secretly wrote about life in the camp while using some of the paper herself to make pretend candles to light on the sabbath. These get-togethers strengthened the morale of the group. It kept alive their hopes of surviving to realise their Zionist dream at the end of the war by eventually moving to a Jewish state in Palestine, which they called Eretz Israel, the land of Israel, where they would not be persecuted.

Rachela never forgot the strength she derived from these occasions. 'Hilde had energy,' she recalled in 1984:

She kept us together, the group. Whoever wanted to join, joined us ... everyone had to get dressed festively, it means not what we dressed every day. If we had another shirt, then that shirt we put on clean, and a skirt ... and Carla she knew Hebrew ... there was a Bible ... there was some verse there and a little we sang and we sat together ... this is how the group was able to survive ... and until this day we are still together.[15]

Anita was a close friend of Hilde but she was no more a Zionist than was Alma, with whom Hilde argued about this subject. Hilde believed that while 'others were fighting for survival; for

Alma she was actually building. She would argue with me, a committed Zionist, for hours to forget going to Israel after liberation as she said she was building an orchestra that she would take on tour of the world after the war.'[16] Hilde knew that Alma had wanted her to be part of this venture. She always resisted.

Fanny Kornblum ('la Grande Fanny'), the Belgian mandolin player and amateur singer, recalled in 1996: 'We all wanted of course to hold on tight to life, and so we imitated the reality outside in that we held comradely discussions.' One onlooker to these debates was Julie Stroumsa, the Greek violinist who had helped the French violinist Violette Silberstein at her audition. 'I remember her as a very gentle, reserved girl who never took part in the sometimes heated discussions which we had,' Fanny told Julie's brother Jacques, who had played in the men's orchestra, after the war. 'Julie was always neutral. She lacked the fighting nature to survive in those shoals of death.'[17] Julie had avoided selection for the gas chambers but died of typhus in Belsen in 1945.

Yet after three months with Alma in charge, the orchestra was able to mask the internal strains behind the scenes and show a public cohesion in their daily performances. This period in the autumn of 1943 also saw a layer of additional brutality in the camp as constant mass convoys of Jews, most of whom were gassed on arrival, turned Birkenau into an ever more ruthless and efficient killing machine. Work had already started on building the third ramp, or unloading platform, which when it was finished in early 1944 brought prisoners directly into the camp, just a short walk away from the crematoria buildings.

Even before the new ramp was finished, the four functioning crematoria in Birkenau (numbered II–V as Crematorium I was no longer in use) were burning almost 4,500 corpses a day and sometimes even more.* These victims were mostly Jews, but the Nazis were also now killing thousands of gypsies and other minorities as well as Soviet POWs and Polish political prisoners selected by physicians in the camp hospital. At times, the bodies of people who had been murdered were also burned on pyres in pits located near Crematorium V. The smell of death was pervasive, and the stench of charred flesh constantly filled the nostrils of everyone in the camp; in addition, ashes from human remains settled inside some of the instruments played by the orchestra, a layer of fine black dust not discovered until after the war.

The orchestra was expected to play on regardless of the carnage all around them. Belgian violinist Hélène Wiernik recalled how on one occasion the orchestra was performing when a group of Belgian women marched past.

> One woman recognised me and cried out: 'Is it you Hélène?' I collapsed in tears. Alma was furious. When we returned to the music block, I was still crying. She slapped my face to calm me down and told me never ever to lose control of my nerves. The show must go on. I never lost control again. I never held a grudge against Alma for I understood the lesson.[18]

Mostly Hélène managed this by trying not to think about what was happening in the rest of the camp even though 'the crematorium was a hundred metres away. Outside our block the barbed wire fence gave off sparks in the night. During the night those selected went to their death in song. It was atrocious,' she said in 1997. 'If we just thought about the work and the music,

---

* According to calculations made by the Nazi *Zentralbauleitung* on 28 June 1943, the crematoria could burn 4,416 corpses per day – 1,440 each in crematoria II and III, and 768 each in crematoria IV and V.

we almost reached a moment of forgetting where we were, if we really concentrated... and then we had to come back to reality.'[19]

But there was no uniformity in the response to such constant carnage and sometimes the women could not avoid the grim truth of daily life in Auschwitz. For instance, on 23 October 1943 a transport of 1,800 Jews shipped on from Bergen-Belsen in northern Germany arrived in the camp. These families had paid large amounts of money for visas to various Latin American countries but on arrival at Belsen had been told they were destined for Dresden and that their luggage would follow. They only realised they had been duped when they arrived on the ramp at Birkenau.

The women were led towards Crematorium II and the men to Crematorium III. As the women were ordered to undress and the SS men began to strip them of their rings and watches, one woman flung her clothes at the head of SS Staff Sergeant Schillinger, grabbed his revolver and shot him three times. She also managed to shoot Sergeant Emmerich. In the ensuing melee other enraged women attacked the Nazis with their bare hands, managing to bite one SS man on the nose and scratch the faces of others. SS reinforcements swiftly arrived and the arrivals were all shot, killed by hand grenades or pushed inside the gas chambers. Schillinger died while Emmerich survived with a permanently crippled leg.

The next day the SS guards took their revenge by firing randomly from the watchtowers at the prisoners below. Thirteen inmates were killed, four seriously wounded and forty-two injured. The music block was immediately beneath one of the watchtowers, meaning it was highly likely the musicians heard the deadly spray of bullets even as they were rehearsing.[20]

Against this background, the sometimes 'heated discussions' in Block 12 often did not get beyond matters concerning daily existence. Helena recalled in old age that within her particular group one of the most popular topics for discussion, after a shared cigarette, was 'everything connected with eating, in other words our favourite dishes and how to cook them'.[21] But she also said that 'there were constant discussions about the moral dilemma and spiritual conflicts over whether or not they should be playing at all', a memory which seems to have been at odds with most of the rest of the orchestra. Anita maintained during an interview in 2022 that she deliberately did not think about such moral dilemmas because survival alone occupied her thoughts. 'Everyone's life was a matter of surviving until the next day,' she said. 'I escaped into music,' she observed. 'There are lots of things I don't remember about the camp. I closed myself into a bubble and played music to myself in my brain.'[22]

It was not that the musicians did not know what was happening as the murder beyond the music block was transmitted via smoke, smell and a strong system of informal communication of information around the camp. News was passed to the musicians partly by messengers such as Renate Lasker, Anita's sister, who had links with the orchestra. In addition, as the Polish violinist Zosia Cykowiak explained, 'from our block, in spite of the so-called *Lagersperre* [camp lockdown] administered during the mass rail transports of Jews . . . through the gaps of the not very tightly set planks, one could see the arrival and departure of the transports of people and the selections, not to mention the view of the flames and the smoke from the relatively nearby crematoria and the stench of the burning corpses spreading through the entire area'.[23] Some days the smoke was so thick it obscured what little sun there was and then, when it got dark, they saw a fierce red glow, like a house on fire, which clouded the stars even on clear nights.

'Occasionally we burst into tears, but not usually,' explained Hélène Wiernik. 'What could we do for the others in the camp?

Yes, there must have been jealousy of us. But you can't imagine what it was like if you weren't there.' She went on to say that by playing music 'perhaps for one moment the other prisoners might have thought of something other than the circumstances of where they were. We didn't speak to the other prisoners. It wasn't my fault I was there. We didn't speak much about the other prisoners. We spoke of other things.'[24]

Alma had no illusions as to exactly what fate awaited her musicians if the orchestra did not live up to expectations. They would all be gassed. As she repeatedly told Hilde, the orchestra 'survives together or dies together. There was no halfway road.'[25]

One subject none of the players could avoid was the music they were forced to play, although they recognised that this was entirely Alma's decision. As long as she did not stray into forbidden repertoire, Mandl did not interfere here. Every day there was march music to play as the work kommandos left and returned to the camp. This was the orchestra's raison d'être however unpopular it made them with the exhausted women passing through the gates, as SS guards watched at the side and punished those who could not keep up with the beat.

Wanda Koprowska, a Polish prisoner who came to Auschwitz in February 1943, gave an account of the terrifying morning marches, intended to speed up the departure of the women prisoners to work in the sub-camps. Most had no experience of marching, so 'when the signal to march out was given, the orchestra began playing marches and the Musselmen [skeletally thin and sick] women, moved their left legs to the beat of the drum . . . Getting one's feet tangled up was not permitted and the sick ones had to grin and bear it.'

At the gate stood a group of Nazi top brass usually including SS *Unterscharführer* Adolf Taube, the junior squad leader with a reputation for randomly beating prisoners to death, and three of the most brutal women guards in the camp – Maria Mandl, Elisabeth Has and the infamous Margot Dreschel.

When marching out one day, one of the women in our kommando stepped out on her right foot instead of her left. Taube noticed. He rushed in between the rows and began kicking the deceased on the rear end, bellowing *Links, Links und Links* (Left, Left, Left). We kept marching and took pains not to get our legs mixed up. The poor woman, she was no youngster. Taube could have been her son.[26]

The marching music, with its pounding drumbeat which easily predominated in an orchestra comprising mainly flutes, mandolins and violins, left negative associations of the women's band in the minds of almost all prisoners in the camp who had to look smart and stick to its rhythm. Maria Zarebinska, a Polish actress born in 1904 who was arrested and sent to Auschwitz for helping Jews get out of the Warsaw ghetto, noticed that although the mandolins softened the overall tone 'on the other hand the drum played threateningly, piercingly . . . the orchestra playing at the gate could be heard from a long way off. The mandolins and violins were cheerful, laughing, rattling like field insects and the drum again was menacing and intimidating: careful, careful, careful, *links, links, links und links.*'[27]

Zarebinska, describing how the exhausted women passed through the gate returning home, trying not to let their heads droop, noticed how

the whole body tenses as the hurriedly straightened rows of five pass through the gate . . . will they make it through or not? A frail little girl did not succeed. She had picked a handful of

Newly shaven women prisoners at Auschwitz-Birkenau ready for work

pinkish white daisies in the field, stuck them in her blouse, and forgot to throw them away before the gate. They pull the girl out of the ranks, pluck the wildflowers away and trample them underfoot, and give the girl a beating. The others march imperturbably. And the orchestra plays on.[28]

For the serious-minded Helena, having to play popular music felt unbearable on occasions. Among the light music that featured in the two concerts every Sunday were hits such as the tango *Jalousie*, *Komm Zurück* and waltzes by Kalman, Lehár and Strauss, the latter Alma's favourite.

That made us think twice and left some of us seriously frustrated. How could we play light music here, against the background of the flames and black smoke that billowed day and night from the crematoria chimneys? How could we play here, in the open space between the Revier blocks, on a sunny Sunday when on the other side of the barbed wire along the nearby camp road, crowds of Jews exhausted by their journey were trudging straight to the gas chamber and crematoria? Yet Alma consistently and firmly inculcated in us, sometimes even using harsh terminology, that 'the Orchestra Means Life'.[29]

Violette Silberstein believed that Alma transformed them all into making 'a unique sound . . . a sound all of its own. A special sound.'[30] Szymon Laks, admitting that his view was partly based on musical rivalry, described the sound of the women's orchestra as 'effeminate' with 'a mild, sentimental quality'.

Yet Belgian Hélène insisted that Alma 'was a great artist' who coaxed us into 'an almost normal orchestra'.[31] However, as the first violin right at the front of the orchestra, she not only saw the suffering female marchers face to face but had to cope with the uncomfortable fact that 'I was seen'. She could not entirely escape from thoughts about whether at least the Sunday concerts if not the marches helped the other prisoners or intensified their suffering.

'Perhaps occasionally it helped,' she told an interviewer in 1997. 'But you had to build a carapace in order to survive . . . it's what you do as an antidote. But a carapace is only superficial. I often thought of my parents.'[32]

It was fortunate she did not know at the time the comments of Charlotte Delbo, the French Communist resister who had arrived at Auschwitz in January 1943, and was especially scathing about Alma.

She parodies the professional she used to be when she led an all-women's orchestra in a famous Vienna café. The waltzes reminded her of an abolished past. To hear them here is intolerable . . . Do not look at the violinist, she plays an instrument that could be Yehudi's if Yehudi were not miles away, on the other side of the ocean. Which Yehudi did this violin belong to? Do not look, do not listen. Do not think of all the Yehudis who had packed their violins when being deported.[33]

Marie-Claude Vaillant-Couturier, a fellow French Communist resister who arrived in Auschwitz with Delbo on the same January 1943 convoy, was similarly disdainful about the orchestra when she testified at the Nuremberg trial of major war criminals in January 1946. The musicians, 'all young and pretty girls dressed in little white blouses and navy-blue skirts, played during the selection, at the arrival of the trains, gay tunes such as "The Merry Widow", the "Barcarolle" from *The Tales of Hoffman*, and so forth,' she said. 'They [the arriving prisoners] were then informed that this was a labour camp and, since the new arrivals were not brought into the camp, they saw only the small platform surrounded by flowering plants. Naturally, they could not realize what was in store for them.'

What Marie-Claude described happening during a selection was interpreted by the musicians in different ways. There is no unanimity in memoirs or accounts by former prisoners or even the musicians themselves as to how the orchestra was used while selections for the gas chambers were being carried out. Some recall that 'the sounds of music could be heard', others that during roll call 'there was a selection for the gas chamber to the accompaniment of the orchestra'.[34]

Sylvia maintained 'We played during a selection but not for a selection. It's easy to misunderstand.' It's a fine distinction but Sylvia was emphatic during an interview on camera in Israel that there was a difference. Playing *during* a selection was coincidental – the orchestra might have just been practising near the ramp – while playing *for* a selection was deliberate, an occasion when they were used by their Nazi overseers as a distraction. She explained that there was one occasion when they had to play outside all night.

> That particular night, when we saw all the convoys arriving, it was different. We were in a lit-up area but everything else was dark. I couldn't see people's reactions. It was dark and we were too far away.
>
> That night was completely different. We were outside all night long. When we had nothing more to play we started at the top and went again. The SS officer just said carry on.
>
> We had to play. We did it as a job.[35]

For all her briskness, as she explains, it is clear how sensitive this issue is. Hilde Grünbaum, who also made her home in Israel and was interviewed alongside Sylvia, did not recall the occasion. There is a discussion, a difference of opinion on camera. Eventually, Sylvia and Hilde agree that as she, Hilde, was inside the block that night, sleeping, she would not have known. It appears to have been a once-only requirement for some of them to play in this way.

Other musicians too were at pains to stress, like Hélène, 'We never played for those going to the gas. We did practise in our block and perhaps we were heard. But I want to explain this,' she told the interviewer emphatically in 1997, 'because it is sad enough as it is.'[36]

Since the band rehearsed at all times of day inside the block, several prisoners remember hearing music when they were first pushed off the trains, persuading them to think that, in a place where beautiful music was played, all must be well. It is easy to see how the belief took hold that playing, or practising, while a selection was happening within earshot of arriving prisoners amounted to the same thing as playing deliberately for a selection in order to make it appear as if they were giving a concert in a place of culture rather than a murder site.

The German accordionist Esther Loewy knew that those arriving at the camp would often hear the girls playing or practising, even before the new railway leading directly to the crematorium had been completed. 'That was the worst as they thought "oh, where music is played it can't be all bad",' Esther recalled in 1995. 'But we knew exactly where the trains were going yet we could do nothing. We couldn't warn them. The SS were behind us.'[37] Esther added that while the musicians found it 'not so bad' playing for prisoners going out to work, it was terrible to see them coming back broken with fatigue or carrying the bodies of their comrades. 'We all had tears in our eyes then.'

Rachela agreed that this tactic meant the orchestra was involved in Nazi deception. 'Yes. Sometimes we played when a transport arrived. They seated us there in the *Vorne* [literally up front or near the gate] and it fooled the people who arrived. They saw an orchestra, so they went on.'[38] 'I remember how Yvette... she always stood and cried. Once a Gestapo man came and said: "We do not want crying girls in the *Vorne*, so get her out, or everyone must smile. You are forbidden to cry here."

'Seeing what we saw, did we have any reason to laugh and smile?'[39]

Around the camp at large, Alma was the subject of prison gossip, accused by some inmates of 'living like a queen'[40] and by others of exerting her authority as a 'Jewish Kapo' harshly. Within the orchestra, many of the performers, particularly the younger players, adored Alma and were in awe of her as a musician. Hélène Wiernik, who had wanted to make a career as a violinist, praised Alma 'for teaching me that a waltz was not something rigid but a bouncing ball'. 'She loved waltzes and for example if she played Sarasate's *Zigeunerweisen* it gave us real pleasure to listen.' Hélène also recognised, as did they all, that their own survival depended on Alma staying the course.

Yet Alma always maintained a certain distance from her troupe. When she entered the practice part of the block from her little room, ready to start a rehearsal, she expected the players to stand, a theatrical gesture in Auschwitz but normal behaviour for any professional orchestra. Yet Polish Helena, who shared the first desk with Belgian Hélène, reflected years later that she had only ever spoken twice to Alma, who did not speak any Polish; once when she was admitted to the orchestra, and a second time when she was recuperating from typhus, grief-stricken from her mother's death, and asked if she might be given lighter duties. 'She showed understanding,' recalled Helena, 'although our conversation was cold and devoid of any kindness.'[41] For several days Helena was excused rehearsals so that she could build up her strength.

'Really there was not much time for conversation in our kommando,' Helena added on another occasion. 'Alma was rather alone and isolated in her separate room.'

Zosia Cykowiak agreed with this assessment, believing that she sought no close contact with any of the other orchestra players. 'She was rather secretive. The music was all. It was her escape, but it was also her biggest drama. She fascinated not just for her playing but her personality.'[42]

Clearly there were several different versions of Alma and her complexity is partly what makes her tragic story so compelling. She was alone yet she was claimed by several in the camp to have had a close relationship with them. She inspired loyalty but she also aroused jealousy. Even those musicians who accused her of being too close to the Germans recognised she was crucial to their survival.

Just as no one individual experienced Auschwitz in the same way, no one saw Alma as exactly the same person. Regina

Kupferberg, the girl from the southern Polish town of Będzin whom Alma had taken on as her personal assistant, supposedly for her beautiful eyes, saw how stressed she was daily from the enormous weight of responsibility she carried. 'She didn't sleep at night because she would write out music from memory,' Regina testified in 1984.[43] 'I liked her but everything was always so tense, which destroyed any possibility of true friendship.' Regina felt she understood from such close proximity what it meant to be an artist like Alma.

> In the morning I would make her food, although there was not much to make it with. Then I would light a fire and make her tea but if the water did not boil for long enough she would be angry. Then she would go crazy and then after that she would say sorry. It was a perfect example of how she was a real artist, also very modest, but it had to be JUST SO and her hearing was absolutely perfect so, sometimes, if the kettle didn't buzz long enough for boiling to make the tea, she would be angry. I wasn't angry with her but it was difficult to live with an artist like that. My friends said to me 'oh you had it so good' but I didn't feel that.[44]

Sometimes Regina felt like an outcast from the troupe of musicians and more of a menial worker tasked with unskilled chores such as cleaning all the muddy shoes.

One who managed a closer working relationship with Alma than most of the other musicians was the guitarist Margot Anzenbacherová, the former Czech Communist resistance activist who also wrote poetry. Alma and Margot worked together to write alternative words to the hauntingly beautiful Chopin Étude in E major, the *Tristesse*, which had become a popular song of the thirties, *Mir klingt ein leid*. The music of Chopin, a Polish composer, was theoretically barred in the camp and when the women performed it with subtly altered lyrics, still in German and with the same title, to convey a message of deep yearning for silence and freedom, the SS forbade its public performance, complaining that it was too sad, and asked Alma to rewrite the lyrics. She refused and the song was performed only occasionally in the privacy of their barracks. Ruth Bassin, the German Jewish piccolo, flute and clarinet player taken on by Czajkowska, commented that she (Ruth) would sing this song, which evoked for her immensely powerful memories of Alma, almost daily to the end of her life.[45]

The woman who probably built the most intimate relationship in the camp with Alma was not an orchestra member at all. Margita Svalbova, or Dr Mancy as she was known in the camp, was a young Jewish medical student deported from Bratislava in 1942, like Zippi part of the early Slovak deportations. Her low prisoner number, 2675, made her one of the camp elite. Eleven years younger than Alma, she became Alma's friend and confidante and, some believed, her personal doctor as well as being able to organise scarce drugs and palliatives.[46] It is not known exactly when the two women met but, as a doctor, even a Jewish one, Dr Mancy was given relative freedom around the camp and attended several of Alma's Sunday concerts. In 1947 Dr Mancy wrote a memoir in which she devoted an entire chapter to Alma discussing their friendship and, in interviews more than forty years later, she said that Alma's loneliness was profound. She was disillusioned with love and longed most of all to play again in a chamber music quartet with her father.[47]

Alma's severity with the musicians extended to the orchestra's copyists, who sat at a long table on one side of the music room. Some of them complained that she was even harsher with them than with the performers, because the paper, with its handwritten staves prepared by the girls in the drawing office where Zippi worked, was so precious that a mistake was unforgivable. Hilde had direct experience of Alma's exacting standards once she gave up playing violin in the orchestra to work full-time as a copyist and harmoniser. For Hilde, one episode in particular epitomised Alma's perfectionism.

Towards the end of December 1943, Alma acquired a grand piano for the orchestra. Szymon Laks, the conductor of the men's orchestra in Birkenau, was aghast that Alma had sufficient prestige in the camp to win the use of a piano, 'whose lack I had so painfully felt at the beginning of my career as an arranger when I had to harmonize and orchestrate by memory the melodies that were supplied to me'.[48] One of the male orchestras at Auschwitz had for a time used a poor-quality piano that had been pulled out of a river where it had been dumped and rebuilt by some prisoners with coloured keys as they did not have any suitable white material. Another inferior piano had been available for a while to provide additional entertainment for the SS officers in the block which Hössler had turned into a brothel, winning him such praise from the authorities. By contrast, Alma's grand piano was a Bechstein, possibly requisitioned by the Nazis from a local family, which could explain why it had to be given back.[49]

Alma had argued to the camp authorities that a piano was essential to create the different parts in such an unusual orchestra where violins were used instead of wind instruments. She was only ever given piano sheets to work from and asked Hilde to do the harmonisation, with Alma standing next to the piano and instructing Hilde what to write. 'She was happy that I understood everything she wanted,' Hilde recalled in 1998.[50]

Alma must have been at her most persuasive when she told Hössler that she needed a piano to coach the girls who were not professionals in order to perform at a level that was satisfactory to the Nazis. Her success in obtaining one may have been connected with another development during these early months of her tenure.

In March 1943 two female Soviet prisoners of war had arrived in Auschwitz: Szura Makarova, born in 1925 in Vologda, approximately 400 km north of Moscow, and Alla Gres, born in 1921 with Ukrainian heritage. It is possible that both women were captured by the Germans in late February following the Soviet army's Donets–Kharkov campaign. When they arrived in Birkenau they were tattooed with consecutive numbers – 38115 and 38116 – indicating they were probably friends by then if not before. Zofia Czajkowska, conductor of the orchestra at that point, was struggling to make a success of it, frustrated by her inability to recruit enough capable non-Jewish Polish musicians. So she decided to visit the block housing the new Soviet arrivals, auditioned Szura on the guitar and accepted her immediately. But Alla, a pianist who had also studied orchestration in Ukraine, was unable to audition as there was no piano for her. Or perhaps, as a professional, she had no interest in joining such an amateur band.

Nine months later, on 19 December 1943, when Alma was in charge, a transport of 234 prisoners from Radom prison in Poland brought more Russian POWs including pianists Sonya (Soja) Winogradowa and her friend, Maria Galewa, to Birkenau. Winogradowa is listed in some archives as being called Soja or Zofia; Sonya may have been a name given to her at the camp through mishearing. She was born in Leningrad in 1921, began learning the piano at the age of six and was just starting out as a professional pianist when she was called up in 1941. She served as a medical lieutenant at the siege of Leningrad where she was wounded and awarded the Red Star for courage under fire. But she was captured by Germans in the autumn of 1943 and, after a month in Radom prison, arrived in Auschwitz in December even though, as a POW, she should not have been in a concentration camp at all.*

Soja and Maria were transferred to the block for Soviet prisoners where they got to know Alla Gres. Most probably Soja and Alla were in communication with Szura, the guitarist who had been part of the troupe since March, and who told them about the new conductor, Alma Rosé, and the sweeping changes that she was carrying out in Block 12, in particular the fact that she now had a grand piano. When Alma discovered that both Alla Gres and Soja Winogradowa were outstanding pianists and that Alla had studied orchestration, she immediately urged both to join the group, bringing to five the number of Soviet musicians in the orchestra. Bronia Labuza, a guitarist, had joined in May and Olga Loseva, a mandolin player, in August.[51]

'The most outgoing of them all was Alla,' according to Helena Dunicz, 'but not to the degree that she ever revealed to us the circumstances and reasons for her being in Auschwitz... We were intrigued by the fact that the troika of Alla, Sonya, and Maria were placed in an ordinary concentration camp rather than an *Oflag*, seeing as how they were all officers in the Red Army.'

It was the piano which now enabled Alma to recruit a small group of singers with whom she worked on arranging duets and extracts from operettas for the weekly Sunday concerts. This in turn required a group of copyists and arrangers to work on the scores. 'One day *Lagerführer* Hössler entered cheerily and said he had "organised" a piano... that piano moved to our barrack. I

---

* According to the Geneva Convention, which Germany had signed, captured Allied military personnel were due a basic level of treatment in captivity which the Nazis rarely upheld. They treated Soviet prisoners of war especially harshly, believing that Communism was in direct opposition to Nazism.

soon had to sit behind it,' recalled Flora Jacobs, who until then had been expected to play the accordion.[52]

Hössler now took great pride in the women's orchestra generally, seeing it as 'his', and was especially proud of Alma's solo violin performances, which he believed reflected well on him. Zosia Cykowiak noticed that 'the highest-ranking Germans even from the men's camp, came to hear her play. On more than one occasion we were amused to see how Commandant Hössler and *Oberaufseherin* Mandl "strutted" in the presence of guests who were amazed and enchanted at Alma's playing.'[53]

Despite her status as the finest musician in Auschwitz, Alma knew that she had to hold herself in check in the presence of her overseers. Dr Mancy recalled a confrontation with an (unnamed) SS officer who accused her of favouring Jewish girls as she was building up the orchestra. According to Dr Mancy, he shouted at Alma: '"Why did you turn away a Polish violinist?" "Because she isn't musical and doesn't play the violin well," replied Alma. "You lie," said the SS. "It is because she is not a Jewess. Now you take her in hand." "As you command," answered Alma – correctly as always.'

Mancy said Alma sobbed as she recounted this story. 'She knew now that elements in the camp challenged her in her music, the one most precious refuge she had left.'[54]

Alma always understood that her position was precarious, and that somebody would be ready to denounce her if she did not do an excellent job. Violette recalled once hearing Mandl say to Alma: '"If you need bread, ask me. I will have it distributed." But we didn't get it. We asked Alma why not and she replied: "You played like pigs in the last concert. To punish you I will not demand bread."'[55] Alma's careful handling of Mandl and other officials laid her open to accusations from some prisoners that by failing to confront the Nazis she was doing their bidding. When she was seen sitting face to face, talking in a friendly way to Mandl, it was bound to fuel camp gossip and criticism. One of the camp messengers, a Belgian Jewish girl called Mala Zimetbaum, who was given considerable freedom around the camp because she was considered so useful, reported what she had seen. 'Alma was talking with Mandl and allowed to sit down. They were having a talk sitting. There was no such example in the history of the camp. THIS IS INCREDIBLE! UNBELIEVABLE.'[56]

Flora Jacobs, the Dutch accordionist, remembered how Alma found one outlet for her anger when something had especially upset her. In the early dawn silence when she might have thought that the Nazis could not hear her, she would play the solo part from the Violin Concerto in E minor by the forbidden Jewish composer Felix Mendelssohn. Occasionally she also played the same piece to the women in her block as a reward if they had performed well. Music rather than food was her chosen battleground where defiance was concerned.

Thirty-three-year-old Lili Assael, the former professional piano player from Salonika, was one of the few musicians who sometimes questioned the musical demands and strict discipline that Alma imposed on the orchestra. She answered back on occasion, which led to further irritation. Lili understood how tenuous the position of the orchestra was but believed that Alma depended on them as much as they depended on her. In some ways it was especially hard for Lili, a strong-minded, mature woman who had previously worked with professionals and who did not like being bossed around. With Czajkowska at the podium, Lili's role not simply as accordionist but as general helper had been important. Now that the younger members of the orchestra, especially the French and German speakers, looked increasingly to Alma as their saviour to be regarded with adulation, Lili was neither needed nor respected in the same way.

Some believed she was actively disdained by Alma. When Anita was interviewed in 2023 she said straightforwardly that Alma might simply not have liked Lili's smell, as the player right at the front. Anita's comment brings us to the heart of the camp. Smell was a key aspect of the horrors of Auschwitz, whether the smell of excrement or urine, rancid vegetables or charred human flesh. Such a basic instinct as revulsion to the smell of another person whose life was in danger may appear at one level shocking when so many worse horrors abounded. But it reveals not only Alma's flawed humanity but also her reverence for life. Alma made sure everyone took a regular shower to try and keep healthy, and punished those who did not. Winning access to these privileges was one of the most significant concessions she had won for her musicians. Lili, used to the warmth of a Greek sun, did not like to emerge cold into a Polish winter and avoided showers if she could.[57]

Zippi Spitzer believed that Lili made 'clumsy mistakes' when she was working on copying. 'Alma screamed at Lili Assael in French because she was clumsy and kept saying do it again. I know because I had to supply the paper to do it again... But Alma kept her.'[58]

For whatever reason, everyone was aware that Lili often had to bear the brunt of Alma's desperation and pain. According to one account, she 'suffered much punishment, anguish and shame... Alma frequently reminded Lili that if she had not been in the orchestra, she would have suffered the fate of death as the Greek Jews very often faced. Lili was hit by Alma many times, but the latter would apologise. Alma even threw her baton at Lili and hit her in the eye. Alma reminded Lili that if she would find a better accordion player, she would send her to the crematorium.'[59] The meaning was plain. If the orchestra was not good enough for the purpose, they would all be gassed.

171

'Oy! how Alma Rosé was always shouting at her,' recalled Rachela Zelmanowicz, the mandolin player from Będzin.[60] Helena too remembered how Lili was often the one 'who felt Alma's rage for playing a sour note – the words *"du blode kuh"* (stupid cow) sounded harsh coming from Frau Alma', she said.[61] Alma threw other insults at the women if she felt they were not playing well. If they missed an entrance or struck a wrong note she might rap them over the knuckles, call them *'Blode Gans!'* (stupid geese) or *'Scheiss Kopf'* (shithead).

Sylvia Wagenberg, despite being only fifteen years old when she joined the orchestra as a recorder player, responded maturely to Alma's explosions. 'I remember Alma falling into a rage over a false note. I just smiled to myself. It became so absurd to me. After all I was only playing a little recorder. Only a person condemned to death, as we were, can realise how the life force, the will to live, permitted us to bear it.'[62]

Violette Silberstein believed Alma's outbursts were occasions which 'annulled her humanity'. Violette remembered how once, before a concert, she spilled some watery coffee on her white blouse and tried to hide the spot with her hands, knowing Alma would be furious. But Alma noticed the forbidden gesture and yelled at her, 'Are you now the one who does the stage directing?'[63]

Lili Assael had another reason for enduring stoically the abuse thrown at her by Alma – she was trying to save her younger sister Yvette's life by preventing Alma from ejecting Yvette from the orchestra. Fifteen-year-old Yvette was now no longer playing the accordion and Lili feared that, after her sister's spell in the infirmary with typhus, she was at risk of losing her place in the orchestra. What instrument could they find for her, especially if there was renewed pressure on Alma to have fewer Jewish musicians? Lili knew that everyone's position was tenuous but, having overheard a conversation between Alma and an SS officer, she was worried that the Nazis might even make the band entirely 'Aryan' by 1944.[64]

Lili proposed audaciously to Alma that Yvette should learn to play the double bass, thus helping both her sister and the orchestra. Since Alma only had one cellist, Anita Lasker, and badly needed to strengthen the bass section she agreed. Yvette had taken double bass lessons briefly for a few months in 1939, but she had soon given up because the instrument dwarfed her and her fingers were not strong enough to make a proper sound. Four years later in Birkenau, Yvette was still not a fully grown adult but was, at least, tall for her age.

There were now enough Nazi officials who wanted the orchestra to succeed that they were prepared to help Alma in myriad ways. It was easy for Josef Kramer to give Hilde a fountain pen to help her write out the different parts so that she did not have to struggle with blunt pencils.* Getting a double bass for Yvette was not a problem either and the senior officer, Franz Hössler, produced an excellent instrument. The next problem was finding someone who could teach Yvette. It was decided that Heinz Lewin, the multi-talented and popular watch restorer in Auschwitz I, who had his own workshop but who had less work at the moment, could be relied on to come across to the women's camp in Birkenau and give Yvette twice-weekly lessons.

'Lewin worked at a large bench in the rear of the barrack,' remembered Auschwitz prisoner Louis Bannet, a virtuoso Dutch horn player who knew him well. 'He was a small, wiry figure with a watchmaker's glass attached to his eye and he always seemed to be hunched over his table talking to himself.'

Lewin was also a musician who repaired instruments, most noticeably an accordion belonging to a young SS guard and music

---

* The fountain pen is now in Yad Vashem.

lover called Pery Broad. Bannet liked to tell the story of how, a few weeks after his arrival at Auschwitz, Broad walked into his barracks and went straight to Lewin's worktable.

'Is it ready?' he asked.

'It' referred to a beautiful deep red mother-of-pearl accordion in a large leather case. Broad ran his long fingers across the keyboard playing arpeggios in various keys while the other prisoners looked on in amazement.

'It seemed that Broad was not just an accomplished murderer but also an accomplished musician.'[65]

He then paid Lewin in cigarettes and asked if anyone else in the barrack knew how to play 'Tiger Rag'. For a while they had one of the most unusual musical sessions ever heard in the camp, since the Nazis officially denigrated this sort of jazz as 'degenerate'. It was yet another example of how, where music was concerned, the Nazis were adept at breaking their own rules. But Broad suddenly stopped playing when he realised the session was attracting too much attention, leaving Lewin to put the newly restored accordion back safely in its case. Lewin was a man trusted by the SS as well as popular with the prisoners. And so they allowed him to come for twice-weekly visits to the women's camp, which involved clearing the gate of the men's camp, taking the road towards the gas chambers and then passing through the gate of Camp B along Lagerstrasse to Block 12. Occasionally he brought Lili and Yvette's brother, Michel Assael, with him. This was highly risky and Michel knew how dangerous his journey would be but could not resist.

I had news from the Maestro [Laks] that someone was teaching my youngest sister the double bass and he offered me to see her. I went shoeless but with an accordion [a cover story]. I go there and inside I see my sisters for the first time. And

I saw they were doing much better than we were. They were in a very much better position with beds and food and we were talking together and suddenly a woman officer comes and she saw me and right away I flew. I started running, she comes after and catches up. She stops me and asks 'what were you doing there' and I explain about my two sisters and she asks how I learned music. I say my mother loved music. And we chatted...

Michel, who knew a little German, had something approaching a normal conversation with Maria Mandl. To his astonishment, he was saved from a punishment because Mandl had a soft spot for his little sister, Yvette, and was fascinated by the idea of a whole family of talented musicians. Like Hössler, Mandl desired the reflected glory from what she saw as 'her' prestige project.[66]

He was lucky not to be punished. A fellow Greek musician, Jacques Stroumsa, a violinist in the men's orchestra but also an engineer, who had a sister in the women's orchestra known as 'little Julie', had been discovered trying to send a note to his sister. As a penalty both brother and sister were punished, Julie with twenty-five lashes and Jacques 'nearly beaten to death' by the guards.[67] Being in the orchestra was no guarantee against being beaten, as Anita Lasker also testified. Asked at a post-war trial why she was beaten, she said: 'In Auschwitz there was no reason at all.'[68]

After two months SS officer Josef Kramer, the Nazi commander who took an active role in selections, questioned the case for Lewin continuing the double bass lessons and demanded to hear if the Greek girl was making progress. Yvette had to play for him, nervously performing a little tune. Alma immediately stepped in to remind Kramer that the child had only been learning for two months and insisted on how essential her instrument was to the overall sound of the orchestra. To her amazement, Yvette passed the test, with Kramer saying encouragingly: 'when you get out of here you will have a career'.[69] Anita often helped Yvette tune her instrument and recalled that Yvette soon became an indispensable addition to the orchestra.

*

Another typhus epidemic raged through the camp in November and December 1943. In early December the mother of the Polish violinist Helena Dunicz died. Helena had been allowed to visit her mother daily in the infirmary so it was hardly surprising that Helena herself caught the disease. As soon as she fainted during morning roll call, her friends sent her on a wooden stretcher to the typhus block. Helena later recognised that 'because I was a member of the orchestra and on top of that an Aryan', she was treated significantly better than other prisoners. 'It was important to the camp authorities to keep the proportion of Aryan women in the orchestra as high as possible... I was placed in a berth that I shared with only one other patient. Three or four women lay, or rather lay dying, in the other berths.'[70]

Helena was allowed nightclothes and a reasonably clean blanket. A nurse came to wash her once a day with water she carried specially for the purpose in a basin. Meanwhile her friends from the orchestra, girls she had only met a month or so ago, brought her something to drink, which involved a dangerous journey for them, going beyond allowed boundaries. Medicine was in short supply for everyone, paper was used to dress wounds and they risked catching the illness. Helena slowly recovered from typhus but in her weakened state was then hit by scabies and scurvy. Luckily, she knew a Polish woman in the infirmary who managed to organise some medicine which finally helped her recover. She was in the infirmary for almost three weeks and remained there over Christmas 1943, her first in the camp. The cards and get well wishes from orchestra friends helped her enormously, especially a note from 'Little' Hélène Rounder, the French Jewish violinist. Yet Helena never got over her guilt about her mother's death. Back in the orchestra, she worried that she should have been able to save her, just as Anita had managed to save her younger sister Renate when she had fallen ill with typhus.

During the epidemic, there was no let-up in December 1943 in the number of transports arriving at Auschwitz,[71] including prisoners transferred from other camps, most of whom were immediately gassed. One transport which arrived on 5 December whose occupants were intended for the gas chambers was nevertheless sent to the quarantine camp BIIa in Birkenau. There, the eighty weakest prisoners were left lying in the ice and snow of the lumberyard by order of the camp commander. Ice-cold water was subsequently poured on them. In the night, the prisoner attendants managed to bring forty-seven of those lying in the lumberyard into a barracks where thirty-two died immediately. Another prisoner who lay buried under the bodies of the others died in the morning when carried away.

Amid this horror, Alma was working even harder than usual to produce a Christmas Day concert in the large sauna for the one day in the camp when none of the women had to stand outside for morning and evening roll call. In addition to the orchestra, there were performances from some Jewish children in the family camp who sang a medley of traditional German hymns. This so-called family camp comprised more than 17,000 people brought from Theresienstadt, the camp in former Czechoslovakia, now housed in camp BIIb in Birkenau. They were given certain privileges for the six months they lived in Auschwitz but were then all gassed. Most likely, they were brought there with the intention of misleading the world should an International Red Cross delegation inspect, intending to prove that the entire place was a benign labour camp.

Sylvia Wagenberg remembered that in addition the SS organised a Christmas party in the sauna and that she was asked to play a carol on the flute.

> They put a pink dress on me and a pink ribbon in my hair and I played the carol, and that night the [members of] the Berlin Theatre Playhouse arrived at the camp and were sent straight to the crematorium. And we were just standing there.[72]
>
> Afterwards we had a discussion about the correct response. Should we leave them in ignorance and say nothing or tell them? We couldn't stop them going to their deaths. They'd find out soon enough from smelling gas. It made no difference to warn them so what was the point?[73]

The concert was disrupted for another reason, by a woman who was widely loathed and feared in the camp, a former prostitute from Bavaria who was a block elder in the sauna and had a reputation as a yodeller. 'Puff Mutti' Musskeller, as she was known, had made many requests to Alma to be taken into the orchestra. All were ignored, despite 'Puff Mutti' being friendly with Mandl.

Now she made a scene. Seweryna Szmaglewska, the twenty-seven-year-old Polish writer and teacher arrested for her resistance activities in 1942, described what happened in her 1946 memoir *Smoke Over Birkenau*. She wrote how, because it was Christmas, the crowd of women were 'excited by the absence of the SS men, by the music and by their own eagerness to forget'.[74] Then the orchestra started up.

The ensemble of women artists collected from all Europe starts to play a sad tune, a tune so melancholy that with its first chords a spell falls upon the crowd standing so densely that their shoulders touch. Musskeller, in her gray dress with the red spot, comes up from the crowd and stands by the leader. She has grown thin and black in the past months and has lost her self-assurance. She raises bloodshot eyes to the leader's face, panting and swaying to the surge of the music. The leader nods and Musskeller throws her head back and with a smile of ecstasy spreads her arms and starts to sing.

The scene was unforgettable for Seweryna Szmaglewska, who was shocked to see how Musskeller was so aroused that she sang over the orchestra.

Her song is the essence of yearning. It seems that the power of loneliness with which the singer invests the unsophisticated words will blow up the walls:

Wien, wien nur du allein? [Vienna, Vienna, only you, city of my dreams]

The writhing of the woman's outflung arms and the passionate animal shouting give a touch of despair to the song... it is not singing, it is the outcry of an individual who defends herself from having her soul deformed.

The orchestra senses the passion of the song. Their playing becomes a cry of despair, wrenched from the bowels of their instruments, and from the depths of their hearts the jungle of yearning as a rule so carefully evaded by the prisoner, suddenly opens and begins to sing with many voices.

However, Musskeller's singing eventually became so hysterical that Alma had to stop the orchestra. Rachela described Alma's reaction as Puff Mutti looked at her with hatred. Alma knew at that moment that she had made an implacable, powerful enemy. 'She [Alma] was so miserable she cried afterwards saying: "What did she [Puff Mutti] do? She ruined the orchestra"... Alma had wanted us to play perfectly,' Rachela reflected sadly.[75]

6

She gave us hope and courage

In January 1944 the orchestra was bolstered by the arrival of an
unusual talent, a classically trained pianist and nightclub singer
in her mid-thirties who became known as Fania Fénelon. Fania,

Fania Fénelon, the Parisian nightclub singer

née Goldstein, was a true Parisienne, less than 5 foot tall but full of sophistication and tales of the French resistance. She seemed to many of the younger girls like a breath of fresh air from the outside world, an inspiration.

'She was intelligent and cultured, she was older and she could recite whole books to us,' is how Hélène Wiernik, still a teenager at the time, remembered the petite French singer who entertained them all by recounting fairy tales, or reciting French poetry, which, for a short time, managed to take their minds off the ever present gloom of their surroundings.[1] 'I was full of admiration not only because she did all the arrangements for the orchestra but because she gave us hope and courage,' Hélène recalled. 'She was *rigolo* [fun], extraordinary, she made us happy. She did tarot or card readings for us in the breaks and asked us what we dreamed of? I didn't dream much. I had nightmares.'[2]

Even Fania, with her wry outlook on life, could not introduce laughter into the barracks. As Hilde Grünbaum insisted, laughter was never present. Violette, the French singer and violinist, tried through making not very funny French puns about gaz/gauze, while Fania, with whom she had a good relationship, managed on occasion to lighten the atmosphere by examining the girls' palms.[3]

Anita, too, was aware of Fania's special talents. 'Fania was a valuable member of our community,' she wrote in her 1996 memoir. 'No-one can recall anything with which to reproach her... she was one of the few accomplished musicians there and I shall never forget the evening when we played chamber music in Auschwitz. Fania had a remarkable musical memory and transcribed the Beethoven *Pathétique* Sonata [for piano] for string quartet. I shall never forget that evening.'[4]

Fania, who was born in 1908, was probably thirty-six – older than she cared to admit – at the time she was deported to Auschwitz under her married name, Fanja Perla.* She was the musical child of a part-Jewish mother and Jewish engineer father, both parents having fled Russia for France, and had first started to learn the piano aged six. Although Fania was talented, her hands were too small to become a professional pianist, so she devoted herself to singing instead. She had studied under the renowned French opera singer Germaine Martinelli, at the Conservatoire de Paris, but had left before graduating. At the time of her arrest in January 1943 she was a popular cabaret singer with a reputation as a Communist. While she may not have been formally inducted into the resistance (few women were), she was arrested and tortured by Gestapo officers who believed the cabaret where she worked was a front for intelligence-gathering activity. Fania herself maintained that when German officers at her nightclubs were so drunk they did not know what she was doing, she would photograph the contents of their briefcases and forward the film. Her last known residence at this time, according to Drancy records, was listed as Rue Fénelon in the 10th arrondissement, which is probably the origin of her post-war stage name.

Fania spent a year in captivity in France, ending up at Drancy from where she was deported to Auschwitz, arriving at dawn on 22 January 1944. After three days in the camp, she was recognised while in the quarantine block by Hélène Rounder, Petite Hélène, the Parisian violinist who had arrived six months earlier. A camp messenger, or runner, was sent for and Fania exerted herself to give a stirring audition performance of an aria she knew well – 'Un bel dì vedremo' from Puccini's *Madama Butterfly* – accompanied on the Bechstein grand piano.

---

* Her pre-war marriage to an athlete was already over but their divorce was not finalised until 1945/6.

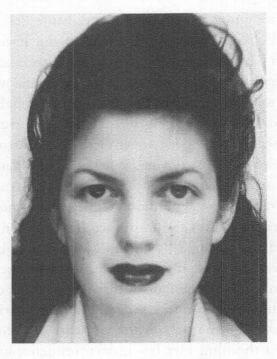

Claire Monis in the photo on her official resistance dossier

Another French singer, Claire Monis, was on the same convoy as Fania. Born in 1922, Claire was almost twenty-two and, according to French official documents, an active and (unlike Fania) official member of a resistance group, listed as a lieutenant for the Free French Forces or FFL. Claire was arrested before Fania and had already spent a year in the appalling conditions of Fresnes prison south of Paris before being sent to Drancy. Although not classically trained, she also came from a musical family of Russian origin and sang with a particularly sweet voice. Her father had played the clarinet and accordion in a klezmer group and the teenage Claire took part in musical competitions organised by the French Federation of Communist Youth. She was just beginning to enjoy a successful career on radio as well as performing at various

Paris venues and nightclubs when she was picked up for resistance activity in June 1942. In her official French resistance dossier photo, she has shoulder-length dark hair swept back high off her forehead with a full, lipsticked mouth. She is glamorous and slim.

The two French women had much in common in spite of the age difference and 'seemed the greatest of friends' according to Ruth Bassin, the German wind instrument player and former kindergarten teacher in the orchestra. Both were in demand from the SS officers and female overseers who, now that the standard of music was so high, started to visit the music block demanding individual performances.

Claire was younger and prettier and had charm. While Fania mostly managed to keep her distance from the Germans, Claire was not so lucky and, on one occasion soon after she arrived in the winter of 1944, her skills not just as a singer but as a sexual object were demanded by some German officers, who forced her to sing to them with no clothes on when she emerged from the shower. Ruth Bassin witnessed it and never forgot what she had seen, as she told the Canadian author Richard Newman when he was researching a biography of Alma.

'They made her sing for them naked. I remember. I watched that. I remember very clearly... she was rather heavy and was devastated.'[5]

Yet Newman did not refer to the episode in his biography of Alma for reasons which are unclear. Quite possibly he felt the story in some way reflected badly on Alma, who was unable to protect her orchestra girls from such sexual exploitation. Or was such cruelty so much the norm in Auschwitz that it was not worth dwelling on?

There was certainly a belief among some in the camp that the price of survival for these women must involve the giving of sexual favours. The Czech teenager Zusana Ruzickova, in

Auschwitz with her mother, was at fourteen a talented pianist who had already performed in the transit camp at Theresienstadt, in former Czechoslovakia. But in Auschwitz, even though she was bored and desperately hungry, she did not volunteer for the orchestra because her mother, fearing what might happen if she were noticed by the Nazis, did not allow it. 'I spent my days half hidden at the back of our bunk on my mother's instructions keeping out of sight to avoid attracting any attention in case Arno Böhm [a convicted murderer sent to Auschwitz by the Nazis in 1940 as a prisoner functionary and renowned as a 'primitive sadist'][6] or one of the guards singled me out. We'd heard dreadful stories from the girls who were taken to his block each night and forced to have sex with SS officers and visiting dignitaries.'[7]

Fear of forced nudity and demands for sexual gratification were rife among female prisoners and a cause of particular anxiety for young immature girls who probably had never been seen without clothes and wondered if this was the price of being saved from the gas chambers. Kitty Felix (now Hart-Moxon) was arrested aged sixteen and sent to Auschwitz-Birkenau with her mother from their home in the southern Polish town of Bielsko. Both survived in the camp for two years, during which time Kitty recalled among many horrors a period of three days when she and fellow prisoners had to go without any clothes. 'For some reason none were available for us,' Kitty remembered in 1981. 'We milled about, teeth chattering, clinging to one another to share what little warmth we could muster . . . the familiar whistles began to sound . . . we couldn't believe we would be expected to line up naked in this terrible cold for the usual evening roll call . . . without a stitch of clothing. But we were bullied into rows of five.'[8] Kitty survived the three-day ordeal and after being assigned a job carrying heavy bags of cement in order to build a ramp for the new railway line,* subsequently managed to get work in various indoor kommandos. But several inmates who endured this same agony did not survive or ended up in hospital.

Alma responded in the only way she knew how to the pressure all the prisoners felt from the ever-increasing numbers of transports arriving in the camp, most sent directly to be gassed, by expanding the orchestra and thus rescuing as many lives as she possibly could. From 1943 onwards Jews were the most numerous group of prisoners in the camp at approximately 200,000. Alma tried to make her orchestra bigger, better and indispensable. She still had no brass players but managed to make her dozen or so violinists and mandolinists somehow sound as if they were playing trumpets and trombones. She also had pianists and accordionists, one bassist, one cellist, two flautists, two recorder players, a percussionist and a cymbalist and now six vocalists and between four to six copyists. It numbered just over forty in all.

Alma embraced the new talent she was acquiring with vigour and ingenuity. She used the wider range of singers now in her orchestra to perform a number of interludes from operettas. Fania was immensely useful to her in helping to transcribe and arrange pieces for which they had nothing written other than that which Alma had created, and sometimes, like Alma, she stayed up all night writing out parts, occasionally from memory. Her role, along with the copyists, was increasingly important because of the odd make-up of the orchestra with its strange collection

---

* Until then the trains, using the main civilian line, passing through the Oświęcim train station, arrived at what was known as the *Alte Judenrampe*, a 500-metre-long concrete platform with powerful beams to light up the nighttime arrivals and selections from trains that passed to the west of the Auschwitz main camp, stopping between it and Birkenau camp, from where the exhausted prisoners walked. The third ramp was not finished until 1944.[9]

of instruments. Whenever possible, Alma also chose Fania to perform, rather than one of the more experienced classical singers such as Ewa Stojowska, the Polish professional, precisely because she knew that Fania's style of popular cabaret would please the Nazi audience. Helena described her as being a 'chanson crooner with a worn-out voice'[10] rather than a professional opera singer. Others were kinder and believed 'Fania brought that spark of colour variety singers have.'[11]

In addition to providing marching music, the performers were increasingly in demand from those Nazis who presumably found music soothing, a reminder of happier days, or a way to convince themselves that the camps were civilised places, or simply a demonstration of their power, because they often called into the music block to listen in on rehearsals or occasionally to request a personal favourite. Many of the SS officers in the audience at Sunday concerts such as Franz Hössler, head of the women's camp, *Hauptsturmführer* Josef Kramer, head overseer and later camp commandant, as well as SS doctor Josef Mengele and Maria Mandl, head female guard, were among those who seemed to derive special pleasure listening to operatic duets or solo performances.

'Sometimes a German would arrive with blood on his uniform. I can never forget the look on German faces, the look that haunts me,' recalled Polish violinist Helena Dunicz. But worse was when she and a small ensemble were ordered in the evening to give a private performance in the SS barrack overseer's guardhouse. Then 'the connoisseurs among the SS-ranks, arriving after the selection, listened to works by Grieg, Schumann, and Mozart, in order to relax'.[12] 'They had very cruel faces especially Mandl. Yet when she was listening to music her face would completely alter. She became beautiful,' Helena continued. 'I used to watch her and Hössler. Five or ten minutes later someone was beaten and kicked.'[13]

Ewa, who also worked as a copyist and the orchestra's 'music librarian', was amazed by Alma's creative treatments of operatic tunes and her ability to coach female singers in ranges traditionally sung by men. Ewa had a strong deep voice, yet she took the tenor parts in operatic quartets which Alma arranged. One of these was the quartet from *Rigoletto*, originally scored by Verdi for two men and two women; in Alma's duo version Ewa sang the part of the Duke of Mantua and Fania the role of Gilda. This arrangement was especially popular with the SS and they were required to sing it on many occasions at the regular Sunday concerts, which sometimes lasted for up to three hours and might also include arias or medleys from *Carmen*, *Cavalleria Rusticana*, *Madama Butterfly*, *The Merry Widow*, and the Bell Song from *Lakmé*. Ewa said that Alma's industry in creating music, or recreating scores from memory, resulted in a collection bordering on 200 passages which the orchestra could perform. Although the work of Jewish composers was officially forbidden, occasionally she managed to slip in among the Strauss waltzes and von Suppé marches a well-known foxtrot tango called 'Josef, Josef!' knowing that tangos were a favourite Nazi musical genre. Yet this particular piece was written in 1938 by not one but four American Jewish composers: Sammy Cahn, Nellie Casman, Saul Chaplin and Samuel Steinberg. It is heart-wrenching to picture this group of mostly young girls playing such cheery accordion dance music, with distinct echoes of klezmer or traditional Jewish folk music, in such a grotesque setting where, far from playing to celebrate, their lives depended on playing the piece well.

In winter, or if the weather was bad, the women played Sunday concerts inside the room referred to as the sauna (the bathhouse), a dank, cement-floored, low-ceilinged room which would have been familiar to prisoners as the room where they were brought on arrival and ordered to give up all their possessions. It could easily take an audience of about a hundred including guards who were usually seated and prisoners who were not. But in summer they played either on the same grassy mound by the gate at the end of the central road between sectors B1b or B1a where they also played morning and evening marches, or, from June 1943 onwards, performed for the patients on the grounds of the camp hospital which was uncomfortably close to the road leading to the crematoria.

Increasingly, as the weather improved, the women played in the square outside the hospital and one chance witness to such a concert recalled how the patients were ordered out to listen. Describing the occasion later, Polish political prisoner Maria Holiczer commented that she did not remember much about it because her attention 'and that of many other women was distracted by the pile of corpses ... that had not been removed that morning and lay outside the hospital barracks'.[14] It is not clear if these hospital concerts for sick prisoners were a regular occurrence and the few accounts of reactions to them are mixed. One refers to how, at the end of a waltz, 'Warm applause broke out and the patients' eyes glistened with gratitude'. But another onlooker remembered a concert during which 'sick prisoners listening to the orchestra were unexpectedly surrounded by SS men before being forced into trucks and driven to the gas chambers'.[15]

Gloria Lyon, a Czech teenager who saw the orchestra when she was sent out to work, recalled years later listening to a concert one summer. 'I'll never forget the cellist with hair shaven and very thin. She fell off her folding chair as the hot sun was coming down and nobody gave a damn ... another time I saw an instrument on the ground, the result of fainting. They were treated just the same as us, but they had uniforms.'[16]

Alma had a reputation in the camp at large for being aggressive when it came to music standards, constantly warning of what would happen if the orchestra was not good enough. She would point to the smoke emerging from the nearby crematorium to say, 'there would be no reason not to send them all there'.[17] But they needed no reminders from Alma about how important it was to work hard as they witnessed first-hand the extent to which they were under scrutiny from the attentions of uninvited SS officers who, as well as attending the concerts, would randomly wander into rehearsals and sometimes 'order' a particular opera or other favourite musical pieces 'on demand'.

Alma and her band immediately stood to attention whenever an SS officer appeared in the doorway to the music block, sometimes after conducting lengthy selections. The Nazi would enter with no warning, tell the girls they had practised for long enough and then order a particular piece.[18] Alma agreed to every Nazi request and her weary musicians obeyed her. Margot, the Czech poet, believed that Block 12 became something of a refuge for some officers, a place to relax and be entertained including, according to her, even Camp Commandant Höss, not known as a particular opera fan.

'Suddenly an SS woman could ask for some Chopin, hear it, and upon leaving kick an old grandmother,' Margot remembered in 1979. 'Commandant Höss would ask for an aria from "Butterfly" then go off on a selection.'

Sylvia, the petite German flautist, similarly remembered an SS man who 'drove Flora [Jacobs] crazy with a tango, making her sing it over and over again'.[19] Hilde believed that sometimes SS men who had to accompany transports or had witnessed something else traumatic 'wanted to recharge emotionally by listening to music'.[20] Zosia Cykowiak and her friend Helena Dunicz agreed with this interpretation and said that SS officers often came to hear the orchestra after hours, when the girls would be 'roused from our nightly sleep with orders to play for SS men returning from duty during mass transports of Jews to the gas chambers'.[21]

Helena described one occasion when an SS man came into the block at night after selecting a transport of deported Jews 'when I think we had already prepared to go to sleep in our bunks and they came in and said "Orchestra – Play". And we had to get dressed and take our places and play something.'[22] Another time, presumably just to keep them on their mettle, the unpredictable Mandl came in saying she had just heard on the radio a performance of Sarasate's *Zigeunerweisen* and that she wanted to compare. The Belgian friend of Elsa Miller, Fanny Kornblum, recalled the terror she felt at that moment, but luckily 'We played like angels. Mandl responded to an anxious Rosé that the orchestra gave a better performance than the one she had heard on the radio. We gave a sigh of relief.'[23]

Once Mandl brought with her a boy, 'a lovely child, very trusting towards her, very open', to listen to them rehearse. Zosia Cykowiak remembered how Mandl requested that the orchestra play a short composition and the child, under the influence of the music, started to dance, 'to move as children do. And what's interesting – the child kept holding her hand. I remember it because after a while, I can't say how long it took, I saw her on the road at the rail side leading him to the crematorium and that paralyzed me.'[24]

By early 1944 constant rumours were flying around the camp about the progress of the war and how long before Germany was beaten. It is not clear how much the orchestra women knew of the Russian advance in the east nor when the Allies would mount their invasion of mainland Europe. But they could see more and more prisoners arriving in Auschwitz, evidence of Hitler's belief that if he could use more slave labour to produce more armaments, Germany could still win the war.

This was Alma's first winter in the camp and it was an especially harsh one with biting Baltic winds and freezing snow flurries striking exposed skin whenever the women went out. Temperatures were rarely higher than about minus 3 or 4 degrees, but Flora Jacobs remembered 'marching out with two stools and a music stand around my neck in the mornings at four a.m. even in 15 degrees below zero... we were waiting for hours by the gate, "*Am Tor*, until the fog cleared.' The extreme cold simply added to the bleak outlook across the camp shrouded by the constant greyness of an Auschwitz winter sky where the sun might appear only briefly if at all in the late afternoon. Alma had requested and was given a wooden floor in the barracks, knowing that a cement floor would have been abrasive for the instruments, but it provided another small comfort for the musicians. The floor was laid by inmates from the carpentry kommando, and included a small podium especially constructed for Alma at one side. Standing on her podium, with the girls in a circular arrangement around her, she could see or hear a mistake more easily. This sharpened her already acute hearing so that if she heard a misplaced tone or if, as often happened, the exhausted flautist Frau Croner fell asleep mid-rehearsal, all the orchestra suffered and would have to start again from the beginning with whatever piece they were practising.[25]

The small stove in the centre of the room was installed out of concern for the instruments but that too offered comfort and warmth for the musicians. Flora Jacobs, the Dutch accordionist, once got too close and she burned her wrist on it so badly that she could not play until it healed. SS *Obersturmführer* Franz Hössler noticed that she was not playing and asked her why, so she showed him her wrist.

'You're lucky I have only two accordionists otherwise I would have you gassed,' he told her.[26]

But although the inmates of Block 12 were, like those working in the kitchens or infirmaries, now excused outdoor roll calls in winter – an *Aufseherin* came inside to count them, a huge privilege compared with most of the other prisoners who were woken at 5.30 a.m. for outdoor roll call or 4.30 a.m. in the summer months – they still had to play outside, often barely able to feel their numb fingers for hours. And although a punishment from Alma – angry words or being made to scrub the floor – was less painful than a Nazi truncheon thwacking them if they failed to work hard enough carrying boulders or cement bags, they all knew that in this febrile atmosphere with German worry about losing the war, their lives were at ever greater risk. Everyone was exhausted from the demands of playing ten hours a day with marches, rehearsals, concerts and private SS requests with so little food, resulting in frequent fainting. Hilde had many intense conversations with Alma at this time and believed she understood how Alma used seeing 'only the music' as her way of surviving.

But Alma was not blind to the intense pressure faced by her girls and eventually negotiated an unprecedented one-hour rest in 1944 in the middle of the day.

The additional playing demands posed severe moral quandaries for all the musicians but it was especially hard for such young girls trying to square what they were doing with their consciences. Hélène Wiernik always insisted that 'I didn't play for the Germans',[27] but in reality they had no choice if they wished to survive.

Helena reflected on how they were used by the Nazis not simply to encourage workers to march more quickly but she believed also to mollify arriving prisoners who did not even get a chance to come into the camp for work. She described it as part of a 'refined confidence trick... that is why thousands of Jews,

including women with babies in their arms, went peaceably to their appointment with death in the gas chamber. Their composure resulted from a lie – that here, in the place they had come to, things must not be as bad if they are "welcomed" with music.'
She went on:

I would like to state clearly at this point that the orchestra was never summoned on purpose to the new railroad platform leading straight to the crematoria . . . the mentions in some camp memoirs of the band playing during the march of transports of Jews to the crematorium should be understood as meaning that the band was already playing at the time that transports walked along the main camp road, between the women's camp in B1 and the men's camp in B11.[28]

But even so Helena had to find a way to live with herself. She is probably correct that they were not positioned deliberately on the final road for the arriving Jews awaiting selection. It was most likely coincidental but, given the vast number of transports arriving daily in early 1944, it certainly had the effect of deception. Survival demanded that she made this distinction.

Anita's version of events is slightly more transparent. When asked at the Lüneburg Trial how it was she saw so many selections she told the judge:

'I used to play in the camp band, and they made us play at the gate. The gate was just opposite the station. At the station arrived the transports and we would observe everything. The transport arrived, the SS people did the selections and we have been just about 50 yards away.'
'Was it known what the selections were for?'[29]
'It was well known what the selections were for.'

There were many different strategies for survival in the camp and this straightforward approach was Anita's. She recalled in her memoirs how she was once asked to play Schumann's *Träumerei*, an exquisitely beautiful and simple piece about dreaming, for Josef Mengele when he walked into the music block one day, and did so because there was no alternative if that was the price of staying alive. 'I played it as quickly as possible. I didn't look at him. I just wanted him to get out,' she said.[30] Asked in 1996 on a radio programme what she felt having to play for such a man she replied:

'I don't think we gave ourselves time to feel anything.'
'You knew what they were doing?'
'Of course we knew what they were doing but what was the alternative?'[31]

It was a typically blunt response from Anita. Allowing herself to 'feel' anything was an unimaginable luxury. 'Surviving the next day was all we thought about,' she said. Anita's story of performing *Träumerei* has captured the public imagination precisely because the concept of such beauty existing in the heart of darkness encapsulates why this is such a difficult story to imagine for those who were not there, and can so easily be misconstrued. Anita says today it should not be given any more weight than any of the other stories of barbarity. She wrote about it simply because 'I thought it worth pointing out that these were educated people. He knew the piece, that's all.'[32]

The intense pressure, which wore so heavily on all the musicians, including Alma, had no outlet or source of mitigation beyond the support they gave each other. Even some of the other prisoners commented on how pale and exhausted they all looked. Yet Alma had to bear it alone.

On 29 February 1944 SS Lieutenant Colonel Adolf Eichmann

made one of several visits to Auschwitz in the early part of that year, ostensibly to view the so-called 'family camp', and Mandl arranged for him to inspect the musicians. Although Alma had prepared the orchestra thoroughly, the visit unnerved her. In the event he did little more than look in and move on.

Ten days later, on the night of 8–9 March, the family camp was almost entirely liquidated and most of the 17,500 men, women and children housed there for the previous six months were gassed in a single night.* Rumours were swirling as to Eichmann's motives but chief among them was his determination to implement the programme for the total destruction of the Hungarian Jews. The new railway line was not yet finished, and he was not happy as he believed he had identified 'deficiencies'[33] in the killing facilities. He had planned to send four transports of Hungarian Jews per day for destruction in Auschwitz. Yet despite the massive expansion of equipment and space for this purpose, Eichmann realised that in practice the extermination capacity did not suffice for the killing of so many people in such a short space of time.

According to Dr Mancy, the Bratislavan doctor who was Alma's friend, events surrounding Eichmann's visit undermined what remained of Alma's equilibrium, her ability to function calmly and continue to produce music while surrounded by ever-increasing madness. Alma watched powerless as day after day new transports arrived carrying Jews from Drancy near Paris and Westerbork in the Netherlands or anywhere else where she knew people, with hundreds of deportees immediately to be gassed. Through the cracks in the wood of the barracks walls all the musicians

---

* The remaining 6000–7000 people in this camp were liquidated a second time over the course of two nights in July. But on this occasion Mengele decided to carry out a selection of the boys from the children's block. At liberation 1,294 prisoners from the family block survived.

could see the new railway lines being built with direct access to Crematoria II and III in preparation for Eichmann's plans. The music block was now just 50 metres away from the ramp, separated by a single barbed-wire fence where thousands of doomed human beings arrived only to be marched to their deaths. The musicians could see and sometimes hear the condemned, just as those condemned could often hear the musicians rehearse.

Zosia Cykowiak, the Polish violinist, recalled one day at the end of 1943 when even the screams of women from Block 25, half-crazed after they had been entirely starved of food and water prior to their deaths, were easily heard. There was a general lockdown in the camp, called a *blocksperre*, a regular occurrence when there was a selection process from inside the camp going on.

'We were hidden on the dark side of the Music Block. I realised that Alma was terrified. Everybody felt that way but practically never said it. It frightened Alma that she would one day see someone she knew selected for gassing and being driven towards the crematoria.' Zosia recalled Alma saying: 'Why are the Germans doing such things? I don't want to die this way,' to which of course she knew there was no answer.[34]

This account was told by Zosia to Jean-Jacques Felstein, the son of Belgian violinist Elsa Miller, when he was researching his biography of his mother. Zosia was especially sensitive to Alma's mood swings and saw how she 'suffered greatly. More than once during the mass transports of [Europe's] Jews to the gas chambers, hidden in the shadow of the block, she watched these scenes with despair, expressing with her whole being her protest of these forms of genocide.'[35]

Felstein, after interviewing Zosia, described this as Alma's 'moment of despair'. She had come out of the music block just enough to lean against the wall and then stuck 'her fingers in her ears so she did not have to hear the heart-piercing cries'.

Seeing Alma start to cry, Zosia took her in her arms without saying a word and calmed 'her by rocking her a little before walking away discreetly to allow her to regain her composure'.[36]

Some days Alma complained of such severe migraines that she asked Fania to massage her neck in the hope of some relief. Nothing helped and the pain appeared to be unremitting. Helena too remembered how downcast Alma had become. 'I can still see her as she walked onto the conductor's rostrum situated right up against the wall of the block. We wait for a sign from her, but she stands motionless for a moment with her arms outspread and then turns her head slightly so that she is facing the sun. She looks as if she is drinking in its springtime rays but there is a look of deep melancholy on her face.'[37]

In the early spring of 1944 the orchestra was rewarded with a walk outside and taste of fresh air. It happened after a visit from Hössler and Mandl. It may also have been given as a reward for pleasing Eichmann when he had visited their block. Mandl had enquired why everyone looked so pale. Alma replied that it was probably because they were spending all their time in an enclosed stuffy atmosphere. But then Zosia, feeling ground down and unable to continue with life, extraordinarily, spoke up and asked Hössler to be permitted to transfer to a different kommando. His reply was succinct: the *strafkommando* or penal kommando. Such audacity had to be punished. However, her request was born of deep sadness not audacity and the terrifying moment passed. Instead Mandl organised for the whole orchestra to be allowed to go for a walk, another unprecedented privilege.

Helena recorded the event:

Getting outside the barbed wire in the direction of the picturesque stretch of fishponds in the village of Harmeze, near Birkenau, came as a shock to us. Of course, it was a walk escorted by armed SS men with their inseparable companions, the fiercely barking dogs... Nature so long denied to us overcame us with its beauty and scents close at hand. At one point Zosia [Cykowiak] dropped to the ground to kiss the grass and one of the dogs jumped at her threateningly and could barely be restrained... fortunately it did not attack Zosia, who miraculously avoided severe bodily harm or even death... they allowed us even to get into the water and to swim.[38]

But the effect of the walk, glorious though it was, did not last long. Life continued in much the same way afterwards with several musicians close to exhaustion and lacking sufficient food to give them energy for such a demanding schedule. As the fainting during outdoor playing continued, the pressure resulted in Alma doling out punishments far stronger than merely making the girls start the piece again if she heard a wrong note. She either made them scrub the new wooden floor for several days or carry the heavy 50-litre soup kettles from the kitchen to the block, a task usually undertaken by the block orderly, or *Stubendienst*. Occasionally she told the girls that they 'played like pigs'[39] or that they were stupid, as Flora Jacobs, the Dutch accordionist, recalled.[40] According to Flora, Alma sometimes also told them they would forfeit extra rations as a result, but this detail is disputed by other witnesses. Zippi Spitzer, the Slovak graphic designer and mandolin player who worked in the camp administration, insisted that for work in the camp office and the music kommando she, Zippi, was allowed two sets of extra rations, which meant she had three rations in all including the basic allowance. But others, including Anita, have no memory of such extra food. When asked about Zippi, Anita questioned how she could possibly manage to be working in the camp office and also be playing in the orchestra, adding:

but none of us remember her. She comes out with a whole lot of information. Now although my memory is not all that good for detail and I had my own method of survival by not seeing things, she says that we got double rations, but I cannot remember that; I rang up my friend Violette recently and asked her if we got extra food.

'Of course not,' she said, 'we got just the same as everybody else.'

Anita concluded: 'If we had all got double rations, we wouldn't have been so hungry all the time!'[41]

The consensus seems to be that they had the same food rations as other women prisoners but often received 'randomly additional portions of bread, marmalade, margarine or canned meat'.[42] This may have been thanks to a passing SS officer if he thought they had played nicely, or thanks to Alma who, according to Rachela, was treated differently in terms of food and given rations from the 'special diet' kitchen, intended for German camp personnel. Rachela said she received her information about this from Rozika, Kapo of the diet kitchen, with whom she became friendly and who offered to help them all.

'So Rozika said "you keep to yourself everything that she gets and I will give her the white bread and send you the onion and garlic, everything you need".'[43]

It is not clear exactly how this worked in practice and whether or not the additional portions came from Alma or Rozika, or even a music-loving Nazi. In any case, they were irregular and meagre but, since the basic camp food ration was 'decisively insufficient even for the most frugal prisoner', as Primo Levi pointed out, 'death by hunger or diseases induced by hunger could be avoided only with additional food and to obtain it a large or small privilege was necessary'.[44]

On one occasion Alma's dispensing of penalties was resisted. Zosia recalled how during one rehearsal three women seated immediately behind the first violins repeatedly played wrong notes until Alma lost her temper and accused the girls of not paying attention. When she threatened a punishment of enforced scrubbing of the floor, one of the three, Jadwiga Zatorska, known as Wisia, the Polish violinist who was a close friend of Helena, resisted as she had in fact been attempting to help Violette with the tune. But also Wisia had just heard about the death of her three brothers in Auschwitz, one of whom, Wladyslaw, had been one of three Polish political prisoners arrested and locked into the punishment bunker of Block 11 in Auschwitz I, the *Stammlager*, and then shot. Once she heard about her brother's death, Wisia, distraught, decided she no longer wanted to live herself. In her distress, scrubbing the floor seemed worse than ridiculous, so she refused. Alma, as Kapo, threatened to report her to the authorities, a threat that implied being transferred to the *Stafkommando*, or penal kommando and almost certain death, just as Hössler had threatened Zosi. The Polish players were all devastated by this prospect. Although Alma backed down when she heard the full story it left a bad feeling. According to Helena, 'The Jewish members of the band regarded Wisia's behaviour as a manifestation of anti-Semitism, treating it as opposition by a Polish Aryan to Alma, the Jew. This was complete nonsense. Yet such was the attitude of some of the anti-Polish Jews, who sniffed anti-Semitism everywhere.'[45] Of course in Auschwitz anti-Semitism *was* everywhere, but Wisia's pain was real too and in a different category. In any other circumstances it would have been treated more sensitively.

At all events, Anita was given an identical punishment after she returned from the Revier in 1944 following her recovery from typhus and played badly, still weak with impaired hearing and eyesight from the illness. Looking back, she believed that Alma's response was her way of trying to keep sane. 'By involving us all in her frenzied pursuit of perfection in our performances of the rubbish we played, she may well have been instrumental in helping us to keep sane ourselves,' Anita said in 1996.[46]

Anita had to scrub the entire block floor for a week on her knees. 'I could not say I loved Alma for this. In fact, I was furious and hated her.' But she concluded, 'Strange though this may sound, I now have nothing less than the greatest admiration for Alma's attitude. I am still not sure whether she took a premeditated line or acted on instinct. But with this iron discipline she managed to focus our attention away from what was happening outside the block, away from the smoking chimneys and profound misery of life in the camp to an F which should have been an F#.'[47]

Anita believes that a key driving force for Alma was the pressure to meet her father's expectations of her. In this way she needed the orchestra to survive and used it to keep her own fear at bay. 'Alma saved the orchestra. It was a prop as real as the prisoners' ultimate need for each other, as real as two sisters holding up one sick sister to prevent her from fainting on roll call. She turned our job into an almost spiritual thing. She might have been as afraid of the Nazis as we were, but she never punished us out of fear.'[48] Moreover, the ultimate punishment, being forced to leave the music block, which would have spelled certain death, although threatened, was never meted out.

As a fellow professional musician, Fania said in a 1977 interview that she could see the increasing strain Alma was under. 'She was conducting a war of nerves in which she was the loser . . .' Under such circumstances any reactions were understandable: 'death, life, tears, laughter, everything was multiplied, disproportionate, beyond the limits of the credible. All was madness.'[49]

Alma with her father Arnold Rosé, whom she adored,
at the Hotel Romerbad in the Black Forest, 1927

Rachela Zelmanowicz, the Polish mandolin player, saw the strain manifest itself in a different way. Recognising Alma was 'a truly fantastic conductor and she succeeded to make something of our orchestra', at the same time even she was occasionally critical of her behaviour since she 'never imagined that professional people could show such jealousy towards each other' as she discovered in Auschwitz. She recounted in her memoir the story of how Szymon Laks, the conductor of the men's orchestra, once came to visit the women's orchestra. He was 'a famous conductor in France and he conducted our orchestra . . . and he brought with him a young boy, 17 years old, and this young boy played. I tell you Alma Rosé ran to her room, locked the door and shouted "this is like in a café".'⁵⁰ For Alma to describe a violinist as 'like a café artist' was the worst insult she could invoke.

Alma did, on rare occasions, offer praise, although the musicians had to earn it. She urged everyone to play the best they possibly could, as if they were living in normal circumstances.

Anita told me that the highest praise Alma would dole out would be to say '"I'm proud of you. You're good enough to play to my father." Clearly, she worshipped him. She used to talk a lot about him.'[51] Anita believed that Alma was unnaturally close to her father, 'turning to him for musical advice as basic as asking for suggested fingering, even as an adult'. Rachela recalled how she used to tell them that practising for eight hours a day was nothing. 'You know I used to play for eight hours a day and if I made one error my father would lift the whole piano in the air.'[52]

Alma's way of rewarding the musicians was to treat them to a clandestine solo performance in the barracks. No Nazis invited. Just the orchestra she had built, listening in rapt silence to a thing of great beauty and enormous courage. Discovery could so easily have led to the gas chambers. Helena believed that the exquisite pleasure of hearing in Auschwitz Alma's beautiful rendition of solo violin works such as Brahms' *Hungarian Dances* or Sarasate's *Gypsy Melodies* was unforgettable as was the 'highly emotional experience' of preparing and playing their own version of Chopin's *Tristesse*. According to Helena 'we played it for ourselves and for women prisoners who sneaked in to listen to something special, something that expressed through music our resistance to the German oppressors'.[53]

These were the only occasions when other female prisoners ever listened by choice to the music that was played in the camp.

Rachel Levy was fourteen when she arrived in Auschwitz in 1944 with her mother and four siblings, the three youngest of whom were immediately gassed with her mother on arrival while she and her older brother were pushed to the left. Rachel remembers being given clean clothes one day and told to sit outdoors and listen. 'I presumed there was an important Nazi coming to inspect.' She didn't mind the popular music but, having grown up in an Orthodox Jewish family in the countryside of the former Czechoslovakia, she knew only religious music. 'This was the first time I had heard an orchestra. What did I know of classical music?' she said when interviewed at her home in North London in June 2022.[54] Listening to the concert neither cheered nor distressed her. It was simply one more thing to be endured.

Young Kitty Felix, after surviving her ordeal with no clothes, was another who wrote critically of the orchestra. She described how two sisters, who had arrived in the camp with her, managed to get her into the sauna for a wash and a change of clothes one day and then 'wangled me into a concert given for the SS and privileged prisoners in the sauna. The camp orchestra played under the baton of Alma Rosé... it was grotesque', she maintained.

'Lesser prisoners were sometimes given orchestral performances but not in the best of circumstances,' she added.

According to Kitty, 'It was quite common for the musicians to play in front of them while they were undergoing "*Sport*" – the term used for a type of Nazi punishment when weakened prisoners were forced to undertake gymnastics until they collapsed on their knees with their arms above their heads.' Kitty was once made to endure this punishment, sitting on her knees holding bricks for hours, while the orchestra played within earshot. Another time the orchestra had to continue playing marches as exhausted women returned from work while one, found to have cigarettes hidden in her dress, was forced to eat the cigarettes.

Kitty was sickened by this and other occasions when they were forced to listen to the orchestra. 'Occasionally... to make up a full audience, a number of prisoners would be rounded up and ordered to attend, maybe along with some of the sick from the hospital. SS officers and privileged prisoners in the front rows might turn and nod condescendingly, especially if they applauded at the right places, and the very next day might send the same people to the gas chamber.'[55]

Kitty's critical attitude to Alma was not uncommon among the rank-and-file prisoners. Yet Alma did not always 'make up to' the authorities. At one Sunday concert a group of SS women in the audience could clearly be heard laughing and swearing. Alma immediately stopped the music, and 'like a bolt of lightning took a deep breath and said "that, I cannot play".[56] The chatting immediately stopped.

There were a few prisoners who saw the performance of music in a camp devoted to extermination in a positive light. Dr Mancy wanted to believe that even though most of the prisoners who crowded into the back of the sauna had to stand for hours during a concert, 'when Alma played her violin, she took them with her beyond the barbed wire to a faraway world of beauty that had vanished for them'.[57]

One prisoner remembered an impromptu serenade when Alma passed by her window and played the traditional German greeting for 'Happy Birthday'.[58] Seweryna Szmaglewska, the Polish prisoner who wrote one of the first eyewitness accounts of life in the camp, left a vivid impression of how it felt to be in Birkenau in the early spring of 1944, hearing music.

As you stand with your back against the wall of the orchestra barracks you can see beyond the line of wires the area between the women's and the men's barracks, then again wires white with frost and again barracks white with snow, separated by more strands of wire. All a white vision, all a tormenting dream. You cannot shake it off and open your eyes, you are not yet ready to wake up.

You can faintly hear the orchestra rehearsing a melody by Grieg. Snowy white strands of small white cloudlets draw up in the winter sky like the feathers of an angel absorbed in listening... the nearest frost-covered strands of wire are like great lines of written music, drawn in white ink against the grey background of the landscape. The eyes roam over them, imagining the various musical notes and symbols on various lines... the orchestra plays on and creates the vision of a white flower lying at the bottom of a lake under a sheet of ice.[59]

It was a gripping if somewhat elaborate account of the sense of hope mixed with fear that stalked the camp in early 1944. Another Polish woman, Jadwiga Bienkowska, agreed: 'sometimes we managed to listen to the beautiful musical works played for the SS by the camp orchestra. We valued highly such moments of spiritual siesta – they took us back to our pasts and made us forget to a tiny degree about our sad reality.'[60]

Critical responses to the women's orchestra were more marked than any responses from men to the music they had on offer. This might well have had something to do with the far greater contrast between ordinary female prisoners and those who played who were relatively well dressed and groomed whereas the men, not being excused outdoor work, did not look very different. Or, as Auschwitz historian Jacek Lachendro writes, perhaps the women prisoners 'took a more emotional attitude to music and to a greater degree pointed out the dissonance between their grim situation and the sometimes merry music played by the orchestra',[61] which made it so unbearable for some.

Sunday, 2 April 1944 was a good day for the orchestra. They had played well in an afternoon concert and in the afterglow of praise Alma had told them she was proud of their performance.

There are different accounts of what happened next. According to Regina and Fania, Alma was called to the SS office and on her return to the music block confided excitedly to a few of the musicians that she was about to be released from the camp to play outside. Fania said Alma told her she was now leaving to play for soldiers of the Wehrmacht, a proposal which met with Fania's disapproval. But Regina maintained Alma had said she was to play in the Katowice Opera House in Poland. Others maintained that any kind of release would have been unlikely.

That night Alma went to attend a birthday celebration for Frau Schmidt, the non-Jewish Kapo of one of the Kanada warehouses. Rachela said she saw her returning from the dinner, clearly unwell, and asked Regina to follow her. 'A few minutes later Regina returned and asked Flora, the Dutch girl who with Hilde, Regina and Dr Mancy was among those closest to Alma, to go inside. Flora went and when she came back she told us that Alma was very ill.'

Regina said that Zofia Czajkowska then appeared and ordered her out of Alma's room.

Among the various accounts of that fateful night everyone agrees that Alma's decline was very rapid. According to Flora, while Alma was still able to speak, she complained of a terrible headache and dizziness. It seemed as if her entire body was gripped by shaking seizures, or rigors. Then she vomited. Flora and the others put her to bed but reported that she was delirious and saying: 'the Russians are coming, the Russians are coming'. Since liberation by the Russians had been her fervent hope, perhaps this was her unconscious optimism speaking.

Soon Mandl was summoned. She arrived with an SS doctor who examined Alma and decided she must be taken immediately by stretcher to the Revier. Under special orders she was given a private room in the medical block, an astonishing concession for somebody Jewish and a clear indication that Mandl viewed Alma's illness with great seriousness from the start. Rumours rushed around the camp and by the time Dr Mancy arrived to see what was wrong with her friend, Alma was covered in bruises and had a temperature of 39.4 Celsius. Semiconscious, she told Mancy that she had drunk some vodka at the birthday party, which Mancy considered a bizarre admission from a woman who had already told her doctor friend that she could not tolerate alcohol at all. Here in the camp, it might have contained anything, but why, she wondered, even if she was celebrating what she hoped would be her release, would an intelligent woman like Alma, a teetotaller, have drunk something unknown and possibly adulterated?

Doctors gave orders to pump her stomach and when her fever disappeared a Jewish woman doctor looking after her suspected encephalitis. There were by this time about six or seven prisoner doctors, as well as Dr Mancy, keeping vigil.

Meanwhile Frau Schmidt was also admitted to another section of the infirmary amid rumours that the camp might be in the grip of a new epidemic, although food poisoning seemed more likely. On 4 April Dr Mengele himself came to see what was happening and ordered a spinal tap at which Dr Mancy assisted, noting that since the spinal fluid was clear Alma probably did not have meningitis.

A number of other tests for possible infections were performed, none of which produced a clue as to what was wrong. Dr Mancy stayed with her friend throughout the night but Alma was drifting in and out of consciousness as her seizures increased. Before dawn on 5 April 1944, Alma Rosé died. She was thirty-seven. Dr Mancy fled in tears, unable to comprehend how in a place where deliberate death was constant and ubiquitous, this particular death, so unexpected and unexplained, had been allowed to happen.

Suspicion of deliberately poisoning Alma inevitably fell on Frau Schmidt as she had organised the food at the birthday celebration. Yet she was also ill. Quite possibly, she had eaten or drunk less and responded better to treatment. Others including Dr Lingens-Reiner thought that 'Puff Mutti' Musskeller, the prostitute yodeller who had disrupted the Christmas concert so forcefully, may have organised it as retribution for the way Alma had treated her. There were even rumours that Alma's immense despair, especially after the destruction of the Czech family camp, may have led to notions of suicide. Nobody knew for sure and for years doubt lingered about the circumstances of Alma's death. Today the mystery remains although botulism, a deadly illness where a toxin rapidly attacks the brain and nervous system, is proposed by Alma's biographer and others as the most likely cause, but that cannot be proved.

Maria Mandl came to the music block to inform the orchestra that they could pay their last respects to their leader in block 4, where Alma's body was laid out on top of two stools covered with a white cloth, a sort of makeshift catafalque. Some women placed sprigs of greenery as a token tribute to their leader but there was not much of that to be found in the camp. And then what happened to Alma's body is disputed. Some orchestra members believed that, on the orders of Hössler, it was taken to the crematorium and disposed of separately and not subjected to a mass cremation. Zippi stated that because of the Nazi fear of public health issues there was an autopsy and that she saw Alma's body, post autopsy, lying on the wagon outside the Revier. 'She was naked, her eyes were sunken. Her abdomen was stitched up crudely as a result of the autopsy.'[62] But there is no official record of this.

Some of the orchestra members declined to see their virtuoso leader in death. Helena admitted in her memoirs that she did not go but did not say why. Hilde did not go because she preferred to seize the moment when the music block was empty to find solace, alone, in Alma's room. While there, she noticed Alma's precious notebook in which Alma had noted the name and address of her Dutch friend, Leonard Jongkees, a doctor and amateur cellist six years her junior with whom she may have been in love. Hilde also saw the banned lyrics written out by Alma for the Chopin Étude in E, which she had been forbidden to perform in public. Hilde took this and hid it carefully.[63]

She had known Alma as well as anyone in the orchestra during the brief period they were together and described her later as like a sabra, a thorny cactus on the outside but inside a refreshingly sweet fruit. Dr Mancy said she was 'like a bird with bloodied wings beating against the bars of its cage. Music enabled her to take flight and leave Birkenau behind.'[64]

Quite possibly, as the musicologist Michael Haas argues, Alma was reckless, a character trait that ensured her arrest and which not only resulted in her being in Auschwitz, but which ultimately brought about her death at a critical moment in the camp, leaving her orchestra 'girls' fearfully exposed and vulnerable.

But she was a complex, multi-layered personality, musically gifted but not a virtuoso, responsive in love but wounded by not having it reciprocated. Above all she was a deeply dutiful daughter. To accept her occasionally aggressive approach to her girls is in no way to erode or invalidate her role in saving them. The reverse. This flawed heroine literally and courageously had embraced the life-giving force of music and, without her, survival for all of them would have been thrown into doubt. Until 1943, Alma's heritage as a member of a famous musical dynasty outshone her considerable musical talent. After she took charge of the orchestra in 1943, until her premature death in April 1944, her star could never shine brightly enough to do justice to her exceptional achievement in saving almost forty lives. Like many in those tragic years her greatness ultimately derived from her ability to transcend her circumstances and show a courage and passion for which nothing in her previous life had prepared her. This was her greatest creative act.

Whether she herself understood the exceptional nature of what she had created by dint of hard work and discipline – an orchestra of mostly amateurs that could play overtures, operettas and marches – is unknowable. But most likely, as she told Zippi and others, 'I will never let these girls go . . . After the liberation I'm not interested in anything else, but I will take these girls and we will travel through Europe.'⁶⁵

It was a dream that for ten short months saved Alma herself.

This was a time of appalling uncertainty in the camp. Two days after Alma's death, the alarms sounded after two young prisoners had apparently escaped, Alfred Wetzler and Walter Rosenberg, later known as Rudolf Vrba. In fact, these two Slovak men, who had been in Auschwitz since 1942, were still hiding in the camp under a woodpile, waiting for three days until the search party was called off, when they succeeded in getting out of the camp and made it home, determined to inform the world about the gas chambers at Auschwitz. And then came the Easter weekend. Easter Sunday on 9 April was a sunny day, not a big deal in Birkenau, and there is no evidence that the occasion would have been marked by special music with or without Alma. But that year, given Alma's death, some of the players felt the need for solidarity more acutely than ever. Little Hélène (Hélène Rounder) prepared a special greetings card for Helena Dunicz, just as she had made her a Christmas card when she was ill in the infirmary. Hélène was Jewish but she had no problem drawing a crucifix for her fellow violinist, who was a Catholic, knowing the sacred occasion would be important for her. Helena kept these cards, commenting in her memoir how 'these little gestures had great meaning in the camp and testified for the human need to bring joy to others'.[66]

7

I felt the sun on my face

In the wake of Alma's mysterious death, the insecure orchestra teetered, threatening to split along national and religious lines. Who could possibly replace Alma? Would the new conductor send the Jewish girls back to the lethal outdoor kommandos – or worse – from which Alma had rescued them?

'The word insecure may seem an odd one to use, but with Alma no longer there it soon became clear she had *been* the orchestra,' Anita Lasker said. 'She had held it all together... with Alma's demise we were deprived of leadership in a much wider sense.'[1]

But the uncertainty did not last long. Josef Kramer, the SS captain who was promoted to Birkenau (Auschwitz II) camp commander on 8 May,* visited the block shortly after Alma's death and unceremoniously announced that Sonya, or Soja, Winogradowa, the twenty-three-year-old pianist, singer and decorated Red Army officer who had joined the band five months before, would be the new and third orchestra Kapo. The Jewish women, having heard a rumour that the Russian element wanted to remove all the Jewish players, feared the worst. According to Hilde, Soja had insisted from the start on no Jews in the

---

* Replacing SS *Sturmbannführer* Friedrich Hartjenstein.

orchestra. 'She set a condition that she would only take over if all Jews were expelled from the orchestra; Jews,' she argued, 'had the best positions in the orchestra first and second violin, singers who were professionals. She wanted to give places to Poles and Ukrainians.'[2] It is quite possible that Soja had argued for this but, if she had, she must have been overruled initially as the Jews continued to play for more than six months in the weakened orchestra. Without them it might have collapsed completely. But for the moment it was business as usual. Or almost.

Soja was good looking, blonde, and, by some accounts, even pretty – something which was considered unachievable by most women in Birkenau. She was also a favourite of the SS. She was a courageous fighter and a talented pianist. However, as a conductor she was 'of very mediocre talent... It was a total disaster,' Anita remembered. 'Nobody respected her and the whole orchestra became a free for all.'[3] Zosia Cykowiak agreed that although she was a very good pianist, 'and Alma Rosé greatly appreciated her playing and entrusted large solo parts to her for performance... she did not have sufficient conducting skills and... She had difficulty establishing herself as an authority in the band, perhaps also because of language barriers.'[4]

Zosia concluded that she distinguished herself mainly by her attitude towards the Germans, emphasising at every opportunity that she was a prisoner of war with the rank of major in the Soviet army, and that she should be in a POW camp.

Giuliana Tedeschi, an Italian Jewish prisoner who arrived that May, described Soja's conducting style as if 'she translated the urgency of rhythm and cadence into hysterical gestures'.[5] Although the orchestra continued to play marches, the Sunday concerts were cancelled, presumably deemed to be of less interest without Alma's solos, and Soja was in no position to fight for additional treats or rewards as Alma had done. In addition, the

SS undermined Soja's authority by reducing the hours the band could rehearse by half, making the musicians undertake 'useful work' during the day which mostly consisted of knitting and mending in the block. The SS maintained that the orchestra could manage without extra rehearsals if all they were now playing was marches which the players knew extremely well. There was no longer a search for perfection, as there had been under Alma, the extra effort to be musical which had given the orchestra its special sound, its soul.

On 6 June 1944, two months after Alma's death, the Allies landed in Normandy. Meanwhile, mass transports of Jews from Hungary were pouring into Auschwitz-Birkenau, as the Nazis raced to make Eastern Europe *Judenrein* (a Jewish exclusion zone) while Soviet forces continued their relentless advance. Starting on 15 May,* thousands upon thousands of Hungarian Jews were sent to their deaths as soon as the trains pulled in along the new ramp which led directly to the overworked crematoria. There were so many Jews to be killed that some bodies were burned in open fields with body fat fuelling the flames. This appalling task was given to the men of the so-called special squads or Sonderkommando who then had to spread the ashes in a deep pit dug especially for the purpose. Within months Hungary's rural Jewry was destroyed as the Nazis cleared Transylvania and the Carpathians. But, just as the urban Jews of Budapest were set on the same path to destruction, the transports ceased. This was partly thanks not only to the heroic escape from Auschwitz in April of Vrba and Wexler but also a further escape seven weeks later of a young Polish Jew, Czeslaw Morodowicz, and a Slovak Jew, Arnost Rosin. The reports from these four eyewitnesses of

---

* There had been two earlier transports of Jews from Hungary on 29 and 30 April but 15 May was the start of the mass killings.

mass murder at Auschwitz eventually led to diplomatic efforts involving the Roosevelt administration and the Pope which halted further Budapest deportations.

Nonetheless, over a fifty-six-day period from 15 May until 9 July 1944, a total of 147 trains transported 437,402 Jews in boxcars to concentration camps, the vast majority to Auschwitz-Birkenau. Most of the approximately 440,000 Jews deported from Hungary to Auschwitz-Birkenau were sent to their deaths in the gas chambers on arrival. Hungary thus became almost completely free of Jews – *Judenrein*, exactly as the Nazis had planned.

The mass murder of Hungarian Jews is widely considered to be one of the greatest crimes of the twentieth century. And yet the catastrophe had one consequence for the orchestra: a handful of talented Hungarian female musicians who managed to escape selection were swiftly recruited. The most notable of this group were the twenty-three-year-old singer Eva Steiner, on the cusp of her career deported with her mother Jolanda, who was allowed to work alongside her daughter in the orchestra as a copyist; the popular violinist and bandleader Lily Mathé; and another classically trained violinist named Ibi (her surname is not known), short for Ibolya, which means violet in Hungarian.

Lily Mathé also remembered how Eva, who had aspired to sing opera since childhood and had just completed her studies on voice and piano at the Budapest Academy three months previously, lied brazenly on arrival: '"My mother is a great musician," Eva said. "She no longer plays, but she can compose our music." Mrs Steiner was not a musician at all [she was a dressmaker] but, as long as we were in Auschwitz, she scribbled notes on paper, and I made music out of it. The girls in the orchestra, Jewish and non-Jewish, played an eager role in that ruse.'[6]

In Anita's view, although Alma was 'irreplaceable ... Lily was a warm and generous person who saved the orchestra at this point.

Her contribution to the orchestra was considerable. We started to play a lot of Hungarian music such as Monti's *Czardas*, and she helped to keep the SS interested in the orchestra for a bit longer.[7] Hélène Wiernik continued to play first violin but there was something about Lily's vibrant personality that the SS found impossible to ignore.

Lily Mathé, born Lidia Markstein in 1910 into a middle-class family in Eger, northern Hungary, arrived in Auschwitz on 7 July 1944 together with Ibi on one of the last transports out of Hungary after having been confined for the last weeks in one bedroom of a so-called 'yellow star' house with approximately eight family members. The Swedish diplomat Raoul Wallenberg, freshly arrived in the Hungarian capital just two days later, immediately began his rescue efforts for some of the few remaining Jews in the country, many of whom were in hiding, but too late for Lily and her family.

Lily had taken up the violin aged six and was a natural performer. In 1926 she and her family moved to Budapest so that she could study with Jeno Hubay, one of the most eminent violinists in the world, at the prestigious Franz Liszt Academy of Music. She graduated in 1932 in both conducting and playing.

Soon after this she married, although the name of her husband has vanished from history. Instead of pursuing a career as a classical soloist, she established her stage name as Lily Mathé and started a band called the Gypsy Boys with approximately thirty or so members recruited by her. The troupe, including her husband who now became her manager, travelled throughout Europe in the 1930s playing to great acclaim in Berlin, the Netherlands, Switzerland, Paris and London, where in the spring of 1939 they were paid £350 for a five-day slot at the Odeon Cinema Forest Gate, around $23,000 (approximately £18,000) at today's prices. This was the first time the cinema had organised a stage show and it was considered a big deal. The Gypsy Boys could not read music so learned the tunes by ear, which added to their fame. One reviewer for the Dutch daily newspaper *Limburgsche Dagblad* wrote enthusiastically not simply about 'Lily's beauty' but about how 'a gypsy never learns music through notes, but only with his heart and hand'.[8]

Even after Europe was embroiled in war, the troupe continued to be in great demand, especially in the Netherlands where they had built up a big following. Yet in 1941, as soon as they could following the German occupation of the Netherlands, Lily and her young husband decided to return to Hungary, partly to support their families and also believing, erroneously, that Jews there were relatively safer than in the rest of occupied Europe since Hungary was not to be invaded by German forces until March 1944. Her husband returned to his family in Ujvidek. Lily never saw him again. She and her parents and young sister-in-law Aranka, who had married Lily's brother Ferenc on 4 July, were deported to Auschwitz on 5 July 1944. Two days later her parents, Sandor and Neli Markstein, were gassed on arrival. Lily later described seeing them led away as one of those moments engraved in her mind for the rest of her life. But their daughter's musical fame – and youth – was such that she had a different experience. She, as well as her brother and sister-in-law, were among the lucky few Hungarian Jews not immediately killed, initially saved merely because they looked young enough to work.

After being taken off the train Lily was led to a barracks. She later told the story of what happened next.

> Then the door opened and in came a man. As I later learned [he] was Josef Kramer, the hated camp commandant. In one hand was a whip.
>
> He quickly walked down the line, asking 'what is your job?'

of each terrified girl. When he came to me, I said: 'I am Lily Mathé. I was the leader of a gypsy band.' Kramer stared at me coldly for a moment. 'Yes, I remember you. I heard you play once in Berlin. We'll see if you can still play. If you can't, I'll have your head off.'

It transpired that Kramer, who regarded himself as a serious music lover, had seen Lily's show in Berlin and had been impressed. So she was taken for an immediate audition and told to play the violin he shoved at her. 'It seemed to please him,' Lily recalled in 1960.[9] She was allowed to join the orchestra.

Yet despite her outstanding musical credentials, Lily did not take over from Soja Winogradowa as Kapo nor did she replace either of the first desk violinists, Hélène Wiernik and Helena Dunicz. Nonetheless, she became the de facto leader of the orchestra. In post-war media interviews and speaking to a biographer of Eichmann following his dramatic arrest in 1960, she recounted how soon after arrival at the camp and the audition with Kramer, she had to have a second audition for Eichmann, Kramer's boss, who was making frequent visits to the camp in 1944 to oversee personally the Hungarian liquidation.

'I remember that beast to this day. In the midst of all the horror and death Eichmann said: "She will do," and to me: "You will lead a camp orchestra to welcome the new inmates and play at the officers' mess."'[10]

But in the same breath Eichmann told her she did not look much like a musician and should get herself something decent to wear. He added menacingly that he still needed to approve Lily's appointment and that if it turned out he did not like the way she played, she would not last long. So she went to the Kanada warehouses and brought back whatever clothes she could carry for herself and some for the others.

Lily could never forget the horror of being ordered to play at raucous Nazi parties, which Eichmann demanded of her. She recalled at least four such occasions, or what she called an 'Eichmann blast', taking place in Kramer's private house. Here she said:

Our gypsy music and streams of alcohol had to bring in the mood (just right) before all the toasts were brought out, (and) we were already there... All of a sudden, Eichmann jumped up. His collar hung loose, and his face was beet-red. He pounded the table with his fist and shrieked, 'Out with the prisoners!'

That was my fourth Eichmann blast. Whenever the bacchanal reached its high point, we were dismissed. A human life was literally reckoned at nothing in Auschwitz. The assembly-line killings seemed to unleash all other instincts in the Nazis...

Prostitutes, who had been taken prisoner because, according to the Germans, they were asocial and antisocial, had to amuse the camp leaders. If this amusement had consequences, girls were shot.[11]

Not only did the musicians have to perform well, they had to look attractive, almost impossible in Auschwitz. '[We] played at these parties with bright bandanas hiding our shaven skulls; Eichmann had said the sight of them put him off his smoked salmon.'[12] For although one of the privileges Alma had won for her musicians was being allowed to grow their hair, this took time as everyone who was not gassed on arrival was still shaven and tattooed, including Lily, and several of them still had unsightly stubble.

'So we wore headscarves, tied behind our ears, like they do in Ukraine,' commented Flora Jacobs, who tried to push hers back so that a few wisps of new hair showed.[13]

We played what Eichmann ordered, rousing marches and his favourite, 'We're marching against Britain'. They all sang to that and the buxom guard girls, some already un-brassiered, leaped within their stiff black jackets as they bounced on the knees of their temporary boyfriends and thumped the rhythm on the table. One night, while Eichmann drank toasts to Hitler, to war, to victory, to the death of pig-dog Churchill, to anything he could think of, and flung glasses against the wall after every toast, Joseph Kramer's mistress beckoned us out. She was the kindest of the guards; she used to give me bread and honey as a present for cleaning her billet. She once gave me a watch and even had two of my cousins removed from the gas chamber list and she had a table laid for us with the leftovers of Eichmann's banquet. We ate all we could and were stuffing the rest into our blouses . . . beef and ham, a pound slab of butter, and I had enough salami for ten lunches.

But that was not the end of the evening, as other guards followed them out.

'Then of course, the Germans jeered. One tried to ram the salami down my throat, and of course we were all ill.'

Two soldiers with their rifles marched the women from this luxurious villa to their loathsome barracks, fifteen minutes and a whole world away.

'A few days later Eichmann stood by the bandstand as we played the girls back into camp from the fields.'[14]

Lily recalled one evening when Commandant Kramer, at a party, hummed a few bars of one of his favourite airs and asked her to play it. He had been drinking heavily, and she could not recognise the tune. She asked him to sing more, but he got angry and cried, 'if you can't play it, you'll lose your head'. Lily made an effort, which luckily satisfied Kramer, who said: 'That was good. You saved your life.' The tune, she later found out, was called 'Little Café'.[15]

According to the author Gabriele Knapp the private concerts mostly took place in the rehearsal room.[16] But as the only rehearsal room was inside the music block itself, these concerts were when SS officers, who were allowed to move freely around the camp, dropped by for an 'informal' request, performances that even Alma had had to stomach. What was new since Alma's death were raucous occasions where small numbers of the orchestra were hand-picked for private parties of the SS, which as Lily stated, were held in villas outside the camp itself.

Sometimes Eva Steiner was required to sing with Lily Mathé and Flora Jacobs, the Dutch accordionist and harmonica player, also regulars. For the rest of her life Flora could never forget the trauma of being forced to play at what were evidently private performances just for Kramer, how 'Josef Kramer would often wake me up in the evening at the music barracks where we were sleeping. Lily Mathé and I had to get up if there were evening arrivals of transports.' According to Flora, Kramer's job on these occasions was to supervise the work of the clothing kommando, tasked with unpicking the seams of the clothes of incoming prisoners.

They were searching for gold and diamonds ... sewn in the seams and shoulder seams. He [Kramer] would get bored or annoyed, and we had to play all night long. Lily on violin, and I on harmonica.

Then he ran around like a kind of power-hungry man or came over for a chat.

[This happened] when it was as late, for example, as one a.m., [and so] Lily and I did not have to appear for roll-call at four o'clock the next morning. Kramer once said: '*Das ist*

Musik einer Jude' (that is Jewish music). I then said it was Wagner or Strauss... and he liked it. I did not know who it was from. I just played it.

I also once played with a pistol at my head. That had a sting. That happened one, three, or four times. I was then asked to play a certain piece of music, to which I said: 'I am an amateur, she is a pro.' Then I pointed to Lily, who promptly had the gun at her head. I will never forget her eyes.[17]

There was one other Hungarian Jewish musician who survived initial selections from the ramp around this time. Eva Benedek was a twenty-three year-old violin student from Budapest, newly married and pregnant. The other musicians did their best to feed and shield the young mother-to-be and after the war, although none of them could recall her name, they had a clear memory of how the entire orchestra helped take care of her, standing around her in an attempt to hide her bump whenever Nazi officials entered the music block.

'We managed to shield her for months. We concealed her and got her food. She received milk and other nourishing foods, which were scarcer in Auschwitz than gold... That pregnant little lady became like a beaming expectant mother in such a camp of living skeletons,' said Lily.

'After eight months we lost her, and after all that we heard that she had brought her child into the world – only to have her child taken away. Both vanished. We could (just) guess where they had gone.'

Dr Gisella Perl, a Hungarian Jewish gynaecologist given the most unimaginable tasks to perform in the camp as the price of survival, recounted what happened in her 1948 book, *I Was a Doctor in Auschwitz*. Eva Benedek was 'a beautiful talented young woman who was separated from her husband only a few days after her wedding ... I bandaged her abdomen and in her formless rags, amidst women whose stomachs were constantly bloated with undernourishment, her condition went unnoticed.' According to Perl, Eva delivered her baby, a boy, during a brief period when the Nazis permitted Jewish children to be born. But immediately 'she turned her back on it, wouldn't look at it, wouldn't hold it in her arms. Tears were streaming down her cheeks incessantly ... Finally, I succeeded in making her tell me what was on her mind.'

According to Perl, Eva said that she dare not take her baby in her arms nor look at him since ' "I feel it, I know it, that somehow they are going to take him away from me ...". And she was right.'

A few days after giving birth the Nazis issued a new order depriving Jewish mothers of additional food, a thin milky soup mixed with flour which swelled their breasts and enabled them to feed their babies. 'For eight days Eva Benedek had to look on while her baby son starved slowly to death ... and on the eighth day I had to take him out and throw him on a heap of rotting corpses.'[18]

Shortly after this Eva Benedek herself was gassed.

Without Alma's protection, the orchestra suffered. The months after her shocking death were among the worst for the orchestra. There was no longer the feeling that playing in the orchestra would be enough to save your life. Some felt nothing could save your life any more or that life was not worth saving. The story of Henriette, known as Jetty, Cantor, a talented Dutch musician who refused a chance to play in the orchestra, is evidence of how much it had declined without Alma. Born Henriette Franck in The Hague in 1903, Jetty was a conservatory-trained professional singer, violinist and actress born into a long-standing musical

Jewish family. By the 1930s, Jetty was immensely successful in a number of genres including as a jazz singer performing in Germany. A fluent German speaker, she loved German culture. 'I always loved Germany. It hurt twice as much that it was Germans who did all this to me,' she said in 1997.[19] Jetty was married at the age of twenty to the cellist Mozes Cantor, with whom she sometimes played in trios. They had a son, Jacob, known as Jaap, born in 1926.

In 1942 she and her husband, her parents, her sister and her sister's children were all deported to Westerbork, the transit camp where Flora had also waited. Her son Jaap, a teenager, managed to avoid deportation. Here she was a leading performer in various cabaret and theatrical activities overseen mostly by camp commander Albert Conrad Gemmeker, a man renowned for his love of watching the comedy performances, although some prisoners believed he was 'star struck' as a result of having so many well-known theatrical names in the camp. But he still sent Jews to be murdered at Auschwitz.

Everybody at Westerbork knew what it meant to say goodbye to loved ones who were constantly being dispatched on trains and told that they were being 'sent east'.

'That was the most horrible thing,' Jetty recalled in 1997, 'how often we had to say good-bye to parents and siblings, to good friends and acquaintances at the train. How can you go back to the stage, be funny and make people laugh afterwards?'[20]

In August 1944 it was her turn. Commander Gemmeker closed the camp theatre and sent its actors on railway wagons via Theresienstadt to Auschwitz. 'He smiled us to Auschwitz,' said Jetty Cantor bitterly. After a few weeks at Theresienstadt, Jetty arrived at Auschwitz apparently still with her violin from Theresienstadt. As a result, she was almost immediately recruited for the orchestra now run by Soja Winogradowa, Alma's successor.

THE WOMEN'S ORCHESTRA OF AUSCHWITZ

But this time, once she learned the fate of her parents, sister and two nieces, all gassed before she had arrived, she could not cooperate with the Nazis.

> First they took my violin away. Then I saw those huge flames and the smoke. I thought that this is the kitchen for all the many thousand people. But it was the gas chamber. And then I was called to the rehearsal. Rehearsal? In Auschwitz? Yes, they said, we should play, in front of the gas chamber. I can't do this, I said. Just imagine: my family or friends go into the oven and I play music to it. Then they fetched me.[21]

Jetty was fully aware of the consequences of her refusal. She was sent to the 'death barracks', the block reserved for those under sentence of death. Against the odds, Cantor did not die in these barracks and nor was she gassed. In January 1945, when the mass evacuations began, hope and a desire to live suddenly triumphed over exhaustion, sadness and pain. Weak and skeletally thin, Cantor managed to jump from a cattle wagon on the moving train sending her to Belsen and survived, although with seriously damaged legs following the fall from the train.*

Jetty's inability to play in Auschwitz once she knew about the murder of her family could be seen as an assertive act or as a demonstration of utter helplessness. Within the camp, the desire not to live any longer was simply described as losing hope or 'going to the wires'. Women (and men) who gave up simply walked to the electric fences surrounding the camp, each carrying 6,000 volts of electricity, and died instantly on contact. Sometimes the

---

* She nonetheless had a successful post-war theatrical and radio career and was able to watch her son, who along with Mozes had also survived, grow up. Her marriage however did not last and she was divorced in 1948.[22]

228

current jolted the corpse away from the fence, but usually their bodies still glued to the wires. 'It was a kind of burning process similar to the electric chair. You weren't allowed to touch them,' remembered Flora.[23] 'We tried to beat them off the wires with pieces of wood. I did all of this too. What haven't I done?'

Sylvia Wagenberg, who went to live in Israel after the war, recalled one such episode in *Bach in Auschwitz*, the 1999 documentary film by French director Michel Daeron. 'One day a woman threw herself against the electric fence while we were playing,' she said. 'But who is responsible for her death? Was the music responsible, would she have done it anyway?' she pondered. 'For me it was not so terrible because tens of thousands were dying every day. It was an organised daily massacre.'

Regina Kupferberg, Alma's maid, interviewed with Hilde and Sylvia in Israel where all three were living, added quietly that she remembered moments when 'I felt I wanted to end it all and would have thrown myself against the wires. But then I felt the warmth of the sun on my face and that sensation stopped me.'

Two additional tragedies hit the camp in 1944. The first concerned Mala Zimetbaum, a twenty-six-year-old Belgian woman of Polish-Jewish descent, known by almost everyone in the camp as she was a messenger who made it her business to communicate information wherever and whenever she could. She was liked by Mandl as she was useful to her and had a strong relationship with many in the orchestra. Mala saw the music block as a meeting place for privileged staff from the camp office as well as prominent prisoners who worked in Kanada or the Revier alongside 'music-loving' SS and tried to help wherever she could. She also had made contact with partisans outside the camp.

Zimetbaum played an active part in the camp's underground and, according to Primo Levi and others, devoted herself to

Regina, née Kupferberg, with her husband, fellow survivor
Aharon Bacia, whom she met in Celle, Germany

helping less privileged inmates in myriad ways. Levi said that
Zimetbaum 'was generous and courageous; she had helped many
of her companions and was loved by all of them'. She interceded
to have inmates sent to easier work when she suspected they were
not fit for harder labour and also warned prisoners of coming
selections in the infirmary, encouraging them to leave to save their
lives if at all possible. Some inmates reported how she sneaked
them family photographs that their relatives had sent but which
were put into Nazi files as the prisoners were not allowed to
receive them in the camp. Zimetbaum also got food and medicine
for people in need.

On Saturday, 24 June 1944 she and her non-Jewish lover, Edek

Galinski, escaped. Mala had hoped to convey to the Allies the truth of what was happening at Auschwitz. There were whisperings in the women's camp almost immediately and word of her escape made those who knew Mala briefly happy, even if not many believed that she could permanently evade recapture.[24]

Two weeks after Mala's escape, on 7 July 1944, American bombers strafed the railway lines to Auschwitz. On 20 August, 127 B-17s, with an escort of a hundred P-51 fighter craft, dropped 1,336 500-pound bombs on the I G Farben Buna synthetic-oil factory that was less than 5 miles (8 km) east of Birkenau, hitting German oil reserves. This gave the inmates of Auschwitz enormous hope. As Elie Wiesel, the Auschwitz survivor and noted Holocaust author, recalled in 1985: 'We were no longer afraid of death; at any rate, not of that death. Every bomb filled us with joy and gave us new confidence in life.'[25] Allied bombardment of Birkenau itself was not given the go-ahead, much as some of the prisoners might have clung to the hope that it would bring an end to their torment. Yet even if the Allies had bombed Birkenau in mid-July it would have been too late to save the approximately 320,000 Hungarian Jews whom the Germans had killed upon arrival at Auschwitz between 15 May and 9 July 1944.

But Mala and Edek were not as fortunate as Wetzler and Vrba, the two young Slovak prisoners who had successfully escaped a couple of months earlier and were trying to alert the world to the realities of the camp. Mala and Edek managed only two weeks of freedom in the mountains before being recognised and recaptured. They were brought back to the main camp, where they were tortured and locked up in separate cells in the punishment block, Block 11, prior to their execution on 15 September 1944. Accounts differ as to the precise nature of their death but while there is no suggestion that the orchestra played during the execution, they and other prisoners were made to watch.

THE WOMEN'S ORCHESTRA OF AUSCHWITZ

According to Helena:

we were intended to be witnesses to the show execution of
Mala. They herded us out into the central street of sector Bıa,
where the gallows had been set up. I stood there a certain
distance away. The execution took place in complete silence,
nothing could be heard but the portentous words of the death
sentence being read out. Suddenly there was a commotion.
In order to elude the clutches of the henchmen Mala had
cut her own wrists and struck an SS man [*Unterscharführer*
Taube] in the face.[26]

This gruesome scene was especially painful for Rachela
Zelmanowicz, the Polish mandolin player who had got to know
Mala well and was grateful to her for trying to help find work for
her brother, Dov, in an office or other indoor kommando since he
could read and write good German. 'She promised me ... listen
I have some connections. I know some people in the camp ...
consider it done,' Rachela recounted. Mala tried but in the event
failed. As she explained to Rachela: 'He stood up in line and they
chose men for the Sonderkommando, which was the cruellest of
all.' But Rachela understood. 'Mala was so miserable. She wanted
to help me so much.'[27]

Now Rachela, along with other members of the orchestra, had
to watch as her friend was killed. 'I saw how they brought her
[Mala] from the bunker. I saw how she took out a razor blade
that she had hidden, and she cut her veins. I was there and I
heard what she said. She yelled at the Germans *"ihr bekomt mich
eine halbe leiche"* [you will get me as half a corpse].'[28] The manner
of her death, cheating the Nazis of their desire to execute her,
added to her mythic status. Both Helena and Rachela were, like

Primo Levi, full of praise for Mala's heroism and the fact that even the brutality of Auschwitz did not corrupt her desire to do good.

On 7 October 1944, Rachela suffered a greater personal tragedy when her brother, Dov, took part in the courageous, but doomed Sonderkommando uprising. For months, several young Jewish women who worked in the munitions factory had been smuggling small amounts of gunpowder wrapped in cloth or in the false bottom of trays to the men of the Sonderkommando who worked at Crematorium IV. They hoped that these small amounts would be enough for the men to blow up the crematorium. The men were at breaking point, knowing they themselves would soon be liquidated because the Germans wanted to remove anyone who had details about their killing operations before they had to abandon Auschwitz ahead of advancing Soviet forces.

On 7 October they started by capturing one of the guards and throwing him into the crematorium. Almost immediately the Germans sent reinforcements and crushed the revolt. More than 250 prisoners died in the uprising including Rachela's brother Dov, who was either shot or gassed just a few days after his twenty-seventh birthday.

According to Rachela, Fania, the older French nightclub singer who helped with musical arrangements, had just warned her of the impending tragedy during one of the fortune-telling sessions Fania gave to entertain the other orchestra members. 'She read my hand and said: "look there is very unhappy news for you, something very sad" and that is exactly what happened.'[29]

Rachela had kept in contact with her adored brother during the time they were both in the camp together thanks to secret letters delivered by Mala, who used her role as an official messenger to help prisoners but had no idea of what he was planning. Most of what she learned about Dov's role in the uprising came after the war. As Helena recorded, Rachela's ability to continue playing after her loss was a rare, important moment of Polish and Jewish solidarity, with the other women helping her through the crisis by reminding her of how brave he had been.

'When Rachela's brother died during the Sonderkommando mutiny Zosia (Zofia Cykowiak) tried to console her by reminding her of the heroism of his act, and that she should be proud of her brother for dying in combat. We were all full of admiration for those who took part in that one-of-a-kind armed uprising.'[30]

Where major tragedies were concerned the orchestra could always pull together. But petty differences, often over food, or perceived favouritism, still divided the Jews from the Poles. On one occasion around this time Maria Langenfeld, the non-Jewish Polish block orderly, ordered that surplus jumpers should be returned to Kanada, the clothing storehouse, but Violette Silberstein selected one to give to a friend working in the kitchen. When Maria discovered that potatoes had been handed over in return, she accused Violette of black marketeering and threatened her with Nazi punishment. Anita, Fania and Hélène Wiernik all insisted it was they who gave the jumper. Confused, Maria dropped her threat.

The francophones were always one of the strongest groups within the block, either singing songs by French popular performers such as Charles Trenet or Jean Sablon in the barracks – *J'attendrai* (I will wait), a big hit in 1940, was a particular favourite – or dressing up. One night, believing that the Nazis were losing the war, which gave them additional courage, one of the French women came up with an idea to organise a beauty contest in the barracks. Categories would include the most beautiful mouth, most beautiful eyes, most beautiful legs, with votes decided by a round of applause. 'The Germans and Poles being either more reserved or more shocked [did not] participate, while the Ukrainians as usual smile and don't understand what's going on. The jury is established and a whole evening passes by ... Fifty years later no one remembered the winners,' concluded Jean-Jacques Felstein, the son of Elsa Miller, having heard the story from Violette. But he added that when he interviewed Yvette Assael, the Greek double bass player, and asked what she recalled of the occasion, she 'confesses and laughs a little saying that she won a prize. "But they were all so nice to me! They made sure my hair wasn't cut too short."'[31]

On 14 July 1944, Bastille Day, the French and Belgian musicians met in the music area to play the *Marseillaise* when one of the Poles walked through the door and asked what on earth was going on?

'As far as she was concerned for Jewish women to sing any national anthem [was] absurd at best and heretical at worst.' Felstein, who recounted the story based on a series of interviews he had with Violette from 1995 to 1997, described Violette as 'small, lively and energetic', never afraid to say what was on her mind. And she wanted to tell him about life in the block after Alma.[32] Exasperated by the attitude of the Poles to their patriotism, Violette and Hélène Rounder decided to get their revenge, fully aware of the dangers of such behaviour. 'One of the best nourished Poles [had] a box full of crumbs and bits of dry cake in her locker, the leftovers of meals and food parcels sent from the outside,' Felstein explained. 'The two accomplices seize the box and empty it greedily, savouring every crumb for its calorific value and ... they share it with whoever wants any.' On this occasion there were no consequences.

Amid this desperation for food – the usual reason for squabbles – Hilde was an exception, constantly trying to do good, bridge the divide and ease the pain. Sylvia recalled in an interview with Felstein how she was 'literally starving' when she returned from the Revier after typhus and 'Hilde simply handed over her food ration to help [me] recover.' Others recall how Hilde always made herself available to translate letters and mitigate any misunderstandings resulting from language barriers and, according to Zosia, 'she did it all for free without even asking for the traditional compulsory ration of bread in return'.[33] Hilde never spoke directly about having done any of this but, when asked by Felstein what had motivated her, she explained that she believed the time spent in her Zionist organisation in a particularly hostile environment in 1930s Germany 'better equipped me than many of my colleagues to be able to survive... I knew that if I didn't do my best to help people then there would be nothing left'.[34]

On 1 November 1944, in the middle of an outdoor roll call for the entire orchestra, the twenty-five Jewish members were all suddenly ordered by SS guards to line up together and told they could not return to their block nor collect any possessions. 'We were ordered to line up Jews to one side, Aryans to the other, it could only mean one thing: the gas chamber,' recalled Anita in 1996. 'I was terribly anxious to contact [her sister] Renate so that she should know what was going on.'[35] Renate, who worked as a messenger in another part of the camp, must have heard about the latest development as she just appeared on the scene. 'The thought of being separated now was unbearable for both of us and it was the most natural thing in the world for her simply to join us, nobody stopped her.'

'We had to lay down our instruments, take a shower and wait for two hours until we received a medical examination,' Lily Mathé remembered. 'The Jewish musicians were then instructed to leave behind their instruments, blankets and any useful possessions, such as combs, toothbrushes or soap and their relatively acceptable clothes.'[36]

'We were issued with real monstrosities,' said Anita, who

recalled having to remove her orchestra clothes. 'It brought home to us that our "cushy" time was at an end.'[37] She did somehow manage to keep a red angora jumper that she had 'organised' from Kanada by exchanging extra bread she had occasionally earned for playing in the orchestra. Whenever it developed a hole, she unravelled a bit of sleeve to patch it and had worn it day and night to keep her warm in the brutal Birkenau winter. Finally, as Lily recalled, 'we got a slice of bread and were put on a train'.[38]

Although it meant disobeying Nazi orders, Hilde remembered: 'I was afraid to lose my friends from the group but somehow I managed to sneak out of the row before the transport and go back to the orchestra block where I took my volume of Faust and all my presents.' Hilde had been given various books from friends in Kanada which she had read from on Friday nights when she prepared her symbolic *Oneg Shabbat*. She could not take the volume of the Austrian poet Rainer Maria Rilke because it was too big but, with remarkable historical awareness even at such a perilous moment, she snatched up the red bag she had made in which to keep sheet music for the orchestra, the Pelikan fountain pen which she had been given by Josef Kramer when he saw her preparing music and doing harmonisation in the orchestra block and, perhaps most important of all, the treasures she had taken from Alma's cubicle on the night Alma had died: Alma's black leather notebook with a small pen and the manuscript of the song which she and Margot had written to accompany Chopin's Étude *Tristesse*, which the orchestra had been forbidden from performing.

Once they emerged from the showers in their new clothes and stood on the station platform they were joined by other Jewish prisoners being sent to Bergen-Belsen. It appears from the differing accounts of how this sudden expulsion took place that there was some degree of chaos, as well as hanging around, as Rachela remembered that one of her friends, Olga Loseva, the Russian mandolin player, ran back to the block to fetch a few special possessions for her while Anita's sister Renate was among several other women who were not members of the orchestra, but joined the Jewish musicians on the ramp. For reasons that are not entirely clear, Ewa Stojowska, the Polish non-Jewish singer, also formed part of the group going to Belsen. Lily Mathé was able to bring her sister in-law, Aranka. Ilse Diament, then aged sixteen, an ordinary Jewish prisoner who had been in several camps since her deportation from Stettin in Germany (now Poland) in 1940, also snuck in with the orchestra women.

Ilse had first got to know some of them when she had been punished for trying to hide a potato in her clothes on her way back from work. The orchestra was playing next to the gate as the potato dropped out and they had to watch her suffer. 'And instead to shoot me, they put me in *strafkommando* [punishment detail]. I was sitting with my knees down [kneeling] where the orchestra was playing and hold here [touching her palms] two bricks and here two bricks for three, four hours. And if I would move, I would be right away killed. But I was so strong. I don't know who gave me this strength, now I understand why I was strong, because my parents are not alive anymore.'

Ilse's testimony, given in California in 1983 as part of a video recording, is powerful and moving. In fluent but broken English she can barely talk about her family without dissolving into tears, forty years after she last saw them. But when she remembers how she owes her life to the orchestra girls her face changes. She does not explain how she got to know them but the implication is that while she was suffering the punishment for the dropped potato the musicians somehow managed to convey sympathy. Now she saw her chance.

On the day when they were due to move the orchestra out Ilse noticed, 'I saw on the right side all the girls from the orchestra were there, and on the left side where I was selected, I didn't see them. So I thought to myself "Come on, they must be dead [going to their deaths], 'cause I went to many camps, I'm sure that where I'm standing is dead" and I smuggled myself to those on the right, and nobody from the people wouldn't say "You don't belong." Nobody stopped me and the orchestra girls, they helped me. They gave me courage, like "Come on, come on!", they pushed me to them. So, we came to the other [camp], Bergen-Belsen, Germany, also in the woods, called Lüneburger.'[39]

Anita recalled, 'We were blissfully unaware of what was still in store for us. It is bizarre that we all thought this was some kind of miracle.'[40] The group, by now swollen to more than thirty, were loaded into a special wagon intended just for the Jewish members of the orchestra. They only had one toilet bucket for them all for the entire journey, but they were not packed in to the point of suffocation like most arriving prisoners.

During the three-day journey north-westwards, the women sang to keep up their spirits.

'We cheered ourselves up by singing our orchestral repertoire, each of us taking her own part. Whether we had instruments or not, it seemed clear that we were going to remain together,' recalled Anita.[41] Others too remembered this moment of hope and desperation: how Yvette tried to imitate a double bass with her voice, Violette to reproduce a violin pizzicato and Lily to simulate an accordion. They even laughed at the cacophony they produced. They understood that their survival up until this point owed everything to being together in the orchestra and so tried to boost morale and keep each other warm now that the weather had turned cold. They had been told nothing about where they were going beyond rumours that their destination was a former military camp.

When the train stopped in the middle of a forest just outside Hanover, they were told to get out and walk in rows of five towards this unknown destination.

'Anita and I walked in front. We thought this was our final stop,' remembered Hélène Wiernik of the hour-long walk. 'This was hell. Anita who always had courage, now she had two big tears. "I don't want to be the last to die," she said to me. "I think this is too hard." '[42] Anita had noticed a signpost written in German gothic script which she thought had said '*Juden Schiesstand*', or Jewish shooting range. In fact, it read '*Zu dem Schiesstand*' or 'To the shooting range'. They all felt enormous relief, but it was short lived. When they saw that there was no barracks for them to sleep in, just a tent on damp ground with a bit of tarpaulin for cover and nothing to sleep on inside, they realised they had swapped one kind of hell for another.

'I was frozen to my core. This was almost worse than Auschwitz-Birkenau. It was completely disorganised, it had all the horrors but now with chaos too,' explained Hélène Wiernik.[43]

'We really thought we wouldn't survive. We were thirsty, hungry and desperately cold. We tried to keep each other warm and to be optimistic. We helped each other. We were no longer privileged. But one just tries to survive. If you give up it's a kind of suicide.'[44]

'For some days we lived like this,' Anita remembered of their arrival at Belsen. 'In a great big heap, on the bare ground in a flapping tent, cold and wretched. But if we thought that these were scarcely the most desirable conditions, and that we had reached rock bottom, we were very much mistaken.'[45]

The women tripped over the exhausted bodies of seriously ill and dying inmates when they needed to relieve themselves in the middle of the night. Anita recalled that she and Hilde had tried, with little success, to create a system of rows in their sleeping tent with a gangway down the middle. 'No doubt it was our Germanic upbringing.'[46]

And then came the storms. After all they had suffered in Auschwitz, this new horror threatened to break them:

One night a terrible storm broke out over Lüneburg Heath, the rain pelting down. It proved too much for the tents. They collapsed on top of us in the middle of the night, and that was that. It was pitch dark and there we were, with the tent flattened, and everybody struggling to get free. Somehow, we managed to untangle ourselves. When we finally achieved this, we just stood there in the open in the pouring rain, the wind howling, for the rest of the night. It is astonishing how much the human body can endure. We were all deeply undernourished and badly clothed – in short, not in the pink of condition. And although it was freezing and we were drenched through, I did not even catch a cold. That would have been out of the question in normal life. One would have caught not just a cold but pneumonia. It will forever remain a mystery to me how we survived that night without serious after-effects.[47]

8

Here you are not going to play

The orchestra girls had been transported from Auschwitz to Belsen as part of a desperate effort by the Nazis from the summer of 1944 onwards to conceal the evidence of their egregious crimes, including but not only attempts at mass extermination of Jews. The Germans feared being taken prisoner by advancing Soviet forces or being put on trial for war crimes by the Western Allies. Nonetheless, deportations to Auschwitz continued through the autumn of 1944, and the gas chambers continued to function until early November 1944. On 30 October 2,038 Jews arrived from Theresienstadt of whom 1,689 were selected to be killed by gas. But then, in November, the SS ordered the dismantling of the crematoria. First the furnaces were disassembled, then the chimneys were demolished. According to one former prisoner used for this work, 'the metal furnace parts were taken after dismantling to the railroad platform and loaded onto cars ... we did this and similar jobs until 18 January 1945.'[1]

And so, with the Russians pressing ever closer towards Auschwitz, the Germans began a steady evacuation of the remaining inmates toward camps inside Germany, including Buchenwald and Ravensbrück as well as Belsen, where they could inflict further death and horror on their captives for a few more months before they had to accept the reality that they had lost the war and would now face world condemnation and punishment for their crimes.

German military authorities had first established a POW camp in 1940 at Belsen in northeast Germany about 11 miles north of the town of Celle and just south of the small towns of Bergen and Belsen. In April 1943, when part of the site was converted into a concentration camp for Jews and other undesirables, the SS took over control, but until the autumn of 1944 the camp complex never held more than 8,000 people. By the end of 1944, Belsen was the main dumping ground for tens of thousands of Jewish prisoners evacuated from Auschwitz and other camps close to the eastern front, as well as many thousands of Soviet and some Polish POWs.* This sudden influx of grossly malnourished and sick survivors of forced evacuations, many of whom arrived on foot, overwhelmed the German authorities who no longer had either the money or men to run Belsen with its expanded population – around 60,000 at liberation.

When the twenty or so Jewish musicians arrived at Belsen in November 1944, they were not immediately assailed by piles of dead bodies; that was to come. But they noticed that the area of the camp where they had been sent was just a collection of tents and had no blocks built. The ground was no longer the yellowish mud of Birkenau, but damp black earth with grass on which they tried to sleep. Auschwitz had been built purposefully, with a different end in mind. Belsen was not prepared for them.

The night after the early November storms, the exhausted women were driven by German blows first into a kitchen tent where they again lay down on the floor; then to some sort of warehouse; and eventually to a so-called small women's camp

---

* It is estimated that by 1945 a total of around 50,000 Soviet POWs had died there.

(*Kleines Frauenlager*) for surviving female prisoners in a dilapidated barracks, intended for forty people but now housing up to 500. The windows were broken, the roof was full of holes and there was no sanitation, lights, bedding or water. Increasing numbers of prisoners kept on arriving bringing the total of women at Belsen to approximately 25,000 by the end of the war.

According to Rachela, the girls had tried, as soon as they arrived in Belsen, to persuade 'the German commander', SS *Hauptsturmführer* Adolf Haas, that they were an orchestra and could be useful. He had nodded dismissively and said, 'Orchestra? Here you are not going to play.'[2] Haas could not have been less interested in the depleted and dishevelled group of young women for whom he had no need whatever, but Rachela said there were nonetheless discussions among the group about re-forming some kind of orchestra, even though they had no instruments. Then, at the end of December, Josef Kramer arrived as the new camp commander and recognised some of the orchestra girls. His eye fell on Flora, the Dutch accordionist, and Lily Mathé, the dark-eyed Hungarian violinist, living in the women's camp. Kramer presented Lily with a magnificent violin in perfect condition and ordered the pair to provide some occasional entertainment at his single-storey wooden home, which was at the entrance to the camp. 'I didn't have time to busy myself with matters of con-science,' Lily said in a 1960 interview when she was asked about the violin, knowing it had been stolen from a Jewish musician. She kept the instrument for the rest of her life.

Flora believed Kramer spotted her because of the margarine grease she smeared on her face, taken from the tiny portion of fat they were all given to eat and which some of the prisoners used to protect their hands or faces from the wind. 'I shined. Literally.'[3] She said of Kramer, 'that man had two sides. Everywhere where extermination was needed Kramer was called in. He was an animal. But they all had a *Schutzhaftling* [a pet Jewish prisoner]. They all picked one for whom they would make an effort.'[4] Flora recalled how on one occasion in Auschwitz immediately after a transport, Kramer came to her and asked if she needed anything. 'I hadn't used a toothbrush for months. I asked for toothpaste and a toothbrush. I would wear it on a piece of string around my waist with my bowl and spoon . . . That man was completely crazy.'[5]

Once Kramer had recognised Flora in Belsen, he kept searching her out, or so it seemed to her. One day, coming across her in the camp, he asked her what she was doing. When she told him she had volunteered for the salt mines, he replied: 'Then you'll be dead in a week.' He told her she was to obey *his* commands in future and put her in charge of a barrack of about 200 women. A few weeks later, Kramer came to her again demanding that she follow him.

'*Sie Komm mal raus*!' ['Get out now!'] 'I was terrified. I had seen how he kicked to death women who had fled . . . my God, I thought what have I done? Would he beat me to death as well?'

Instead, Flora was introduced to Kramer's wife, Rosina, as '*Das madel von Birkenau*' – the girl from Birkenau – and employed as the family nanny for his three children. 'I was being picked up by two SS men every day and taken to his bungalow outside the camp. "Here's a cup of soup for you," he would say, while he would let hundreds starve on the other side of the fence. He gave me a raisin bun or *Schwein fleisch im Schmalz* [pork meat in lard] . . . I wasn't allowed to mention that I had real coffee there.'

Over several winter weekends, Flora, Lily Mathé, Violette Silberstein and Hélène Wiernik were taken back to the villa to play for Kramer's wife and children. Lily remembered once playing the 'Teddy Bears' Picnic' for the children on her violin. Kramer gave the prisoners food again, but with no spoons. 'We ate like pigs. He went and played Bach suites on his record player while we listened. He was a schizophrenic.'[6] Flora remembered trying to bring back some of the food to others she knew in the camp, in particular her brother-in-law Appie Schrijver, whom she discovered at this time in a different part of the camp in a terrible condition suffering from what she later described as hunger oedema (a swollen stomach from starvation) and typhus. But there was nothing to carry it in.

To celebrate Christmas 1944, Kramer hosted an evening party for SS officers and summoned a small group of the musicians to play, including Fanny Kornblum, Hélène Wiernik, Fanny Rubak and Elsa Miller. Everyone was exhausted, both physically and emotionally. Somehow, they managed to clean themselves up and perform.

According to Fania, when the musicians returned 'I asked how it had gone, and they answered laconically that it had gone well. Do you know, Fania, they applauded us.'[7]

Flora's nanny job lasted only a few weeks as Kramer was nervous, correctly, that the camp was so disgustingly filthy that she might be bringing germs into his house. Both Lily Mathé and her sister-in-law Aranka fell ill with typhus at this time and were removed to the camp hospital. Aranka soon recovered, but Lily was seriously ill for days. 'Then all at once, a gigantic guy stood by my bed, a German doctor, who said, "The Commandant has sent me to treat you." Now, that was a real example of how amazing Kramer could be, so inhumanly cruel and then so un-expectedly kind! The doctor gave me an injection, and I got better,' Lily recalled.[8]

Meanwhile the other orchestra women were given what they considered useless tasks that threatened to separate them as they were sent off to different parts of the new camp. Yet they fought to stay together in one block and at first they slept two in a so-called bunk, which was little more than a few planks of wood but was at least off the ground and kept them together.

'Although we were no longer an "orchestra", we continued to function as a group,' Anita wrote in 1996. 'It happened quite naturally and without any discussion and was undoubtedly one reason for our continued survival. We watched each other like hawks for any signs of giving up.'[9]

One of the tasks some of them were assigned at Belsen involved weaving strips of greenish cellophane paper which was used as camouflage netting by the German army, with Hilde responsible for counting how many workers were present and how much each one produced.[10] They sat in a room called the *Weberei* and, presumably because they were unsupervised, 'did not do anything. We just sat and waited,' according to Rachela Zelmanowicz.[11]

The few orchestra women who later described how they managed to endure Belsen agreed that Hilde was a natural leader and crucial to the survival of those who were able to remain in her block. Since there was almost no water, clean or otherwise, they washed in the weak early-morning coffee.

'Everyone received in the morning a portion of coffee and that is all because of Hilde. She was a genius!' remembered Rachela. 'She said: "Every time two girls will give up the coffee and every day another girl will wash in it." We used to wash our hair... and we drank together each one of us a little from the coffee we received. We drank only half of the coffee.'[12]

Hilde also organised how her group ate in their block, gathered around the beds.

'Let's say we cooked some potato soup, so she organised this,' said Rachela. 'I learned from her justice. Everyone received two spoons of that soup. We always sat in the same places, in a circle, so when the soup ended on that day by a certain girl, tomorrow the next girl was the first to eat. This is how it went about everything. And she, Hilde, was the one who sent us to get things. She sent Carla to [the Belsen version of] Kanada and Carla brought underwear. She did not give Carla the underwear but whoever of the girls needed the underwear, that girl received it."[13]

Without any music to study and play, boredom was a new difficulty on top of everything else. Violette Silberstein was appointed a Kapo in a different block in charge of almost 200 women, largely because she spoke French, German and Hungarian (thanks to her Hungarian Jewish parents). She made Fania, the older French singer and arranger, her assistant, so these two women who had always got on well could continue to help support each other in ever more challenging circumstances. Fania was good at entertaining them all with her fortune telling and, even at Belsen, managed to find a pack of cards. One day a Nazi female guard noticed the game and, after slapping Fania across the face, asked her to predict her own future by using the cards. According to Violette, Fania spun her a yarn about good fortune ahead to keep her happy.[14]

Anita and Hilde, already close, formed a special bond at Belsen. Hilde taught Anita English and together they devised a way to make little chess figures out of bread, however precious it was to eat, so that they could play chess together. They felt that any kind of brain game was essential for making it through until liberation, particularly as they could no longer play music.*

The main problem now, though, was enormous hunger, verging on starvation, which afflicted everyone at Belsen during these harrowing months. Desperate prisoners hovered by the side of dying bodies collapsed in the street, knowing that bread held

---

* Anita's uncle, Edward Lasker, brother of her father Alfons, was a chess grandmaster in America where he had emigrated many years previously.

in the hands of these victims would be wasted unless they took it. Flora Jacobs and Anita both spoke of cannibalism at Belsen. 'Hollowed out people have cut out the livers from dead bodies and eaten them,' Flora recalled.[15] While Anita saw a man on his knees being punished because he had 'a human ear in his mouth'.[16]

Captain Derrick Sington, a British officer serving in the Intelligence Corps who was later to write one of the first published eyewitness accounts of Belsen, also recalled in graphic detail how he too heard for the first time of people having eaten the flesh of dead bodies. 'There were lungs, hearts and livers missing from some corpses, and pieces cut out of the thighs and buttocks.'[17]

It was thanks to the combined efforts of Hilde and Anita that the orchestra girls managed slightly better than most. They were able to get hold of a little more food and some clothes for the small group, largely because they were extremely resourceful and also spoke German as their mother tongue. They worked as a team, as Rachela later recounted.

'Hilde decided that we must "organise" [procure] blue shirts for the men from Holland who worked in the *BrotKamer* (bakery) providing the bread,' Rachela recalled. '[She and Anita] were two girls from Germany and they always went with an SS woman. Anita was telling the SS woman some stories, keeping her busy, while Hilde went off to get the bread.' In this way the SS woman did not notice how much bread they managed to persuade the bakery team, presumably pleased with their new shirts, to let them take away. 'The men took out the bread counting like this: "One two three three four five five six seven seven eight." And that is how she got a few more loaves of bread home. She was wearing a coat over a coat and she hid there two loaves of bread and that's how she walked... she kept us alive.'[18]

Reading about what Rachela described as 'the heroism of Hilde' and 'her innate belief in justice', it seems that trying to do good, to behave well, was of even greater importance for the women's survival in Belsen than it had been in Auschwitz. Here, the total breakdown of order meant that they had to scavenge and use whatever opportunities they could to stay alive, keeping the group together and supporting each other in this common cause.

Even so, in their weakened state, they were highly susceptible to rampant typhus, diphtheria, tuberculosis and a host of other potentially fatal diseases at Belsen. Those who had recovered from a bout of typhus in Auschwitz, such as Anita and her sister Renate, now considered themselves relatively fortunate as they were probably immune. However, they were all vulnerable to other illnesses, especially because the sanitary conditions in the barracks and around the camp were deteriorating by the day. 'It was too filthy for words,' Flora remembered. 'There were no toilets in the barracks, everybody had all kinds of diseases. If I climbed down from the third bed to go to the toilet, I was done by the time I got down. I then just went back up.'[19]

She went on: 'The women undressed the dead bodies and took their clothes. That clothing was riddled with typhus lice... we were riddled with lice... if I had nothing else to do, I took off my vest so I could check the seams. The lice with a small red line, those would infect you. I squeezed them between my nails.'[20]

Ilse Diament, the teenager who had managed to escape Auschwitz by getting on the train with the orchestra, was separated from them once they arrived at Belsen and put in a hut with a group of other Germans and Dutch. She was desperately alone, trying to make friends with new people, only to see them dying all around her. Waking up next to a stiff, dead body was a common occurrence in Belsen. Ilse started crying out loudly that she too wanted to die. 'I don't want to live anymore,' she wailed.

And somehow that is when Hilde found her. Later, in 1983, telling her story from her home in California, Ilse recalled: 'So she said "don't cry, I am your big sister and I'll watch over you and look, here are five, six children, girls from the orchestra". And she introduced me to all those girls and said "we will help you. You've come to us," and took me away and put me up next to where they were sleeping.'[21]

Hilde, simply by talking and sharing food, was able to boost Ilse's mood when the girl felt she had nothing left to live for. But soon Ilse too succumbed to typhus and was very sick. She recalled how Hilde protected her even then 'because sick people wouldn't live there. There was no medicine available. Every time that they [the Nazis] were counting, she put her body over me, or somebody else did, because everything was okay, she was from the orchestra, they trusted her.'[22] She was not discovered.

Yet others from the orchestra who had earlier been protected from the gas chambers at Auschwitz by Alma Rosé, died before Belsen was liberated. More than 35,000 people perished between January and mid-April 1945 from starvation, overwork and disease, including latterly a typhus epidemic which among many other victims killed fifteen-year-old Anne Frank at the end of March. 'Belsen was truly a living hell,' said Hélène Wiernik, the Belgian violinist, as she remembered being desperately ill there from typhus. 'What I never understood was the Red Cross. Why did they never come to us?'[23]

The Greek violinist Julie Stroumsa, engaged in Salonika to David Perahia* before the war, also succumbed in the final days before liberation. As did Lola Croner, the younger of the two spinster Croner sisters, who had been a professional flautist before the war and was called Tante Croner by many of the teenage orchestra girls for her motherly kindness towards them. Ibi, the

---

* Father of Murray Perahia, the American-born pianist and conductor today considered one of the world's greatest pianists.

Hungarian violinist who arrived at Auschwitz in July 1944 with Lily Mathé, died from typhus. Lili Assael fell and broke her leg at this time. With little strength to recover, she became seriously ill too so Yvette, fraught with anxiety, now tried to repay the elder sister who had done so much to save her. She did not seek help from Hilde and her small group, perhaps because she and her sister were no longer in the same barracks.

Instead, she approached Irma Grese, one of the most brutal and sadistic former guards at Auschwitz, for help.

Irma Grese had left school at fourteen and worked as a camp guard since she was nineteen, quickly acquiring a reputation for sadism and brutality at Ravensbrück and Auschwitz, where she had walked everywhere with her fierce dog, instilling fear among the women. In March 1945, still only twenty-one, she was posted to Belsen. Since Grese had made it her business to know many of the orchestra girls by name in Birkenau, Yvette took a gamble that she would remember her now. With trepidation, she went to the Nazi officers' building to ask Grese if she could possibly arrange for her to have some kind of job at Belsen that would enable her to earn extra food to help her dangerously ill sister. Grese initially claimed she did not know who she was and did nothing.

Some time later Yvette saw Grese walking through the camp and once again summoned up the courage to ask for her help. This time Grese recognised her and, when Yvette explained her sister's worsening situation, Grese asked to be taken to see Lili. As she entered the block everyone stood to attention, terrified. However, on seeing how sick Lili was, she ordered the block leader to give her two extra life-saving rations of soup a day. She then took Yvette back to the office and organised a job in the kitchen for her. After three days, however, Yvette had to beg another favour from Grese as she found even the work in the kitchen too hard. Emaciated and weakened, she could not lift the heavy pots. Instead Grese now gave her a cleaning job, which she just about managed and for which she received extra rations. Yvette then set about exchanging these in the kitchen where she had worked for more nutritious foods to help Lili. Yvette knew that without this extra food certainly Lili, and possibly Yvette herself, might not have survived.

In a 1995 interview, Yvette, wanting to believe the best of her captors, concluded that these were humane actions by Grese.[24] Anita however believed Grese's behaviour in Belsen had an ulterior motive. 'In reality, she was as mean and vicious as the rest of them.' Anita wrote of how when Grese 'came up to me one day in Belsen and started to make "friendly" conversation... I recall that she used the word "we" (me and her) as though we belonged to the same species... there could be only one explanation for her sudden friendliness: she was trying to create a space for herself in my heart by being so pally... It was obvious: the end must be near.'[25]

9

I have never seen anything like this

On Sunday, 15 April 1945 the British Second Army liberated Belsen. The British troops who first entered the camp were stunned by the sight and smell of what they saw: 60,000 starving, emaciated and desperate human beings crammed together or left in piles by the roadside without food, water or basic sanitation. It was clear that many were suffering from typhus and dysentery as well as starvation and were on the edge of death. The scale of the grotesque scenario was beyond any of their imaginations. Flora overheard a British general say, 'I have experienced battlefields for five years, but I have never seen anything like this.'[1]

Attached to the division which entered Belsen was a young BBC radio broadcaster, Richard Dimbleby, not yet thirty-two. Dimbleby's task was to reveal to British listeners something which he knew, even after five years of gruesome war reporting, they would find hard to comprehend. The resulting broadcast, graphic and laced with fury at the hideous spectacle all around him, had to be deeply factual. Nonetheless the BBC initially refused to play it, believing the public did not have the stomach for Dimbleby's words and images of horror and not entirely sure whether such a grim account was wholly reliable.

On 19 April, several days after his first visit to the camp and only after Dimbleby had threatened to resign, his story was finally transmitted.

'I passed through the barrier and found myself in the world of a nightmare,' he told British listeners in a sombre eleven-and-a-half-minute report.

Dimbleby spoke of 'dead bodies, some of them in decay [which] lay strewn about the road'; of 'a whirling cloud of dust, the dust of thousands of slowly moving people, laden in itself with the deadly typhus germ'.

And with the dust was a smell, sickly and thick, the smell of death and decay, of corruption and filth.

Along the rutted tracks on each side of the road were brown wooden huts. There were faces at the windows.

The bony, emaciated faces of starving women too weak to come outside – propping themselves against the glass to see the daylight before they died.

And they were dying, every hour and every minute.

I saw a man wandering dazedly along the road then stagger and fall. Someone else looked down at him, took him by the heels and dragged him to the side of the road to join the other bodies lying unburied there.

No one else took the slightest notice, they didn't even trouble to turn their heads.[2]

Dimbleby's grim picture was soon corroborated by others as the British army took over running the camp. Lacking manpower, the British agreed a temporary arrangement under which 200 SS troops, 400 German guards and 4,000 Hungarian soldiers fighting for the Nazis would remain at the camp to clear it of corpses and clean up the site. In exchange, the British granted them eventual guaranteed passage back to their own lines, which now scarcely existed.

Brigadier Glyn Hughes was the first Allied medical officer to enter Belsen. He saw immediately that the two main issues were the control of disease and the distribution of food. Hughes acted decisively, taking charge of the local hospital and removing German patients in order to treat desperate prisoners, mostly Jews, in urgent need.*

The first necessity was clearing up the piles of dead bodies and human filth, a foul job assigned to the remaining German guards, and to organise as much medical care as possible. The guards were put to work carting dead bodies and digging mass graves. According to Renate Lasker, sister of Anita the cellist, the SS had tried in a desultory fashion to move the bodies a few days before the British arrived, and for this purpose had given the prisoners 'some string to tie the arms of the dead together and then drag them along the main thoroughfare in the camp. But we did not have the strength. The operation was discontinued, and the bodies remained where they were.'[3]

Ensuring an equal distribution of rations was a far greater problem. With only 120 British troops, the Germans were initially ordered to assist in the control of food in the camp. On the first night, a riot broke out among the inmates over limited rations and the German guards reacted by shooting and even killing several of them.

The British army had arrived just in time to rescue the Assael sisters and the young German orphan protected by the orchestra, Ilse Diament. In mid-April, before she had recovered, she had heard shooting and the other girls wanted to run away. 'But Hilde was firm; "No, we cannot leave Ilse alone. We stay together."'[]

---

* The hospital was later renamed the Glyn Hughes Hospital in his honour.

And at that moment, they looked out of the window, saw British tanks and heard someone speaking through a loudspeaker.

> And they [the British] came right way and asked: "Who is sick?" and right away Hilde said me [Ilse] and took me and gave me all kinds of shots or whatever and they cleaned us up . . . I was lucky. I couldn't eat because I was sick, and I just wanted to drink. And I remember they gave me cans of pears. Oh, it was so delicious . . . And until today, when I open a can of pears, I remember how the British doctor gave me the first can of pears and I loved it.

As she starts to remember how close she was to death, Ilse's voice breaks again and the smile disappears.[4] Ilse was taken to a makeshift infirmary and began her long road to recovery.

Despite the occasional extra food from Kramer, Flora, like most of the others, was seriously ill by the time of the liberation. She clearly remembered the day itself, 15 April, for the rest of her life. As soon as the British had taken control, she discovered strength she did not think she possessed and chased after any of the female guards she could reach, since in her experience 'those SS women were even worse than the men. I got hold of one . . . I managed because she was alone and lost apparently. Despite being severely weakened, I pummelled and screamed and took her shoes.'[5]

Fania too, on the brink of death from typhus, recalled the euphoria of the liberation. She weighed just 65 lb (29 kg). 'I shall never forget it. A soldier carried me outside where the SS were being arrested. We had savoured this moment for so long and with such passion,' she recalled. Someone handed her a microphone and she summoned up enough energy to sing the *Marseillaise*. 'When I discovered the microphone belonged to the BBC I sang "God save the King".'[6]

Meanwhile, Kramer was put in ankle chains for two days before being taken to the POW cage at the nearby town of Celle to await trial along with forty-eight other Nazis who had worked at Belsen. Flora was one of the former prisoners brought to Celle to identify Kramer as part of the process of preliminary evidence.

Many of the women prisoners, if they were in reasonable health, were given jobs as interpreters. But first they had to endure one more indignity. If they could stand, once again they had to get undressed and stand naked in front of British soldiers. 'They deloused us with DDT,'* Flora remembered. 'Afterwards I received a pair of trousers from an English marine and black turtleneck. The oedema made me very swollen. Clearly those making up the packages had no idea what the prisoners had been through as they were given mirrors and lipstick. I felt like a chimpanzee, I looked ridiculous. They gave us cans of corned beef even though we had not had fatty foods for years. It gave me jaundice.'[7]

Flora's most urgent requirement was to see a dentist because her teeth were falling out. 'I drove that man [a British officer she identified as 'dressed in stately blue with impressive decorations'] crazy [until] he took me to the army as they had dentists there.' While there, she was asked if she would like to be an interpreter for Margaret Montgomery, sister-in-law of the field marshal as she was married to his brother, the Reverend Colin Montgomery, an army chaplain. Margaret Montgomery was among the first party of Red Cross nurses working in Belsen and subsequently in charge of entertainment in the camp. Flora agreed immediately as it was a good job. Mrs Montgomery was very popular and she hoped it would bring her closer to her brother-in-law, Appie, to whom she was trying to take food and medicines.

---

* Dichlorodiphenyltrichloroethane, a toxic man-made pesticide used in the 1940s to control insect-borne diseases such as typhus and malaria.

British Red Cross nurse Margaret Montgomery,
much admired by several orchestra survivors,
painted by prisoner Piri Hevizi

A forty-two-year-old British rabbi, Leslie Hardman, who accompanied Dimbleby into Belsen, had the grim duty of officiating at the burial of tens of thousands of the corpses of his co-religionists. This Orthodox chaplain from Liverpool, his faith in God severely tested by what he saw, got on with the job. From then on, Hardman believed it was his duty to bear witness to this horror and to assist in the establishment of an independent Jewish state. 'His Judaism and his Zionism were inseparable thereafter,' his obituary in the *Guardian* noted in 2008.[8] As he did his best to honour the dead, Hardman asked for English-speaking volunteers from among the survivors to compile lists of people who had relatives in the United States, British-mandated Palestine or elsewhere. Hilde, ideally suited to this work, volunteered. One of her first tasks with Hardman was to go to the men's camp with him to see who survived and where they could be sent.

It took weeks to impose order on Belsen. Along with the

International Red Cross, castigated by Belgian violinist Hélène for making what she believed was a belated appearance, scores of international aid organisations such as the UK-based Jewish Rescue Unit sent volunteers. In mid-April a group of young British medical students from the London teaching hospitals arrived. One of these volunteers, Gerald Raperport, wrote of his shock at what faced them despite being trained as medical students 'to meet bad smells unflinchingly... The stench in these huts was almost more than we could bear... Universally the floors were carpeted, literally, with a thick, glutinous layer of weeks old excreta.'[9] Even though all the outside toilets were blocked, 'the SS guards had forbidden the inmates to defecate or micturate outside the huts on pain of death should they be caught'.

Physically the most startling sight was the degree of emaciation to which all prisoners had been reduced, literally skin and bone. 'Their heads were no more than parchment covered skulls, their thighs could be circled by finger and thumb... Their muscles were mere fibrous strands and the women's breasts just wrinkled flaps of skin.'[10]

Reading such graphic eyewitness descriptions reinforces the astonishing strength of the desire to live displayed by any survivors who had come through the war to this point. The courage of the orchestra girls, like everyone else who survived Belsen, demands to be recognised.

By mid-May, helped by reinforcements, British forces had managed to impose some order in the camp.* In the late spring

---

* By this time my father, Major Eric Rubinstein, had arrived in Belsen, along with the tanks which formed part of the 31st Armoured Brigade. His list of instructions for the Military Government made clear that the problem of what to do with the Displaced Persons (DPs) was immediately recognised as uppermost, second only to 'the restoration of law and order' and above the requirement to apprehend war criminals.

of 1945 after the unconditional surrender of Germany to the Allies on 8 May, the British military government together with the various international aid organisations now at Belsen tried to look beyond the immediate bleak necessity and, with input from the prisoners, transformed the camps into active cultural and social centres. There were theatre and musical troupes which toured the camps while athletic clubs from various DP centres challenged each other. The British army created a music room at Belsen and procured gramophones and other musical instruments so that the prisoners, once again, were soon performing.

1. QVERTURE   CELLE CAMP BAND (Polish and Czech).
2. 11TH LIGHT FIELD AMBULANCE DANCE BAND
                                    (90 Swingtet).
3. MLLE KRONENBERG,
   MR. OPASTOWSKJI ....Tap Dance.
4. EVA STOJOWSKA ......" Mattinate " (in Italian)
                                            Leoncavallo
5. LILI MATHÉ ....Hungarian Czardas.
                        (Solo Violinist)
6. EVA KOLSKA.........." Whispering "
                        " South of the Border."
                        (Solo.)
7. QUARTET DANCE ......" Hokey Cokey."
8. EVA STEINER........." Madame Butterfly."
                        Rosina Aria (" The Barber of
                        Seville "), *Rossini*.
                        Viliah Song (" Merry
                        Widow "), *Lehar*
9. EVA STOJOWSKA.......Kujawiak (words by Christina
                        Krahelsk, who died in the
                        Warsaw rising of 1944).
                        (Solo Song and Dance.)
10. JETTA JANOWSKA......2 Russian Songs (*Donajewski*).
                        (Solo.)
11. SELINGER SISTERS......" Ha'beit m'schomajim "
                        (" Help' us, Heaven.")
                        " Eli, Eli."   (Duets.)
12. DIANA RUBIN ...." Waltz François." (Dance.)
13. MICHLA GOLUB ...." Noch einmal das Leben."
                        (Solo.)
14. CELLE CAMP BAND.

Announcement of a Red Cross concert with some orchestra survivors
on 24 May, the same day Belsen huts were being destroyed

At first these were informal, revue-style events and recitals with a military band as well as impromptu choirs, dance groups, a Polish-Czech band from the DP camp in Celle and several amateur musicians. On 24 May the British Red Cross organised something more professional. Ewa Stojowska and Eva Steiner, the Polish and Hungarian singers who had performed at Auschwitz under the baton of Alma Rosé, were persuaded to sing opera arias alongside Russian, Yiddish and Hebrew partisan songs. Lily Mathé played a dramatic *czardas* violin solo, a traditional Hungarian piece.

Afterwards she was approached by a British soldier who, according to Lily's later version in 1960, spoke to her first in English, and then French. 'Finally, we managed in German because amazingly enough he was a native Austrian. He had been imprisoned, had escaped, and (then) fled to the British.'

More than a decade later she enjoyed telling the story with considerable flourish.

He asked me if I wanted to dance and I said that I wanted to, but I could hardly walk. We talked until two in the morning. He promised to come back the next evening with some clothes and a pot of jam.

I waited and waited until another soldier asked: 'Are you here for Eddie?' Then he started to laugh. 'So you are the bird he went out with last night. He got back too late – (and for that) seven days hard labour. But I need to give you this...' A pack of a hundred cigarettes! Enough to buy all of Belsen. And Auschwitz included.

Day by day, life was visibly improving for the orchestra girls, as it was for the rest of the inmates.

German farmers came to the camp to trade some potatoes, and a girl somewhere got hold of a boar's head, which we cooked out in the open air. The wood from our beds served as fuel.

All over Belsen you saw those fires burning. We sat around and realized that we had a future again. The most difficult part was learning to laugh again.

We didn't realize that we now had food aplenty. We were still working with [our] 'campmates' and gave away pieces of boar's head as if they were precious treasures. I put a piece of meat under my bed and ripped off strips for a whole week, morning, noon, and night.

Then Eddie came back. And with him life came back. He gave me lipstick and powder and cold cream and I stared into the mirror; I could not believe my eyes.

And he asked: 'Will you marry me?' I really wanted that. But it wasn't that simple. The Nazis had put me through this hell because I was not German, but in the eyes of the British I remained, for the time being, 'technically' a German. Eddie was a British soldier of Austrian blood. And British soldiers were not allowed to marry German girls. Not yet at that time. It took us fourteen months to get married.'¹

*

Anita Lasker was only prevented from joining the Red Cross concert on 24 May, the same day that the huts were finally burned down, because until the end of June 1945 she lacked a cello. However, aged only nineteen – 'but I felt like ninety' – she made herself heard in other ways. On 11 May the BBC was looking to interview witnesses in and around Belsen. As she later explained, 'someone told me there was a jeep and some journalists who wanted to interview people'. Anita went over and with great composure started by explaining that she and her sister Renate were political prisoners who had been incarcerated for the last three years. She recalled that 'it was no easy task for me to be confronted with a microphone and talk',[12] especially as she had only just recovered from serious illness.

Instead of discussing the present horrors of Belsen, she suddenly felt an urgent responsibility to represent those who had suffered in Auschwitz, both victims and survivors. She said, 'I want to say a few words about Auschwitz. The few who survived fear that the world won't believe what happened there. They threw healthy people into the ovens and burned them alive. The screams reached our barracks. I was in the orchestra... music was played as a background during the most terrible times.'

As she spoke, she was joined by some of her orchestra friends. 'We stood next to her and sang there,' recalled Rachela.[13]

It was a powerful monologue delivered from the heart by a young girl in a lucid and confident voice in German, her first language.[14] Her comments were prescient. Afterwards she found an unwillingness in her adopted country, England, to hear the truth of what she had seen and experienced first-hand.

Anita's message, which was rebroadcast many times, led swiftly to contact with what little family she still had. A neighbour of her eldest sister, Marianne, now Mrs Adlerstein, married and living in Redhill, outside London, heard the broadcast and told Marianne the good news: both her sisters had survived. Marianne had escaped Germany in 1939 en route to Palestine. Eventually their uncle, Edward Lasker, the chess champion in America who had emigrated in 1914, was also involved. But Renate and Anita wanted to come to Britain not the US.

'I have often asked myself how Marianne must have felt when she heard my voice,' Anita wrote in 1996. 'She had never dared hope for one moment that we had survived and there was no postal service yet, as the War was not over. The first return message from her came courtesy of the British Army.'[15]

Anita and Renate's life in Belsen was now 'quite congenial' as official interpreters attached to the British army, she wrote later.[16] The position gave them various privileges and passes, and they were in effect 'free people'. Yet leaving Belsen proved a complicated business for the Lasker sisters who were stuck in the camp for a further eleven months after liberation. Unlike Marianne, who had been en route for Palestine in 1939 when she got stuck in England, Anita had never been a Zionist. Anita wanted to go to England with Renate and began her life as a professional cellist there.

But the sisters faced many obstacles getting the necessary documents and believed that the Home Office made 'pathetic difficulties . . . before finally granting us permission to come to England'.[17] Meanwhile, Anita's life became progressively less 'congenial' as one by one all her friends departed. 'Tomorrow will be a sad day,' she wrote to Marianne on 4 June 1945 as Hélène Rounder, 'yes, this little Hélène of mine, is going back to Paris tomorrow hoping to find her sister . . . I was together with her during all my KZ [*Konzentrationslager*] times and we are good friends. When one has spent months and years lying in the same shit and has shared every piece of bread and every cigarette this is a very special kind of friendship.'[18]

By July, Anita had at last been given a cello after a British army officer found one on top of a local mayor's cupboard. In August, she played in a concert organised by Mrs Montgomery with Eva Steiner from Auschwitz and Giuseppe Selmi, an Italian POW who before the war had been principal cellist with the Radio Rome orchestra. Anita opened the concert with Schumann's *Träumerei*. She never described suffering emotional turmoil playing that particular piece, in spite of her strong memories of being forced to play it for Mengele in Auschwitz. On the contrary, she has always insisted that 'Music is Music' and nothing the Nazis did could destroy music for her.* In the second half of the concert she and Selmi played Bach's Sonata for Two Cellos and she commented later that 'Selmi was such a nice man and he helped me a great deal with my cello playing. He was after all a most accomplished cellist while I was merely a student who had never had an opportunity to study seriously.'[19]

On 27 July, Yehudi Menuhin and Benjamin Britten gave two concerts as part of a short tour they were making of various DP camps, an uplifting occasion for Anita and her fellow prisoners, but all they really wanted was to be free of camp life.

Renate wrote to Marianne on 30 August 1945: 'We are sick and tired of the camp. It gets worse every day. The whole atmosphere is so depressing I cannot stand looking at those faces any more.'[20]

In September Anita was called as a witness at the Belsen Lüneburg trial in a British military court held in a converted school. Officially called the Trial of Josef Kramer and forty-four others, Anita was asked to testify against Kramer, who had been camp commander at both Auschwitz-Birkenau and Bergen-Belsen, Fritz Klein, camp doctor at Belsen, and Franz Hössler, deputy camp commander at Belsen who had been so key to getting the orchestra underway at Auschwitz. All were charged with war crimes according to international law.† Anita's command of English was good enough by then for her to give evidence in English. 'It was,' she wrote in 1996, 'the big distraction from the endless waiting for the end to our domicile in Belsen.' However,

---

* However, Schubert's *Marche Militaire* is a tune she hoped never to hear again post-war.

† Being a British military tribunal, charges such as crimes against humanity and genocide could not be brought. These were reserved for the high-level trials at Nuremberg which began two months later.

she found it hard 'to reconcile myself to the fact that these criminals actually had a counsel for their defence just as in a British law court. That made me very angry indeed... it was sick making for the likes of us who had been at the receiving end of this murder machine... at that instant I understood for the first time how incomprehensible to the rest of the world were the events which had led to the Lüneburg trial.'[21]

Josef Kramer, former camp commandant, in leg irons under British guard at Belsen in April 1945

On 17 November 1945 Kramer, Klein, Hössler and eight other defendants including Irma Grese were found guilty and sentenced to death for crimes both at Auschwitz and at Bergen-Belsen. On 13 December, the eleven were hanged in Hamelin prison by Britain's chief hangman, Albert Pierrepoint. Another eighteen were found guilty and sentenced to prison sentences of one to fifteen years. Due to clemency pleas and appeals, many prison sentences were eventually shortened considerably. By mid-1955, all those sentenced to prison had been released.

Maria Mandl, the Nazi guard who had had closer connections with the orchestra than any other Nazi, was not on trial here. In November 1944 she had been transferred from Birkenau to Mühldorf, a sub-camp of Dachau, near Munich. She managed to escape from Mühldorf into the mountains at the end of the war and was not captured until 10 August 1945, while hiding at her sister's farm. Her father had refused to help her. She spent another two years in prison before she was eventually tried in Poland.

By the end of 1945, Anita recalled, she and Renate were 'desperate to get out of Belsen and start a new life'.[22] But it was only in March 1946, after the sisters had bought slightly forged papers paid for with fifty NAAFI* cigarettes and spent two and a half months marooned in Brussels, that they were finally able to board a ship for England. Renate, having turned twenty-one in January 1945, was over the age required for DPs to join their relatives in Britain while Anita, like many former prisoners, did not have 'a scrap of proof as to my identity' and so officials at the registry office in Belsen were bribed with the cigarettes to create two new birth certificates displaying suitable dates of birth. However, by the time they arrived their sister Marianne had already departed for Palestine since an opportunity had arisen for her to emigrate which could not be postponed. 'She had to leave prematurely because the Home Office refused to give her permission to extend her visa,' commented Anita sadly.[23]†

While Anita and Renate were struggling to get to England, the orchestra girls in Hilde's Zionist group who wanted to emigrate to Palestine were facing their own difficulties. One of them, the

---

* The British army catering services which supported troops on active service.

† Although there was eventually a post-war reunion with Marianne, this was short lived as she died in 1952 shortly after giving birth to her second child.

mandolin player Rachela Zelmanowicz, remembered how 'an international committee' came to Bergen-Belsen 'in order to send us back to Poland, so everyone would return to where he originally came from. And we ran from place-to-place shouting: "We want to go to Israel! We will not go back to Poland. This is not our country, we will not go there!" And wherever they [the committee] went, from one camp to another, we were together as a group, with Hilde and everyone, we went after them and we shouted: "We don't want to return to Poland." '24

After this Rachela said that she and Hilde and the handful of women from the orchestra who had always wanted to make their new life in 'Eretz Israel' simply decided they would start walking there, hitchhiking if they could, but staying together until they arrived. In the event it took longer than they expected partly because they joined up with some young men along the way with the same idea.

'So two young men went forward twenty km. They rented an apartment, and they came back to take two women... they arrived at Celle. They took two [more] women. After these two got organised, the guys came back to take another two women.'25

While they were in Celle, Regina Kupferberg, Alma's former maid, now twenty-three, met her husband there. Aharon Bacia was an enthusiastic Zionist and economist who had been deported to the camp at Mittelbau-Dora prior to Belsen. 'It was love at first sight,' recalled Rachela, who also met her future husband, Rafael Olewski, Director of Cultural Activities of the entire British zone, on the same day. Both Regina and Rachela were married in 1946, Aharon and Regina in Palestine but, because of Olewski's work, Rachela remained in Germany until 1949, longer than she wanted, and gave birth to her first child, a daughter, Jochi, at the Glyn Hughes Hospital in the Bergen-Belsen DP camp.

This group, so strongly glued together in Auschwitz, now

started to splinter. In this way the orchestra girls were emblematic of the wider problem of the thousands of former prisoners who all had different hopes and needs. In the drive for normality, and an urgent desire to recreate a new family, many swiftly found boyfriends and husbands and now had to consider their hopes and needs too.

The Belgian and French girls, Hélène Wiernik, Violette Silberstein, Claire Monis and Fania Fénelon, wanted to go back to their original countries. 'We were talking a lot in the orchestra,' Rachela recalled. 'We sat and discussed why "Eretz Israel"? and why we have to go there? And she [Fania] would say, "Listen I don't understand why I should not live in France. France is my homeland. I was born there, I studied there and I had a good life there. Why shall I leave France? This is my homeland I don't think that I should betray her. Never." '26 Either through a feeling of patriotism or hoping to find surviving family, they returned to Brussels and Paris as soon as they could leave Belsen in early May 1945 by plane. Once back in France, Fania joined some American entertainers touring GI bases in occupied Germany for a few more weeks.

Hilde Grünbaum, now twenty-two, who had done so much to hold this group together at Auschwitz and Belsen, had always believed in the ideal that Jews should have a Jewish homeland in what was then British-controlled Palestine. It was what had sustained her throughout her ordeal at Auschwitz and Belsen, especially after she had rejected a place on the Kindertransport to Britain in 1939 in order to help her mother. Now the prospect of emigrating to Palestine at last seemed realistic and she was determined not to miss her chance. A few months after the liberation of Belsen, she met her husband on a visit to the men's camp with Rabbi Hardman. Ernst Zimche, a Polish Jew from Poznań, was one year older than Hilde and had been deported to Auschwitz in 1943 with his family. After they were killed he was sent to work at the I G Farben plant Buna Monowitz until 18 January 1945 when he was sent on a death march over 80 km from Auschwitz to Gleiwitz and from there to Belsen. The pair were married in August 1945 but did not attempt to go immediately to Palestine because they were both immersed in the challenge of helping the DPs at Belsen. Eventually Hilde's deep desire to establish a new home and family in Palestine won through. But it was not to be a straightforward journey for her and her husband.

*

In newly liberated Belsen, still awaiting freedom:
Hilde Grünbaum (right), Anita Lasker (middle)
and 'Little' Hélène Rounder (left)

What had become in the meantime of the Polish and Russian non-Jewish musicians in the orchestra who had been left behind in Auschwitz in November 1944 when the Jewish girls had been suddenly transported to Belsen? They scarcely had an easier time of it.

Helena Dunicz, the Polish violinist, was upset she and her Christian friends had not been allowed to say a word of farewell or make a single gesture to their former Jewish comrades despite Olga Loseva, the Russian mandolin player, having bravely managed to hand Rachela Zelmanowicz a few precious things before she left. The other non-Jewish musicians simply went back inside their barracks in stunned silence, convinced that the Jewish girls were being led to the gas chambers.

'Our remnant was soon transferred to sector B11c, which the men had vacated,' Helena recalled. 'To the great satisfaction of *Rapportführerin* Dreschel, the women's orchestra in Birkenau had ceased to exist. She and [SS Adolf] Taube had always regarded the orchestra as freeloaders and harassed us in any way they could.'[27]

All the instruments, sheet music, music stands, everything connected with the functioning of an orchestra, were left behind in Block 12 when they moved out, including their blankets, sheets and mattresses. The remaining women snatched whatever personal treasures they could, such as letters, but otherwise were allowed nothing. The block they were moved to just as another winter approached was as filthy and cold as all the other blocks in the women's camp. 'We noticed that there were not many of us because all the Russian women had vanished,' said Helena.[28] They never saw them again, nor were they told where they had gone.

The handful of Polish musicians stayed only a few weeks in Birkenhau and in mid-December 1944 they were transferred again, this time to Auschwitz I. Helena was shocked to hear that a call went out for musicians to re-establish the women's orchestra in the main camp. 'What a sick idea to organise an orchestra in the face of a general retreat all along the front. Who were they trying to fool? Themselves?'[29] The conductor of the principal men's camp orchestra in Auschwitz I, Adam Kopycinski, held several rehearsals with this small group of Polish women (only three volunteers had come forward – two mandolin players, Janina Palmowska and Janina Sosnowska, and one singer, Janina Kalicinska). But it was a fiasco and the group was swiftly disbanded. After that they were given various more or less useless tasks involving cleaning and moving bricks and planks of wood around the camp by yoking them to carts as if they were beasts of burden.

Helena was right that there was a 'general retreat' and sense of confusion in November 1944. Prisoners were constantly being moved around even as hundreds of prisoners were still arriving, mostly from other camps. Some female prisoners were transferred from Birkenau to Ravensbrück, north of Berlin, and others to the main camp, or Auschwitz I. At the same time, there were still around 300 women in Dr Carl Clauberg's pseudo-medical experimental block. On 2 November the use of Zyklon B gas in the Auschwitz gas chambers was 'probably discontinued', according to Danuta Czech, the Polish Holocaust historian and deputy director of the Auschwitz-Birkenau State Museum in Oświęcim, Poland, author of *Auschwitz Chronicle 1939–45*.[30] Yet that did not mean that mass killings ceased. Instead, the selected prisoners were shot to death in the gas chamber or in the grounds of Crematorium V.

In early November, having overseen the extermination of thousands of Hungarian Jews at Auschwitz, Rudolf Höss and his family left the villa where they had been living on the periphery of the main camp and moved to a house close to Ravensbrück. Four freight cars were required to move the abundant furnishings of the villa and the many possessions the Höss family had acquired. Höss took up a new job in Berlin but fled the city to join Hedwig and the children before the Russians arrived.

Christmas 1944 was miserable and muted for those orchestra girls who had been left in Auschwitz. There was no music but Helena and her friends were ordered to decorate a Christmas tree. 'They gave us coloured paper and scissors. No one was even watching us.'[31] On 5 January 1945 the Polish orchestra women had to endure one more horror, along with the other prisoners: the public hanging of four of the girls from the munitions factory who had aided the Sonderkommando revolt by smuggling gunpowder to them.[32]

This barbarity was a belated attempt to show the remaining prisoners that even at this late hour, sabotage would not be tolerated. It was already clear to most of the women that for the past month at least the camp was being prepared for evacuation, as the Soviet army was approaching and the war would soon be over. On 18 January, a freezing cold and snowy night, several hundred women were force marched out of the camp as the main evacuation of all remaining inmates got underway. They included the Polish women Zosia Cykowiak, Wisia Zatorska, Marylka Langenfeld, Marysia Mos and Helena Dunicz. Later they were joined by the three Janinas – Kalicinska, Palmowska and Sosnowska – the Polish women who had been part of the final orchestra in Auschwitz I for just a matter of weeks. Zofia Czajkowska, the orchestra's first conductor, now aged forty, was no longer part of the musical group, having been transferred at her own request to a different kommando months previously. But she too was force-marched out of the camp on 18 January.

All these women, wearing rags and with nothing more to sustain them than a loaf of bread each and some sugar cubes, were the last of the orchestra whose movements can confidently be traced on what became known as one of the death marches to Ravensbrück inside Germany, a journey of 600 km.

Stories of these death marches – the Nazis referred to them as evacuation marches – in some cases lasting for six days and seven nights to the various camps, make for almost impossible reading. As Jacques Stroumsa, the Greek violinist, recalled of his own almost 400 km march from Auschwitz south to Mauthausen in Austria: 'anyone who stumbled or lingered was shot and the SS men escorting the exhausted and poorly clad prisoners insisted on a rapid pace constantly barking orders "*Schnell, Schneller*" . . . It is incomprehensible what people can endure.'[33] Jacques had last seen his violinist sister 'little Julie' from the women's orchestra several months previously. He had no idea where she had been taken, since they had not been able to say goodbye, but he said that hoping to be reunited with her gave him strength as he was force-marched to Mauthausen.

As the Polish female musicians straggled on to Ravensbrück, where they arrived five days later, they were barely recognisable as human beings. They had had to trudge along rural side roads covered in thick snow, aware of fellow prisoners constantly falling by the wayside and either kicked to death, beaten with a rifle butt or shot, but not daring to turn and help. 'We heard gunshots every few moments,' said Helena. 'Yet we had to keep going.'[34]

Zosia could barely stay upright. 'Wisia put an arm around her and held her up the whole time.' On the first day, around midnight, having covered about 20 km from Auschwitz, they finally sat down in an enormous barn to eat bread, Wisia usually the one who took on the role of dividing it fairly. They had nothing to drink and a raging thirst which handfuls of melted snow failed to quench.

As they passed through friendly Polish villages, they realised that one or two prisoners had managed to escape, hoping the locals would take pity on them. But this was a huge risk as Nazi guards pointed guns at stragglers they thought might bolt or at villagers who came too close. Although some of the latter, shocked at the abuse they witnessed, threw bread or potatoes at the eerie columns, that was usually the extent of any help. Occasionally prisoners were lucky and found refuge. However, 'escaping was only possible alone, and the decision had to be taken immediately,' said Helena Dunicz. 'We were trying to stick together, although Wisia would have had a good shot at getting away because she knew the area well . . . But Wisia never even mentioned the possibility, knowing that Zosia would not make it without her help.'[35]

Eventually, having covered a 'murderous marching route' of 63 km with nighttime temperatures of minus 20 Celsius while 'the SS men continued to zealously carry out their bestial mission', they were shoved into open railroad cars for the final two days of the journey. They arrived at Ravensbrück on 23 January 1945, but after three weeks they were moved on again, this time further east to Neustadt Glewe, a satellite camp where women were used as slave labourers to make aeroplane parts. It was at this camp, with neither bunks nor blankets, that the group of hitherto tight-knit Poles, starving and totally exhausted, started to unravel and finally erupted in conflict. Helena, describing the tragic feud much later, said only that 'a bitter dispute flared up between Zosia and Marylka. Zosia "went off on her own" and our paths would not cross again until several years after the war.'[36]

Just as the Jewish girls at Belsen had found, they too were expected to work until the end, digging trenches or unloading potatoes for the local German population. They were exhausted, famished and in the grip of yet another typhus epidemic in the camp when, on 2 May 1945, two American soldiers approached to announce that Russian troops were on their way to liberate the area. This news meant that the trauma was not yet over, for they were terrified of what was in store from the victorious Soviet army, well known for violent and drunken rape attacks on any women they came across. After all that the women had witnessed in Auschwitz and Ravensbrück, it was now soldiers from the Red Army they feared most. 'I was scared to death of them,' Helena

Dunicz wrote in 2014, with memories still fresh of their cruel and violent behaviour in her hometown of Lwów before she had been deported to Auschwitz. She now decided she must avoid them at all costs but did not know where to go: west to the territory occupied by the Allies or east to liberated Poland?

Neither choice filled them with optimism and yet, before the month was out, a group of seven Polish women, all of whom had some connection to the orchestra, eventually decided to try and walk home to Poland. They had lost both Zosia Cykowiak and Marysia (Maria Mos), but in addition to Wisia there were the three Janinas and Irene Walaszczyk, who had briefly been a room elder in the music block. One night, on the road to Poland, they stopped to sleep in a deserted German house near some woods and dreaded a visit from Russian soldiers. Sure enough, the men soon arrived with meat and alcohol and demanded to 'celebrate'. Knowing what that meant, the women tried, while accepting the food, to keep their distance. According to Helena 'they accepted our demurral, which we justified by our long stay in the concentration camps'.

What Helena remembered above all from that night though was finding a white satin wedding dress in an otherwise empty wardrobe, and a memory of cooperation.

'I decided to make brassieres from it. In the orchestra block one of the violinists, a Greek Jew [Julie Stroumsa], had shown me how easy it is to make a brassiere . . . it didn't come out badly and one by one we added that accessory to our wardrobe.'[37]

The seven, attired with brassieres for the first time in months, split up in Poznań as four went towards whatever was left of their homes, leaving Wisia, Marylka and Helena together to board a train to Krakow.

On 29 May 1945 these three reached Krakow where their cruel reckoning with the post-war world began. Just as Helena had known that night of the fateful Beethoven sonata it was the safety of her own group that had given her strength. Now, aged twenty-nine, with no family of her own to return to, she once again felt deeply alone and so remained forever grateful to Wisia, just a year younger, who took her in to live with her own grieving family. Three of Wisia's brothers, all active members of the Polish anti-Nazi underground, had been killed in either Auschwitz or Gross-Rosen. Yet Wisia's parents warmly welcomed Helena into their grief-stricken home.

In the early days after the war Helena could not bear to listen to music at all and for more than ten years she would force herself to attend concerts only to return home physically ill. 'Time eventually healed,' she told Jean-Jacques Felstein, son of the Belgian violinist Elsa Miller, when he was researching his mother's story in the 1990s. But not entirely, because Helena's playing days were over.[38] Music nonetheless remained a part of her life. Within months of returning to Poland she found a job working for the Polish Music Publishers. As the company grew, she moved from secretary to director of department and finally deputy director before retiring in 1975.

10

Someone three quarters destroyed by her experience

Hilde Grünbaum Zimche started on her own post-war career helping refugee-survivors, who were officially designated 'Displaced Persons' (DPs) by the British in Belsen, rather than refugees. Jewish and other aid agencies had long since realised that this ocean of homeless, damaged people was going to cause the most acute crisis whenever the war ended and did their impossible best to plan for it. From 1945 to 1952, more than 250,000 Jewish DPs lived in camps and urban centres in Germany, Austria and Italy. These facilities were administered by the Western Allied authorities and the newly established United Nations Relief and Rehabilitation Administration, UNRRA. But deciding who was a worthy DP became immensely controversial as some former Nazis and Nazi sympathisers, disguised as Polish resisters or even Jews, slipped under the wire.

Helping the DPs establish a new life was painful and desperate work since most had no homes to return to and were often the sole survivors from their families or communities. Few were able to contemplate returning to their countries of origin, fearing for their lives either because houses had been destroyed and possessions looted or else, in the case of Poles, Ukrainians, Belarusians, some Czechs and Hungarians, they feared persecution from

Communist regimes now installed in their former homelands. These traumatised survivors, who had suffered so much and witnessed atrocities beyond imagination, assumed that the victorious Allies would surely want to right these wrongs and cushion their re-entry into what remained of the civilised world. But numbers allowed to emigrate to British-controlled Palestine had always been severely restricted by the British, even during the war, when Europe's Jews were trying desperately to flee Nazi persecution. The British had governed a deeply unsettled Palestine under a League of Nations mandate since 1920 and had in 1917 promised in the Balfour Declaration 'a National Homeland for the Jewish people'. They were also anxious not to antagonise the Arab world, in particular the Egyptians and oil-rich Saudis, and so had similarly made promises to Arab nationalists about an eventual united Arab country.

After the war, despite the pressure of world opinion – in particular repeated requests by US President Harry Truman to admit 100,000 Jews to Palestine – the British under Prime Minister Attlee felt unable to lift the ban on immigration as Truman called for. Jewish survivors chose British-controlled Palestine as their most desired destination in increasing numbers between 1945 and 1948, their nationalism heightened by lack of autonomy in the DP camps and having few destinations available. But getting to the US, which some DPs would have liked, was also difficult since each individual was required to have a sponsor and a place to live before their arrival, as well as a guarantee that they would not displace American workers; a relative who was an American citizen was helpful too. The DPs stranded in Europe became an influential force in the Zionist cause and in the political debate about the creation of a Jewish state. They condemned British barriers to open immigration to Palestine but were blocked for fear of antagonising Arab nationalists who now saw their own homeland being overrun. Since there were very few legal possibilities for getting to Palestine, and the illegal routes were fraught with danger, many Zionists, having held off opposing the British while the British were engaged in fighting the Nazis, now turned to armed resistance against them in Mandated Palestine.

The immediate post-war era in Europe was one of confusion, homelessness, hunger, looting, disruption, devastation and divorce. The suffering for those who had lived through the daily horrors of a concentration camp did not end with 'liberation'. They may have slowly grown physically stronger, or rebuilt some sort of life, but the shadow of that experience loomed over them and took up space inside them for the rest of their lives. Each survivor was marked in different ways, but none was unaffected. There were few places where survivors felt comfortable talking openly about their experiences, often sensing in their listeners who had not lived through the camps a mixture of shame, guilt and incomprehension.

'Nobody wanted to know. It's a complete fallacy to say we did not want to talk about it,' is how Anita still remembered that time in an interview in 2022. 'We were dying to talk about it, to tell the world. We wanted to change the world, we thought it was the end of anti-Semitism, that's how naïve you can be when you are young.'[1]

In her 1996 memoir about her experiences, Anita elaborated: 'When we first came to England, Renate and I badly wanted to talk but no one asked us any questions. I know very well that, on the whole, people want to protect themselves from too much knowledge. Under the pretext of not wanting to bring back memories in case they should be upsetting, they allow silence to prevail.'[2] But slowly things changed.

One of the first tasks Anita set herself immediately after she arrived in England in 1946 was to visit Arnold Rosé, Alma's father, then living in Blackheath, southeast London. Alma had repeatedly talked about her father to the musicians and asked that if any of them survived they should try and find him and tell him about the orchestra, a request which revealed Alma's despair that she might not survive and also her pride in what she had created.

Anita's conversation with the legendary musician was not easy. 'I was told that he was old and frail and I must be very careful with him. I didn't know what he knew about his daughter or the orchestra,' she recalled.[3] The Mahler family had been told about Alma's death a month after the end of the war through Alma's Dutch connections. But the garbled account they were given at first indicated suicide as the most likely cause of death. Arnold, now in his early eighties, was in such pain at hearing that his beloved daughter was dead that he could barely speak about it. He wrote to his son, Alfred, in America that 'my only consolation is that she had achieved martyrdom'.[4] Then, one morning later in 1945, two nuns dressed in long black habits called at Arnold's door in Blackheath, handed him a violin case and mysteriously departed without a word. The case with its satin-lined, red velvet cover decoratively embroidered with the initials AR contained Alma's precious 1757 Guadagnini violin which she had used before the war and had given to her Dutch friend, Dr Leonard Jongkees, the ear, nose and throat physician whom she had met in the summer of 1941, to hide from the Nazis. Having survived the war, Jongkees now saw to it that it was restored to her ailing father courtesy of the two nuns.*

---

* Needing the money, and knowing he would never play again, Arnold Rosé sold the violin to the Viennese-born concertmaster of the Metropolitan Opera in New York where 'Its sweet tone was heard for two decades', according to the story told to the music journalist Norman Lebrecht by Alma's cousin Eleanor Rosé. 'The true humanity of Alma Rosé', 5 April, 2000.[5]

Anita, like Jongkees, wanted to fulfil her promise to Alma and tell Arnold the truth about Auschwitz and Alma's astonishing achievement. 'I spent an afternoon there. That I will never forget. I told him what a wonderful disciplinarian Alma had been.'[6] Most importantly she wanted to tell him that his daughter had died peacefully, not suffocated in a gas chamber, and that what she had meant to all the orchestra girls was life itself. Arnold listened, perhaps relieved, but he was in fragile health and died, aged eighty-two, on Sunday, 25 August 1946, a few weeks after Anita's visit.

Such difficult conversations were the price of survival as the Holocaust – though not yet called that – bled into the liberation and attempts to start new lives. The talented Belgian violinist 'La Grande Hélène' Wiernik had to tell her parents, Chune and Etka, who had only been thirty-eight and forty-five when she was taken by the Nazis, that their only son, Hélène's eleven-year-old brother, had been gassed immediately after he arrived at Auschwitz in a hospital train. 'I remained silent because for my parents it was too much to hear about my brother,' Hélène recalled in the 1999 film *Bach in Auschwitz*.

Hélène gave up her beloved violin playing after the war. She was too weak, too damaged physically; she said she simply did not have the endurance to continue playing. She also suffered serious emotional issues from hearing, in the music block, the nighttime noise of a lorry disgorging its human cargo. 'In the night I heard chanting, living skeletons singing hymns and praying. That will be a vision I will never forget. They were directly en route to the crematorium. We probably all thought that one day our time would come.'[7]

In 1946 Hélène married fellow survivor Léon Minkowski (born in Chemnowitz in 1925; deported from France to Auschwitz in 1942), with whom she had two children, Danielle and Yves. She rebuilt her life in Belgium, supported by her continuing friend-ship with the violinists Fanny Kornblum (later Birkenwald) and Violette Silberstein (later Jacquet).*

Hilde and her new husband Ernst Zimche spent six months 'on the road'[8] after leaving Belsen in 1945, travelling southwest until they reached Antwerp, Belgium. Here they stayed for four months in two big houses which had been made available by various Zionist organisations to young survivors, would-be immigrants to Palestine who were given agricultural training before heading to Marseille. In March 1946, she and 700 or so others climbed aboard a cargo ship called the *Tel Hai*, purportedly going to Panama, and hid below deck. All 736 stowaways were attempt-ing to get to Palestine. However, the ship was intercepted by the British destroyer HMS *Chequers* 140 miles out at sea as it approached the Palestine coast. Fortunately, the refugees were then sent to a detention camp in Palestine called Atlit, rather than to Cyprus, where most illegal immigrants ended up, or Mauritius, another destination. Eventually, Hilde and her husband received permission to remain in Palestine and for the next two years lived on different kibbutzim until after the Arab-Israeli war of 1948, when they moved to their present home, a kibbutz in the centre of Israel, which was founded by a small group of Holocaust survivors in Germany immediately after liberation and originally called Kibbutz Buchenwald. By the time they moved there Hilde was pregnant and her first son, Amnon, was the first baby born on the kibbutz. Uri followed soon after in 1950.

Today the kibbutz has a new name, Kibbutz Netzer Sereni – in memory of an Italian Jewish Socialist, Enzo Sereni, captured by

---

* After her husband was killed in a car crash in 1965, she remarried, becom-ing Hélène Schepps. She died of cancer in 2006.

the Nazis and executed in Dachau. Hilde and Ernst Zimche and their families, as well as Regina and Aharon Bacia, made their lives here and both still have many descendants living on the kibbutz.*

Esther Loewy, the first accordionist in the orchestra under Czajkowska, had left Auschwitz for Ravensbrück in 1943 persuaded by a Red Cross deal for those who were not 100 per cent Jewish that life would be better there. When Ravensbrück was evacuated near the end of the war she was sent on a death march from which she and several other prisoners fortunately escaped, ending up in a market square in the small town of Lübz, about halfway between Berlin and Hamburg. Here she celebrated the Allied victory over the Nazis by watching a picture of Hitler being set on fire by American soldiers, one of whom then handed her an accordion, which she played as soldiers and other camp survivors danced in the street. Esther had survived but was now, at the age of twenty, totally adrift with no family to return to in Germany.

She made her way to a displaced persons camp near Belsen where she learned that the Nazis had deported her parents in

---

* After 1945 more than 100,000 people attempted to illegally enter Mandated Palestine. There were 142 voyages made by 120 ships with more than half of these stopped by the British patrols. The Royal Navy had eight ships on station in Palestine, and additional ships were tasked with tracking suspicious vessels heading for Palestine. The British held as many as 50,000 people in camps, mostly in Cyprus. More than 1,600 drowned at sea. Only a few thousand entered Palestine. The pivotal event which brought the issue to world attention was in 1947 when the SS *Exodus* was intercepted, attacked and boarded by a British patrol. Despite significant resistance from its passengers, *Exodus* was forcibly returned to Europe and its passengers were eventually sent back to Germany. It took several more decades before there was widespread discussion of the Nakba or Palestinian catastrophe, when Palestinians were expelled from their homes and which accompanied the creation of the State of Israel.

1941 from their home in Saarlouis to Lithuania, where they were shot and killed. Her sister Ruth, who had fled to Switzerland, had been deported and killed at Auschwitz just before her own arrival there. Esther had one other sister, Tosca, who was already in Palestine, so she decided to try and get there. She hitchhiked to Frankfurt and from there took a train to Marseille where in August 1945 she boarded a boat to Haifa.

Esther was briefly interned on arrival but was allowed to stay and then fought hard to restart her life in the new land. She studied singing, joined a choir, gave music lessons and in 1950 married Nissim Bejarano, a truck driver, with whom she had a son, Joram, and a daughter, Edna. She eventually met up with Hilde in Israel but, because of both illness and her transfer from Auschwitz to Ravensbrück in 1943, was not remembered by many of the musicians who arrived later and had bonded over their memories of playing under Alma's baton. In 1960, Esther returned to Germany, partly because she and Nissim were pacifists who could not face fighting again after the Second World War. She had German nationality and so settled in Hamburg, running a laundry service with her husband and barely eking out a living.

She was never comfortable in Germany either. 'Whenever I saw a German in uniform a chill ran down my spine,' she told the newspaper *Süddeutsche Zeitung* in an interview in 2015.[9] She found it difficult to discuss the Holocaust with anyone in Germany and was appalled by what she saw as a resurgence of anti-Semitism, which she felt the German government was ignoring. It was an event in the 1970s, when she watched German police officers shield right-wing extremists against protesters, that turned her into a political activist. She joined the Association of the Persecutees of the Nazi Regime and for the last forty years of her life told her own story in schools, delivered protest speeches and sang resistance songs with a band which she formed with her own children in 1989.

Once she had found her voice, she performed on stage and regularly gave interviews, appalled by violence against Turkish immigrants in Germany and what she perceived as the resurgence of the far right. Esther explained how she wanted to use music to act against fascism. In 2009, when she was eighty-five, Esther's musical career took a further turn. She was invited to join a German hip-hop group called Microphone Mafia, with whom she continued to spread her message against fascism and intolerance to young audiences in Germany and abroad, touring from Istanbul to Vancouver. Onstage she was an unusual figure: a tiny woman with a snow-white pixie haircut, singing in Yiddish, Hebrew, German and Italian. She joked that hip-hop was not her natural choice and she had to persuade her bandmates to lower their volume and stop jumping around on stage so much. But she believed that hip-hop's influence on young people could help counter a rise in intolerance. 'We are three generations of musicians on stage, with three different religions. The message is self-evident: music unites us, regardless of language and origin,' Esther said.[10]

The life lessons about human behaviour in extremis which she had learned in the camps became a reason for living and spreading her message. Shortly before her death in 2021 at the age of ninety-seven the German government awarded Esther an Order of Merit. Microphone Mafia wrote on its website after she died about how they would miss her after twelve years and almost 900 concerts together. 'All this thanks to your strength... Your laughter, your courage, your determination, your loving manner, your understanding, your fighting heart.'[11]

*

In 1952 Anita Lasker married the pianist Peter Wallfisch, a child-hood friend from Breslau who was a few months older than her. Aged eleven, they had even played in school concerts together.

'I didn't take any notice of him then,' said Anita in an interview for the Royal College of Music. 'He was rather a fat little boy!' Peter had managed to escape the war living in Jerusalem, where he was taken in 1939 as part of a scheme to rescue talented Jewish children. He then moved to Paris once the war was over. A mutual friend suggested to Anita who was about to go to Paris – to visit her sister Renate who had married a Frenchman – that she look him up while she was there. She did and found 'we now had a lot in common'.[12]

The pair settled in London where Anita, as a founding member of the English Chamber Orchestra, became the professional cellist she had always dreamt of being and also mother of two children, the cellist Raphael Wallfisch, and the psychotherapist Maya Jacobs Wallfisch.

Today, in her late nineties, she is still brisk and straight talking with an impressive presence and stature as she welcomes me one hot summer's day into her home. As she takes up her position in an armchair overlooking a small garden, I find myself looking at the same face, now fringed with grey hair, that I have looked at for the last few years as she stands between her friends, Hilde Grünbaum and Hélène Rounder, all three smiling in a photograph taken at Belsen after liberation. She has everything to hand, phone, pen and cigarettes, one of which she now lights, as she tells me with an understandable weariness how many times since then she has been called upon to tell her story about surviving Auschwitz. I apologise, but she is kind and indulges me.

Anita has never had time for discussing feelings such as survivor guilt. As she explained in her memoir:

my main aim when I started building a new life for myself after the war was to catch up on the lost years and provide normality for my children. I believe most survivors felt the same way. It took me many years to understand that normality is not something you can create out of nothing. How can there be normality when you hesitate to answer your children's questions about where their grandma and grandpa are for fear of traumatizing them beyond redemption... providing normality for my children meant that among other things they should not feel different or isolated. Now, fifty years on, I know that this was all a pipe dream. There is no place in normal life for stories which are so outrageously horrendous that they seem like fairy tales at best and gross exaggerations at worst.[13]

Her children, to whom she always spoke in English – to speak in German would have been totally impossible, she explained to an interviewer[14] – saw it slightly differently. Anita's daughter Maya said in the 1996 BBC documentary *Playing to Survive*: 'She wasn't like other mothers... if we asked her a question she'd say, "I'll tell you when you're older." I think the fact that my mother has now written her story has helped her a lot,' Maya added.[15]

Maya, born in 1958, was the only member of the family who did not play music professionally, which may have complicated her childhood responses to her parents' war. But as she explained in an interview, she believed many of the children of survivors suffered from their parents' unimaginable experiences in the camps.

If you are a child and you feel ill, and then it is said to you, as it was several times to me, 'Are you about to die? Have you got parents? Are you starving? What's your problem?' – you're left with complete confusion. How do I figure out what I feel, need or want when I'm being told those things don't exist? It's a complete disavowal of one's experience, which becomes irrelevant or inconsequential; and although not intended, that has the impact of making one struggle for identity and any kind of legitimacy about one's personal needs. If everything is recorded against the backdrop of what my parents had been through, you can just forget it.[16]*

Anita shared with me, in one of our interviews at her North London home, how she thought Alma was excessively close to her father.[17] 'She even asked him for fingering as she played...' I wonder if what Anita is actually revealing here is the answer to my nagging question throughout the research on this book: what special qualities enabled a teenager without either of her parents to survive prison and camp life of the most brutal kind and emerge to lead a full life, just as she did? Was Anita born with a will to survive or was that will forged in Auschwitz?

'I'm a very positive person,' she said in a radio interview in 1996. 'I wasn't going to let the Germans, who'd destroyed my family, destroy me as a person who is embittered and full of hatred... I wanted to live.'[18]

Asked in the same interview if finally returning to Auschwitz 'had helped in any way', Anita sounds almost affronted by the question. 'I don't need any help in that sense. I'm way past that. I go back now out of curiosity to see what's happened there.'[19]

Some former prisoners of Auschwitz seem to have been able to survive extreme traumatic experiences and yet managed to rebuild

---

* Today Maya is a psychoanalytic psychotherapist and educator who has written a book, *Letter to Breslau*, exploring the intergenerational Holocaust trauma she experienced.

their lives afterwards. Others appear to be carrying the trauma with them, haunted by it and unable to shake it off for the rest of their lives. The women's orchestra contained both. Again and again, survivors tell interviewers that only those who were there, who experienced Auschwitz first-hand, can understand what it was like and what it took to survive.

In November 1947 the trial of Maria Mandl began in Krakow. Officially known as the First Auschwitz trial, any thoughts that the appetite for hearing about the horrors of the gas chambers had waned were to be disproved here in Poland. This was partly because the large number of defendants on trial (forty-one senior Auschwitz staff were indicted) included several female guards, whose salacious private lives the international press found of particular interest. Best known among the defendants were Arthur Liebehenschel, former commandant November 1943–May 1944, Maria Mandl, head overseer of the women's camp, and SS doctor Johann Kremer. The forty-one represented a small fraction of the total of approximately 7,000 SS men and about 170 female overseers who worked in Auschwitz during the period when the camp operated. Maria Mandl was given, like the other females in the dock, a plain grey suit and white blouse to wear. She had to listen as she was accused of causing the death of hundreds of thousands of women and children, and additionally by several survivors of specific instances of brutality, including selecting prisoners to receive lethal injections, and branding, beating and kicking individual women. The eyewitness description of how Mandl killed a newborn baby was especially gruesome. One survivor, Janina Frankiewicz, spoke of Mandl on the ramp awaiting trainloads of Jews and being responsible for their selections to the gas chambers along with SS officer Adolf Taube, renowned for inflicting random cruelty on female prisoners, and Therese

Brandl, a senior female guard.* Others, including non-Jewish survivors of the women's camp such as the Polish writer Seweryna Szmaglewska who in 1945 wrote the first non-fiction account of the camp called *Smoke Over Birkenau*, bore witness to Mandl's wild beatings, kickings and selections which had her signature attached on the paperwork. Mandl admitted, 'Yes... I was signing the lists of those destined for death... but it was only

Maria Mandl, the Auschwitz-Birkenau guard who promoted the orchestra, shortly before her execution for crimes against humanity in 1948

---

* Brandl was convicted of crimes against humanity during this trial and executed in 1948. The fate of Adolf Taube, considered one of the cruellest SS men in Birkenau, is unknown.

pure formality,' but otherwise consistently denied all the accusations, insisting she was at the ramp only to put into practice what the doctors or her superiors ordered. Her defence lawyer made the tired arguments that his client was simply a slave in the system. But the evidence was damning. Maria Mandl was 'a demon in a human body... When she ruled the camp, we thought it was the end of the world for us,' said one witness, referred to only as Marchwycka.[20]

To the orchestra Mandl was both benign and malign. Without her support, irrespective of her motivation – rivalry with Margot Dreschel, her fellow senior female guard, or a desire to prove to a Nazi lover how cultured she was – there would have been no orchestra and its members would not have survived. Equally they knew the base cruelty of which she was capable. The three Polish members of the orchestra who attended the trial (Wisia, Helena and Zosia) heard accounts of how Mandl would stand at the camp gate as the exhausted work details returned and were expected to march in time to the music. Any who were out of step or did not start with their left foot would be hauled out for a beating accompanied by great laughs on Mandl's part. The court was told things which they all knew first-hand.

During breaks in the trial proceedings one of the three, the violinist Wisia Zatorska, tried to get close to Mandl – the defiant Wisia who had been made to scrub the floor after she refused an order from Alma, the same Wisia who had carried the ailing Zosia on the death march, who had lost three brothers in Auschwitz and the Gross-Rosen camp during the war and felt bitter hatred towards Mandl and the other Nazis at the trial. Perhaps she did not know herself exactly what she hoped to achieve from approaching Mandl beyond a recognition that she had suffered. Zosia Cykowiak, with Wisia in the courtroom, tried to restrain and calm her friend, fearing a hysterical scene which would result in the judge removing them all from the courtroom. Finally, Zosia, on Wisia's behalf, got close enough to Mandl during one of the breaks to ask 'if she recognised us. We were from the orchestra. She kept looking at us, but she wouldn't say a word.' By then Wisia had lost control of herself; 'she started pulling at me and we led Wisia out'.[21]

All these women wanted was some recognition that Mandl knew them, acknowledged what she had done to them and recognised that they too were human beings she had all but destroyed. But they were denied that. Zosia returned to the court on 22 December 1947 for the verdict. Mandl was found guilty of participating in mass murder and hanged on 24 January 1948, aged thirty-six.

But even that did not bring any long-term relief for Zosia, who found she could never entirely lift the weight of the camp off her shoulders. She remained tightly bonded to the violinist Helena Dunicz Niwińska as well as the other Polish women from the orchestra. It was Helena who looked after the physically and emotionally broken Zosia, despite suffering emotional torment herself for what she perceived as her own failure to save her beloved mother. Helena regularly visited Birkenau to pay homage to this mother for whose death in Auschwitz she felt responsible. While she was a prisoner, she had 'forgotten' that her mother understood music sufficiently well that she too could have been a copyist in the orchestra. She blamed herself for not doing what Anita had done for her sister, Renate, by getting her a job which protected her. But as others had to remind Helena, it was not her forgetfulness that killed her mother. It was the Nazis.[22]

In 1961, there was one more sensational trial which grabbed world headlines. Adolf Eichmann, who had regarded the destruction of the Hungarian Jews as his personal mission, had briefly been arrested by Americans in 1946 but had escaped and evaded recapture before fleeing Germany with his family in 1950. On 11 May 1960 he was dramatically kidnapped by the Israeli secret service (Mossad) in Buenos Aires and brought back to Israel.

His trial before three Israeli judges in Jerusalem intensified scholarly interest in trying to understand the Nazi attempt to exterminate all the world's Jews. The most famous account of the trial came from the German Jewish political thinker and philosopher Hannah Arendt, whose controversial articles in the *New Yorker* magazine saw Eichmann not as a monstrous psychopath but as an unimaginative human being who, in her words, was 'neither perverted nor sadistic . . . but terribly and terrifyingly normal'.[23]

Lily Mathé, having been able finally to leave Belsen in 1947 and come to England to marry her Viennese-born British army rescuer, Eddie Bernstein, was now desperate to appear as a witness at Eichmann's trial. Until this moment, Lily had never spoken publicly nor written about the gruesome nightmare she endured in Auschwitz and Belsen. She had carved out a double life for herself as both Mrs Bernstein, living quietly in suburban North London with the man who had fallen impetuously in love with her at Belsen, and Lily Mathé, the virtuoso performer who played regularly at Lyons Corner House café on the Strand in central London, using the beautiful stolen violin that Josef Kramer had given her at Belsen.

When she heard about Eichmann's capture, she was roused to anguish once again and agreed to give various interviews, including one published in October 1960 as a four-part serial in the British tabloid *News of the World* under the headline 'I too was Eichmann's Victim'.[24] Lily's horrific account prompted a British Independent Television (ITV) one-hour special documentary about Eichmann in which she featured as the main witness. But, much to her chagrin, Lily was not summoned to testify in person against

Eichmann because the prosecution had already compiled enough evidence against him. During his trial, which lasted from 11 April to 15 December 1961, Eichmann gave evidence from a glass cage, insisting doggedly that he had just been following orders. He was found guilty of crimes against the Jewish people and sentenced to death, the only capital sentence ever imposed by an Israeli court. He was hanged on 31 May 1962, and his ashes were scattered at sea.

I too was Eichmann's victim

Lily Mathe today —with her violin and a future. In Auschwitz there was no future— just survival

Lily Mathé after telling her story in 1960 of being auditioned by Eichmann at Auschwitz

*

In 1976, thirty years after liberation, Fania Fénelon, as she now was, became the first of the orchestra girls to publish a book about their experiences. Her semi-fictionalised memoir, in which most of the protagonists were given invented but easily recognisable names, was initially called *Playing for Time* or, later in the UK, *The Musicians of Auschwitz*. While the book caused pain and anger among the surviving protagonists, it brought this hitherto almost unknown story into the open. Fania maintained that she wrote the book because she could not get Auschwitz-Birkenau, where she spent eleven months in the orchestra, out of her head, and had based her story on the 'tiny, tattered notebook' secretly brought with her from Auschwitz to Belsen, in which she had written details of her time in the camp.[25]

'Particularly at night. I can't help it. I find myself back in the block at Birkenau and it all happens without any help from me. It never starts in the same way, someone shouts . . . Florette or Irene . . . someone is crying, Anny perhaps, there's a shower of insults, blows . . . I spend every night there – every night.'[26]

Asked why she had waited thirty years to tell her story, she said that she had had to live, 'to have the youth we never had; we looked like old women, and we were in our twenties [sic]. I needed to bask in other people's warmth, to eat, to make love, to love . . . to recover. I had to get over the camps. That took years. After thirty years of silence during which I tried to forget the unforgettable, I saw that it was impossible. What I had to do was to exorcise the orchestra.'[27]

Fania saw her time in the Auschwitz orchestra as 'both an oasis and a ghetto . . . a sort of sandwich; a slice of music between two slices of wretchedness'.[28]

She added that she wanted the world to know about the wretchedness and the compromises, as she saw them, that they had had to make in order to survive, including allusions to lesbian relationships among her fictional cast, the latter removed from subsequent translations. But there were other reasons too. She maintained that it was experiencing a resurgence of Nazism in

France that had pushed her to write the book. Another factor, which she did not mention, was that she needed the money.

Post-war life had not been easy for Fania. Divorced from the Swiss athlete Silvio Perla almost immediately, she then travelled around Europe giving cabaret-style concerts with various productions. One of those she accompanied was the African American baritone singer Aubrey Pankey, who had been accused by the US House Un-American Activities Committee of being affiliated with 'Communist-front organizations' and who could not live in France after the French government refused to renew his residence permit and ordered him to leave the country. He moved to East Berlin in 1956 and Fania, 'who was very enamoured of him',[29] moved there soon after and taught in a high school for music in East Berlin. In 1971 Pankey was killed in a car crash in East Berlin after which Fania returned to Paris, where she lived alone in a modest apartment.

Stories about the concentration camps were a relatively new publishing genre. Fania's book, written with the help of French journalist Marcelle Routier, was a highly novelised account of her eleven months in the orchestra but with enough true facts in the narrative to make it a gripping read for an audience who were not well versed in the reality of Auschwitz, Belsen and Ravensbrück. These facts, she insisted, came from the notebook of her time in the camp. Alma Rosé remained 'Alma' and Fania's jealousy of her is plain in the book, criticising her for her obsequiousness towards the Germans and for her harsh punishments of the girls. 'Wrong notes seem to be your only recurrent nightmare,' was one accusation she threw at Alma.[30]

'How loathsome Alma was, lording it on her platform, masterful and self-confident. Or was she? If I was her, I'd be ashamed [a reference to the way Alma had refused to ask for more bread] . . . an admission of pride and powerlessness?'[31]

After Alma, the cruellest portrayal was of Claire Monis, the French singer and resistance fighter who had arrived with Fania. Claire, barely disguised as Clara, was described negatively throughout the book as being obese 'with enormous breasts flopping down on her fat stomach'[32] and constantly exchanging sex for favours in the camp with both male prisoners and the SS. One reason why Fania singled out Claire and Alma may have been that both were dead at the time of publication and would therefore be unable to respond. Or perhaps Fania was jealous of Claire as well as Alma since Claire had a fine voice when her own was well past its best. Claire had also played an active role in the resistance, which was better documented than Fania's rather vague activities. The real Claire 'had the very pretty face of a young woman',[33] according to Helena. Anita was also outraged by Fania's description of Claire. 'The worst distortion was that of Claire, who was no longer alive when the book came out,' Anita recalled in 2014. 'But her son was still alive . . .' In another interview, Anita said that 'absolutely UNFORGIVEABLE [sic] is the portrayal of the girl who becomes a prostitute. It is not only tasteless but UNTRUE.'[34]*

In 1980, four years after publication, Fania's book became an even more controversial film, produced by Linda Yellen, with a screenplay written by Arthur Miller. Now it was Fania's turn to be angry. She bitterly opposed what she described as a sanitised rendition of life in the camps and was especially upset by the casting of British actress Vanessa Redgrave to play her. Redgrave was a controversial choice after her 1978 award acceptance speech when she referred to the actions of 'a small bunch of Zionist hoodlums'[35] and also because, standing close to six feet tall and

---

* Claire's figure, well rounded by camp standards, may have been as a result of hunger swelling or starvation oedema.

with blue eyes, she bore little physical resemblance to the petite Fania, who was barely five foot.

'I do not accept a person to play me who is the opposite of me... I wanted Liza Minnelli. She's small, she's full of life, she sings and dances. Vanessa... doesn't have a sense of humour, and that is the one thing that saved me from death in the camp,' Fania said in an interview. She even attacked the tall, fair-haired Redgrave in person during a US television interview on the popular *Sixty Minutes* programme, but ultimately lost the battle over casting. Redgrave insisted she was not anti-Semitic. 'How could I be?' she said in the programme. 'Everything that I have done shows that I have fought fascism and racism.'[36] Jane Alexander, the American actress who portrayed Alma, was widely praised.

Many of those from the orchestra who were still alive at the time felt betrayed by Fania's account in one way or another. In public the responses were somewhat muted. Even Lili Assael, who

The Assael family in New York: Michel, Lili and Yvette (far right) with Fania Fénelon between the sisters

did have reason to criticise Alma's treatment of her, did not make any public statements supporting Fania's version. Hélène Wiernik strongly defended Alma, whom she adored, in an interview in 1997.[37] However, she was still not prepared to attack Fania, insisting that 'I liked her a lot' and 'she had a special voice'.

Hélène Wiernik's daughter, Danielle Minkowski, said that what her mother most objected to was not only the 'untrue notion' that the women did not get on but Fania's failure to make clear for posterity where they played. According to Danielle, her mother 'wanted it made VERY CLEAR that this orchestra NEVER played outside the gas chamber. They ONLY played marches when the prisoners went to work and when they returned.'[39]

Anita Lasker-Wallfisch wrote her own version of the camp orchestra, called *Inherit the Truth*, published in 1996. 'It is very important not to underestimate the mutual support we gave one another,' wrote Anita. 'I think we all contributed a little to each other's survival. We watched everyone and bullied people when for example we noticed the first signs of slacking in personal hygiene.'[38]

It is a rich irony that Fania Fénelon, although not equal to Alma in musicianship nor leadership, helped immortalise her. In the wake of the scandal, Richard Newman, a Canadian journalist and music critic, began work on a biography of Alma Rosé to which many of the surviving members contributed. There was general consensus among the core Jewish and non-Jewish groups who were now interviewed by Newman that they must speak out to convey not only the rigorous determination of Alma to save them all but to make clear the enormous help and assistance they had given each other in Auschwitz, and counter Fania's account of division and squabbling. But in their determination that Fania's version of this appalling time in their lives should not remain for posterity as the prevailing narrative, the women who made their views known did not completely deny that alongside the sisterly support, mostly between small groups, there had also been petty arguments and mutual distrust.

Fanny Birkenwald, in Auschwitz the Belgian mandolin player, Fanny Kornblum, wrote in 1996 when she was seventy:

> I have a wonderful memory of the marvellous understanding that reigned among us. Particularly the brave little gestures by which we gave each other the courage to hold out; the hope we gave each other when there was no longer anything to hope for; and the bread we shared. We remained human beings and for those who lived through the life of the camp, it is a great achievement to have been able to preserve their dignity. I am proud to have been part of the orchestra. In my opinion we were all responsible for each other's conduct.[40]

Fanny's comments, written deliberately to rebut the image of division among the orchestra members, may have exaggerated the cooperation. Not all the members of the orchestra were always prepared to share bread or look out for each other in a wider sense. But from Fanny's perspective, reflecting on her arrival at Auschwitz in a family group and how her mother Frieda pushed her to audition for the orchestra even though she was hardly a talented musician, it was precisely the brave little gestures – a slice of potato here or comforting hug there – that made all the difference between life and death. Frieda, along with Fanny's grandmother and sister, were all gassed.

There were some positive results from the publicity given to Fania's book. Anita in London and Helena in Krakow now began a halting personal correspondence, although it took until September 1994 before they were able to meet up again. 'I am glad that I am in contact again with two of the Polish members of the orchestra, Helena and Zofia,' Anita wrote in her 1996 memoir.

> Still somewhat hampered by the language difficulties, we managed to talk to each other in spite of it and in place of mutual distrust we have established a good and honest relationship ... what I really want to say is that, contrary to the way in which we were portrayed in Arthur Miller's film version of the camp orchestra, we were far from being a vindictive mob of unruly girls who stole from and betrayed each other at every opportunity. In spite of many differences in character and background, we were a very positive small community of people sharing a miserable life and the prospect of a miserable end.[41]

Helena (Dunicz Niwińska) with Anita (Lasker-Wallfisch) and Zofia (Cykowiak) in post-war Europe

*

Flora Jacobs, later Schrijver, told Newman what Alma meant to her. She argued that even though Alma personally suffered extreme nervousness as to what might happen if they failed to perform well, she imbued her charges with courage that they would survive. 'She promised me, never be afraid of the gas chambers because if that happens, I will get you out.'[42]

But she said it was watching the film which compelled her to start talking about her experiences because it was 'not a true reflection of reality . . . until that time I shied away from publicity. The film was the decisive factor. I had to honour Alma Rosé posthumously. The woman who saved our lives was being portrayed as a woman who mistreated us. We wrote to Arthur Miller saying if you have to make a film listen to our stories.'[43]

Flora needed half a century before she was ready to publicly share her experiences by cooperating in the writing of a memoir called *Girl with the Accordion*, published in 1994, based on a series of interviews she gave to the author. She told how in 1945 she had arrived back in the Netherlands, a twenty-one-year-old widow whose husband, Emmanuel van Praag, the German Jew she had hastily married in Westerbork camp in 1942 hoping that marriage to a Dutch woman might save him, had been deported and killed. She was destitute and miserable, with an impossible desire to return to normal as the sole survivor of her large family.

In August 1945 she returned to Amsterdam, which was almost unrecognisable, felt aimless with nowhere to live but dependent on the kindness of distant relatives as she was insistent she was not going into another camp. She could not find any work until she went to the British Embassy and explained that she had worked for 'Lady Montgomery', as she believed she was, in Belsen. 'From that moment I was welcomed with open arms,' said Flora.[44] Before the end of the year she had married Appie Schrijver, her brother-in-law, after discovering that her sister had been murdered in Sobibor, and had two children with him.

'We went to the town hall to sort everything . . . I was still officially married to Emmanuel van Praag. We looked for someone who would confirm that he had seen Emmanuel had died.' She had last seen her brother-in-law Appie in Belsen when she tried to bring him food. Later she was appalled by her own haste.

In hindsight it's wrong, of course. In 1945 you're liberated then meet your brother-in-law, you marry and think 'oh well, there have been so many murdered now we'd like to have children'. But when you're pregnant in 1946 your brain is still in 1945, right in the camp. You pass it on to your children in their blood. I have two daughters to whom I never spoke about the horrors of war.[45]

My [second] husband wanted to give our children all that we had lost in our youth . . . so my daughters, Jettie and Phyllis, can look back on a carefree childhood.[46]

Although Flora too tried hard not to share her trauma with her children, she could not help herself. Her hatred for Germans knew few limits. 'Once I was on the Côte d'Azur and a German couple with two adult sons kept staring at me . . . I walked over to them and said "listen you weren't aware of course just never ever look at me. I go crazy when I see a German . . ."' This particular couple said they had both been doctors who had been part of the German resistance.

In 1981, still traumatised whenever she met Germans and now a widow again, Flora was on a cruise when the purser put her on a table with other Germans. 'Do you want a third world war?' she asked him.

I got another table. Opposite me was a group of Englishmen. One of them had performed bombing missions over Germany during the war. I told [him] about Birkenau, about the orchestra, about Bergen-Belsen. I told him that I had lost track of Lily Mathé, that I thought she might have married an English officer.

I did not know that this man took a picture of me during the cruise. He later placed it in various English newspapers, with the text: 'Flora Schrijver, played in the orchestra in Birkenau, later in Bergen-Belsen, looking for Lily Mathé.'[47]

One week later I got a call. Lily Mathé was in London. Anita Lasker was in London too, he told me. I went there. It was a reunion of graying ladies, who saw each other again after thirty-six years. Later I discovered a few other survivors of the women's orchestra in Brussels.

*

Eventually, at the end of the twentieth century, several of the women found ways to meet up with each other even though it was almost too late. Anita bumped into Lily Mathé in a London department store but the women were never close. Their musical styles were different and Lily had only known the tail end of a dwindling orchestra, a very different creation from the cohesive unit that Alma had moulded them into. Helena Dunicz Niwińska wrote that every contact re-established after the war, including the ones with some of the Jewish members of the orchestra, became a very important event for all of them. 'One of the first Jewish girls in the band with whom I managed to get in touch was my concentration camp English teacher, Margot Anzenbacherová, later Větrovcová. Unfortunately, we never met again. Margot died in 2007.' Thanks to the Auschwitz Museum, she was put in touch with Rachela (Zelmanowicz) Olewski when Rachela paid a visit to Birkenau in her eighties. 'She called me from her hotel in Krakow. I went there immediately.' The women agreed to meet again in Israel in 1992 but Rachela died just beforehand. However, Helena used that opportunity to meet Regina, saying later that 'the joy of this reunion after so many years assuaged the loss of Rachela'.[48]

And then came one of the most powerful reunions for Helena, in Germany, with Esther now Bejarano, even though the pair had not been in the orchestra at the same time. They nonetheless possessed a strong thread of connection which pulled them towards each other, aware that they had both survived an experience which united them in a uniquely compelling way. As Helena wrote in her memoir after meeting Esther: 'I realised that the Pole, Zofia Czajkowska, was just as much a figure of salvation in the life of Esther, a Jewish woman deported from Germany to Auschwitz, as Alma Rosé, a Jew, was for me, a Pole.'[49]

One of the most obvious physical scars that all the women bore was the tattoo on their forearm.

Esther Bejarano suffered from much hostile questioning from strangers about her tattoo in Germany in the 1960s after returning to live there. Once she was asked 'Do you have the number (41948) so your husband can put you in the washing machine? And in Berlin a man on the subway said I had the number because I was an easy girl and would like to be called.' Eventually she underwent a painful removal process but decided, given her ambivalence towards Germany, that she did not want it done there and returned to Israel to have it removed.[50]

Flora decided after six years, in 1952, to have her tattoo, number 61278, removed partly because she too could not tolerate the constant questioning as to whether this was her telephone number and also because it was a permanent reminder of her suffering. Later she admitted she regretted it; with or without the number, she could not get the camp out of her mind. And she still had the scar on her wrist from burning herself on the tiny stove in the middle of the music block.

Murray Perahia, the son of Greek Jews brought up in America and today one of the world's greatest pianists, tells a similar story of ignorance about tattooed numbers on the arms of survivors. In the early 1970s, he met Anita through the English Chamber Orchestra and noticed the numbers on her arm. Puzzled, he said this reminded him of his first piano teacher and the numbers on her arm and wondered what they were.

'Nobody talked about Auschwitz then ... as a child I certainly didn't ask my piano teacher why she had numbers engraved on her arm,' Perahia said in an interview.[51] By an extraordinary co-incidence, this piano teacher had been Lili Assael, the older sister of Yvette, who had emigrated to New York after the war following her brother Michel who had won a music scholarship to study there. She was in her early fifties when she became Murray's first piano teacher. She taught him from the age of about five until seven in the early 1950s when, realising how talented he was, she had insisted to his parents that he needed to find a more advanced teacher. 'She was generous in that regard and did not try to hold me back,' recalled Perahia. Lili and young Murray spoke only Ladino together, the Judaeo-Spanish language spoken by some Sephardic Jews, which was probably, he thinks today, why she had been chosen. There were not many Ladino-speaking piano teachers in the Bronx.

Murray did not grow up in an especially musical family, although his father David, a garment maker by trade, liked opera. They were part of a close-knit Greek community in the Bronx, where David had moved in the 1930s with his family for economic reasons. He had returned home to visit Salonika at the end of the 1930s and it was on this visit that he became engaged to Julie Stroumsa, the violinist, who had died of typhus in Belsen.

Yet Murray knew from an early age that he wanted to learn the piano. His inspiration came from Lili's brother.

'I was in awe of a man called Michel Assael, who seemed to play, compose and improvise all the music in the synagogue. That was what I aspired to. But for some reason Michel was not available to teach me although Lili was.' So Lili became his first teacher and, twenty years later when he met Anita, he was able to put the two women in touch again.

Lili Assael giving a piano lesson in post-war New York

Lili did not remarry after her young husband, Sam Hasid, was gassed on arrival at Auschwitz, but made a life for herself as a successful piano teacher. Her younger sister, Yvette, still a teenager when the war ended, tried to return to her roots in Salonika from Belsen but found it impossible. At first, she worked in a nightclub for Allied servicemen but there was no Jewish community left and she was despondent and lost.

Her life was saved by an Irish soldier, Sergeant James Lennon, working on assignment with the British army to help with re-settlement of DPs, who in 1946 heard her performing. It was his love that saved Yvette now. 'She really did not know if she wanted to continue living,' said her daughter Peggy. Michel and Lili, both living in New York, were extremely worried about their young sister. In 1947, still only twenty, she married Lennon and after five years in London they too went to live in New York where they had two children. Lennon 'spent his entire life getting her through and helping her to live again', according to Peggy.[52] Yvette's son David recalls that in the 1960s a family doctor was regularly summoned to treat his mother. 'We were told she was suffering a nervous attack, having nightmares about the camp.'[53] Both Peggy and David believe that while their mother felt 'sadness, Aunt Lili was angry. She would often laugh as she told stories of life in the camps. I think she laughed a lot because she saw the ridiculousness of the situation,' said David.[54]

Yvette's 1947 wedding to Irish soldier Sergeant James Lennon

In addition to the Greeks, isolated in Auschwitz and continuing to support each other post-war, the two core groups who eventually managed to stay in regular touch with each other were Anita Lasker (later Lasker-Wallfisch), Violette Silberstein (later Jacquet-Silberstein), Hélène Wiernik (first Minkowski later Schepps), Fanny Kornblum (later Birkenwald) and to an extent Hilde, and in Poland Helena, Zosia and Wisia.

But there was one other who, strangely because she was very much part of one of the orchestra's sub-groups in Auschwitz, seems not to feature in the memories of others: Elsa Miller, the violinist who saved Hélène by telling her to apply to the orchestra so that Hélène could in turn save Fanny, thus creating the Belgian group. Elsa's son, Jean-Jacques Felstein, set out on an odyssey in the 1990s to rediscover his mother, who died tragically of cancer at the age of forty-one in 1964 when he was just sixteen. She had never talked to him of her time in the orchestra and her violin was put away at the back of a cupboard never to be played again. She was, he felt throughout his childhood, 'a quasi-absent mother, someone three quarters destroyed by her experience'.[55] Jean-Jacques spoke to Hélène about his mother but 'she's made it clear to me what the cost of bringing up these memories in front of me does to her'.[56] He was distraught at discovering how other colleagues from the orchestra – Hilde, Regina, Sylvia and Yvette – could not remember Elsa.[57]

In an imagined conversation with his dead mother, Jean-Jacques said: 'Back in Auschwitz you ate at the same table as Carla, Sylvia and Ruth, the German-speaking band. But you were the link, the hinge with the French and Belgian group! Not anymore. I finally realise that it's no wonder she [Hilde] has forgotten about you. If you had had a designated function in that group beyond your place at the second violin desk it was to smooth out the rough edges and erase any conflicts. You weren't one of those people everyone remembers for their energy and loud-mouth, like Violette, or for their talent as a musician like Big Hélène. From what I know about you,' he continued, 'it was your discretion and concern not to cut corners or to clash with the others that prevailed the most.'

There was one other factor that gave Elsa additional strength in Auschwitz. According to Anita, a key to her survival may have been simple luck. Another factor must have been Dora, a fourteen-year-old girl she tried to protect who was not part of the orchestra.[58]

Elsa was twenty when she arrived in Auschwitz in 1943 along with Dora who had been arrested with her in Brussels. The girls knew each other because they lived in apartments on different floors within the same house and Dora had had a bit of a crush on one of Elsa's brothers. While they were being guarded by Belgian guards before deportation Dora had wanted to escape but Elsa had been too afraid. Piecing together his mother's life after interviewing her friends in the 1990s, Jean-Jacques concluded that Dora was the key to Elsa's survival. From the moment they arrived in the camp 'she felt responsible for the child ... in the camp Dora did not stop crying. She's afraid of everything and everyone and snuggles up against her. Elsa pretends to be calm and confident about the future in order to reassure Dora. But now she'll do for the other girl what she thought she could never do before. She'll fight for survival.'[59]

At London's Imperial War Museum, new Holocaust Galleries opened in 2021 full of poignant sepia images recreating pre-war Jewish life in Europe, a red jumper in one of the glass cases stands out. It is Anita's much-mended red angora pullover, the life-saving sweater that somehow came with her from Kanada in Auschwitz to Belsen and then London. It had cost her 'a lot of bread' – the Auschwitz currency – to 'organise' but it was so precious that she wore it incessantly, a symbol of a brighter future, perhaps, or simply a means of keeping herself warm. Anita has no answer as to why she, let alone the jumper, survived, a particular oddity given how much she (like most of the orchestra girls) smoked. Cigarettes, or part of a cigarette, offered a brief moment of pleasure, little more. While she recognises that music was the key to survival for some, it was not a guarantee. For Julie Stroumsa and Charlotte Croner, it merely postponed death. Anita insists there is no recipe for survival, beyond luck. Everyone did whatever they could for as long as they could.

Once people learned about Auschwitz one regular follow-up question was: 'How on earth did you manage to survive?' Szymon Laks, conductor of the men's orchestra, wrote of how he answered one woman who, with resentment in her voice, asked this question: '"So many people died but you survived. How did you do it?" I flushed, felt guilty and blurted out though not without some affectation, "I'm very sorry . . . I didn't do it on purpose."'[60]

Returning to Auschwitz was a hurdle for many survivors. Hélène recalled how she had always resisted going back but in 1995, for the fiftieth anniversary of the liberation, agreed to go when asked by the Belgian army. 'I couldn't find our block. The immensity had gone because the block had been destroyed. It was very hard to return like that. It was a big empty space, not like it was, just full of distress and memories.'[61]

When French film director Michel Daeron decided he wanted to record on film this unusal story of survival through music, he gathered as many orchestra survivors as he could including Hélène, Anita, Violette, Margot, Eva, Flora, Regina, Sylvia and Hilde and interviewed them in their hometowns. This sensitive approach helped the musicians to talk openly about their experiences, some for the first time on camera. Daeron also took Helena and Zosia back to Auschwitz together to relive their experiences. He called his film *Bach in Auschwitz*, a reference to the Chaconne played by Hélène for her audition. Flora, with some misgivings, agreed to be a part of it, saying later, 'I only do interviews for television to honour Alma... I have to think about it all and then I don't sleep. 48 hours later, I am still crying.' She explained how one television director had proposed an idea for eight survivors of the orchestra to play together for a film he had in mind, offering a large payment. She saw him off abruptly. '"Are you crazy," I said, "we had to play for our lives."'[62]

Anita finally agreed to address the German parliament on 31 January 2018, having said when she left Belsen that she would never set foot in Germany again, how it appalled her to be thought of as a *German* Jew.[63] She went with her sister Renate – both women now widows – to remember the victims of National Socialism with a special ceremony at the Bundestag. Following an opening address by Bundestag President Dr Wolfgang Schäuble, Anita gave the commemorative speech.[64]

Speaking in German, which with the passage of time she was able to do without suffering, she recounted clearly her life in Breslau before the war and the beginnings of anti-Semitism leading up to her arrest and time in a prison before arriving in Auschwitz.

She gave an account of how 'the orchestra was based in Block 12, close to the end of the road into the camp, just a few metres from Crematorium I and with an unobstructed view of the ramp. We could see everything: the arrival ceremonies, the selections, the columns of people walking towards the gas chambers, soon to be transformed into smoke.

Even if you were not sent straight to the gas chamber, no one survived in Auschwitz for long – the most you could expect was about three months. But if they needed you for some reason, you had a tiny chance of survival. I had that chance – I was 'needed'.

We played marches at the camp gate for the prisoners who worked in the nearby factories – I G Farben, Buna, Krupp etc. – and we gave Sunday concerts around the camp for the people who worked there or anyone else who wanted to hear us play. For many, hearing music being performed in this living hell was the ultimate insult. But for others, perhaps, it was a chance to dream of another world, if only for a few moments.

And then she moved into a higher gear by speaking about the present day.

Anti-Semitism is a virus which is two thousand years old and apparently incurable. It mutates to take on new forms: religion, race. Only today, one does not necessarily say 'Jews'. Today it is the Israelis, without really understanding the context or knowing what is going on behind the scenes.

Jews are criticised for not having defended themselves, which simply confirms how impossible it is to imagine what it was like for us back then. And then the Jews are criticised for defending themselves. It's scandalous that Jewish schools, even Jewish kindergartens have to have a police guard.

Sometimes, I think that the orchestra in Auschwitz was a kind of microcosm, a society in miniature that we can learn from. All the nationalities were represented. It was a Tower of Babel. Who can I talk to? Only to people who speak German or French. I can't speak Russian or Polish, so I won't talk to them. So instead, we eye each other mistrustfully and auto-matically assume that the other person is hostile; we don't think to ask why the other person has ended up in Auschwitz as well.

And as for the resurgent anti-Semitism: ask yourselves who are the Jews? Why do we come across them everywhere? Is it perhaps because they were driven out of their homeland two thousand years ago and dispersed across the world, and have been searching ever since for a place where they hoped to live in peace and not to be murdered? 'Jews' does not work as a collective term. Jews are just people – people with a very unusual history, it's true – so often the scapegoat, persecuted, murdered, defamed.

What is positive is that on the 18th of this month, this House unanimously adopted a resolution stating that anti-Semitism must be combated resolutely. We can only hope that you win this fight. The future lies in your hands.

For those who survived beyond the fiftieth anniversary of the liberation of the camps, Anita became the living link, or, as she described it, 'the moving target'. Because she played in many concerts touring around Europe she saw her friends from the camp orchestra more than others. Slowly other documentaries were made about those who survived, including one with Anita and her daughter Maya where they went back to Auschwitz together, called *Playing to Survive* (BBC, 1996), and another called *The Maestro and the Cellist* made by German television in 2022 which attempted to compare Anita's war with that of Wilhelm Furtwängler, the German composer and conductor who, in spite of his professed opposition to anti-Semitism, remained working in Germany throughout the war.

Also that year Anita had her portrait painted by Peter Kuhfeld, the only son of a German prisoner of war. It was one of seven portraits of Holocaust survivors in the UK commissioned by the then Prince Charles for the Royal Collection Trust.

Having started to talk she has never stopped. Anita rarely refuses an interview but knows you cannot change anything and despairs at the ignorance.

I have been asked: 'How is it possible that so and so managed to survive this or that camp?' To me it has implied that 'survival' was somewhat suspect and must have been achieved by foul means such as collaboration with the Germans. Such questions sadden me greatly. The short answer is . . . if you did witness the day of the liberation you were simply lucky. You were a survivor.[65]

Why did I survive? I came to the conclusion that it's better somebody survives to tell the story. I don't need to feel too guilty about that.[66]

EPILOGUE

If we forget, we are guilty, we are accomplices

On a cold January morning in 2023 I leave London and fly to Israel to meet ninety-nine-year-old Hilde Grünbaum Zimche. I wonder what sort of discussion about grief and trauma I might have with this woman who has seen so much of both. Hilde is a stranger to me and yet one whose life I have been thinking about for many months before we actually meet.

I am worried I have left it too late for a meeting of any depth with Hilde. As I will discover, I am underestimating the strength of mind needed to survive in a concentration camp and help lead others, character traits which I am about to encounter face to face.

When I started my research for this book, I had believed various newspaper accounts of the orchestra which commented that there was only one member still alive – Anita Lasker-Wallfisch in London. Anita herself, who had been exceptionally close to Hilde in Auschwitz, believed this to be the case, having lost contact with her friend a year or so previously when Hilde, requiring more care, moved to a different section of her kibbutz. As soon as I learned Hilde was alive and well, I made plans to go and meet her.

My taxi driver, who is taking me from my Tel Aviv hotel

on the half-hour journey to Hilde's kibbutz, wants to be chatty but struggles to speak English. As we move out of the city in the early morning sunshine, he asks why I am here. When I explain he immediately takes his right hand off the wheel and taps repeatedly on to his left forearm. 'My mother...' he tells me, his voice trailing off.

Nothing else needs to be said. I am overly conscious of how many survivors or children and grandchildren of survivors walk these streets, each with a story to tell of coming to terms with grief and trauma. 'My answer to Hitler,' as many say. I feel an interloper.

Hilde, in a wheelchair pushed by her carer, is waiting for me at the entrance to the kibbutz, as well as Sivanne, the granddaughter of another orchestra member, Regina. Hilde, dressed in a sweatshirt and comfortable trousers, looks well groomed, her nails beautifully manicured with pink polish, her face obviously older but instantly recognisable from the picture of a smiling young woman in a photo taken after VE Day with the world awaiting. All three make a fuss over me as they lead me into a large room marked Day Care with balloons on one pink-washed wall and a garland spelling Merry Christmas (a nod to the many foreigners who work on kibbutzim) – nearly a month after the event – festooned on the other. I wonder how to start the conversation. I need not have worried as Hilde is full of smiles and happy to answer whatever it is I want to know. When I compliment her on her English, she tells me proudly, 'I translated for the British in Belsen.'

So I show her the photograph of my father in his British army uniform at the time he was there, more by way of explanation of my interest in Belsen than because I expect any recognition from her. She seems to have a clear memory of that camp. 'Yes, I remember the concert there on 24 May. I think it was meant for the Polish people in Belsen but Anita and I, we went anyway.'

My task then is to steer her back to Auschwitz and ask her what she remembers of her time there.

Random memories emerge, punctuated by repeated urgings for me to eat more biscuits.

'I know in wintertime at the end when we couldn't go out, so we did knitting, knitting of socks for soldiers.

'I remember Anita used to say to me: "Who can understand these people? One moment they want Schumann's *Träumerei*, the next moment they are putting people in the fire."'

She recalls how Alma used to talk to her and Anita about books, literature and the circle of artists and writers, such as Jakob Wasserman and Franz Werfel, that she used to move among in pre-war Vienna. 'You see we could speak to Alma in *Hoch Deutsch* [formal German, the opposite of colloquial, indicating a high-quality education],' she told me.

When I ask her about fear in the camp, she has no hesitation in telling me about the time in 1943 when she had an abscess in her neck and could no longer play the violin. 'I did not want to go to the Revier . . . a doctor came and gave me medicine and I got better. I was frightened then because I was not good enough for the orchestra so I copied out the music. I was so afraid.'

As the patchwork of memories tumble out, many of them stories she has told before, she says she cannot remember what she wore in Auschwitz, although she does remember that she had shoes. 'I was the only one who had shoes . . . a friend gave them to me. So I slept in my shoes.'

I keep questioning her, but I can see she is tiring. The carer warns me that soon she will need a rest. Hilde wants to tell me something about her journey from Belsen to Palestine and how her belief in Zionism never wavered. She asks me if I know about how this kibbutz began as Kibbutz Buchenwald in Germany at the end of the war in 1945 where a group of them had lessons in agriculture, how they then made their way to Antwerp where they had more agricultural instruction. 'And then we had to cross the border from Holland to Belgium and our driver was an English soldier.'

However, I am determined not to be sidetracked into a discussion about Zionism or Israel today. Gently, I bring her back to the camps and ask her, as she looks back on her life, if she understands what factors kept her alive, what made her want to go on living, having witnessed so much horror?

I remind her of a striking comment she made in a 1997 interview: 'I knew that if I didn't do my best to help people there would be nothing left.'' She now tells me repeatedly it was hope that sustained her. 'Hope was my religion, and my faith in Zionism.'

That is what she thanks her parents for most of all, as well as for giving her a good education where music and languages played such an important part.

'We earned our life because we could play. I often think that what my mother taught me – "all what you know you can take with you, material possessions are of no value" – she was right. [It was] the two and a half years living on my own which helped me to survive and everything that I learned in books and from poems, that is what helped me to survive.'

But after the war, she tells me, she never played music again. There is a silence in our conversation. I do not feel a need to ask her for any explanation and let the silence sit. After all, most of the musical troupe were not born to be musicians, they simply used music as a tool when it was offered.

While some of the orchestra women, like Hilde, turned away from playing music after 1945 others embraced it with a passion and passed a love of music on to their children and grandchildren. Violette Silberstein reinvented herself as a nightclub singer with her husky smoker's voice – a potent reminder of how cigarettes were such a vital commodity in the camp – and insisted that she always had a strongly positive reaction to hearing music played after the war. 'I feel fine. I am saying I am still here,' she said in 1999.[2] Similarly Anita, who is always ready to proclaim robustly that whatever else they killed, the Nazis could never kill music, has in addition to her successful cellist son, Raphael, several grandchildren who also perform professionally. Simon Wallfisch is a baritone living in Germany, Benjamin Wallfisch is a composer of film scores in California and Joanna Wallfisch is a singer composer and multi-instrumentalist. Other descendants play for pleasure, which proves her point.

In April 2022, Deborah Assael-Migliore, the cellist daughter of Michel Assael and niece of Lili and Yvette to whom she was close, arranged a concert in New York's Carnegie Hall for a piece written by her father in 1947 called 'Hymns of Auschwitz'. Deborah had never heard the music played before and believed that it encapsulated 'his whole experience of what he told me when I was growing up, all the stories I'm hearing in his musical language'. Michel Assael, who died in 2006, wrote the piece soon after liberation as a tribute to all those who did not survive. It was dedicated especially to the memory of Lillian Menasche, the Greek teenager who was gassed after being sent away from the women's orchestra by Zofia Czajkowska to be replaced by one of her Polish teacher friends. Lillian's father, Dr Albert Menasche, a flautist and practising physician, was a friend from Salonika who had continued to play alongside Michel Assael in the men's orchestra long after he knew about his daughter's death. Michel and Albert were 'inseparable companions... after evening roll call one could often see them rooted to the spot, arm in arm just before the barbed wires', the orchestra's conductor Szymon Laks recalled. 'They would stare at the neighbouring women's camp where the doctor's daughter and Michel's two sisters were... Other times they waited in vain for the appearance of their dear ones.'[3] Music was in this case a way of remembering, of commemorating.

My interpreter during my brief visit to Hilde, barely necessary but helpful in case the ninety-nine-year-old lapsed into Ivrit or modern Hebrew, the language of the kibbutz, is Regina's grand-daughter Sivanne, a vibrant Israeli married to a Dutch man who, with her children, has returned to live on this kibbutz steeped in so much Second World War history. Sivanne is actively researching her own family story since, when she was young, it was never discussed.* Slowly, over lunch in the vast kibbutz com-munal dining room, and later walking in the fields picking up clementines from the ground, I realise why. She tells me how her own mother was too close to her grandmother Regina, who felt beaten down by the story. Sivanne has learned much of what she knows from books. But she grew close to Regina herself before her death in November 2014.

'I learned from my grandmother that even though Alma was difficult as her artistic temperament made her a perfectionist, she was also like a mother to her so that when Alma died it felt like her own mother died again,' Sivanne told me. 'My grandmother always felt unhappy because when the orchestra went out to play she was left chopping wood, clearing up, feeling she was nothing more than a maid, Cinderella.'

When Elsa Miller's son, Jean-Jacques Felstein, met Regina in 1997, she opened up to him further about experiencing a sort of double guilt. She suffered for years over the privileged status she occupied in Birkenau but in addition 'she'd been angry at Hilde

---

* It was thanks to her discovering my interest in this story and reaching out to me that I discovered Hilde.

for having been the one responsible for her joining the group'. Only when she was ill and on the verge of death was Regina able to talk to Hilde about it. She never ceased feeling herself to be an outsider in the group but, finally, she let go of this remorse, recognising how being part of the wider orchestra group saved her life. According to Felstein: 'Regina tells me ... that she no longer wants to remember anything and besides since she was nothing more than a simple orderly her story is of no interest. She fears she's been forgotten by comrades.' But of course, her story is interesting precisely because 'she experienced the scandal of music at Auschwitz on a daily basis, this human activity that was carried out almost normally in what was otherwise generalised madness'.[4] She was saved by music in the widest sense, irrespective of whether or not she played an instrument in the orchestra.

Among so many atrocities in the camps, the worst fear for many male prisoners in Birkenau who were kept alive to work and not gassed immediately was that they might be selected for the Sonderkommando, the so-called special squads whose task was so horrific – removing dead bodies after gassing to be burned – and who were then killed themselves because they knew too much. The women's orchestra had a particular link to this appalling squad because Dov, the brother of Rachela Zelmanowicz, spent time doing this work until he was killed following the October 1944 revolt.

But each work kommando brought its own terrors. As Krystyna Zywulska, the Polish-Jewish writer who had taken on an assumed identity to hide her religion and was sent to Auschwitz in 1943 as a political prisoner, recalled, 'We were frightened but we always arrived at the same conclusion: "They will get rid of us in the end, it makes no difference where we are."'[5] Zywulska managed to survive disguised as a non-Jewish political, who was given work in Kanada, or the *Effektenkammer* – widely considered, along with the kitchen, laundry, office and hospital, to be among the best kommandos in the camp. Prisoners assigned to this type of labour squad were safeguarded against harsh physical labour outdoors and, unlike the musicians, had ample opportunity to illegally obtain food, clothing and other valuables. They slept in smaller barracks, were allowed to wear civilian clothes and grow their hair and were released from both roll calls and selections. Yet, for all of their privilege, even the Kanada workers, located adjacent to the crematorium, could not escape the possibility of illness or the sight, screams and stench of the relentless, daily mass killings taking place just a few yards away.

Perhaps the most important privilege which being in the orchestra gave its members was hope, hope that as long as the Nazis needed them or enjoyed their concerts they would survive. As Anita recognised, 'all we could hope for was to live until tomorrow'. Holding such a precarious hope helps explain how they lived with accusations that they were privileged, which they knew they were. They shared the same fear as other inmates and pretty much the same hunger. Unquestionably they worked hard, crucially not outside, and with a bed, blanket and access to a toilet at night.

And it was precisely these small, practical privileges which underpinned another hope, not grasped by all of them, that 'someday this will all be over, someday this will come to an end, for better or for worse, someday'. Even while hoping for a good end, survival and new life, Rachela was never entirely optimistic that she would avoid death in the camp. It would be an end but not the one she wanted.[6] Ordinary prisoners who marched out to work on demolition jobs or hauling boulders had no real basis for any kind of hope for a post-war life.

Other prisoners in privileged kommandos such as Olga Lengyel, a Romanian-Jewish Auschwitz survivor who worked in the infirmary, believed that 'The greatest crime committed by Nazis against the prisoners may not have been their extermination in the gas chambers but the frequently successful endeavour to form the prisoners after their own image, to turn them into bad persons.'[7]

This too was Primo Levi's belief, that the establishment of the Grey Zone, where some prisoners had to work for the continuation of the Nazi system, becoming privileged prisoners, was the most wicked of all Nazi actions, forcing inmates to make a choice if they wanted to survive.

'The hybrid class of the prisoner functionary [in the camp] constitutes its armature and at the same time its most disquieting feature. It is a grey zone with ill-defined outlines which both separate and join the two camps of masters and servants. It possesses an incredibly complicated internal structure and contains within itself enough to confuse our need to judge,' writes Levi. He goes on to say that any moral judgement is 'imprudent' since 'it must be clear that the greatest responsibility lies within the system'.

In general, he concluded, prisoner functionaries were

poor devils like ourselves, who, for an extra half litre of soup, were willing to carry out these and other 'tertiary' functions; innocuous, sometimes useful, often invented out of nothing. Their privilege, which at any rate entailed supplementary hardships and efforts, gained them very little and did not spare them from the discipline and suffering of everyone else; their hope for life was substantially the same as that of the unprivileged.[8]

My own belief is that any mention of the meagre privileges available in a place like Auschwitz should always remain within this Primo Levi framework: 'That their hope for life was substantially the same as that of the unprivileged.' And not everyone,

329

even those in a so-called privileged kommando, could always summon up the will to live, the ultimate rebuke, in order to triumph over this obscene system.

I have constantly questioned what special characteristics imbued the survivors with a strength and desire to go on living; what were they able to grab onto that enabled them to live for something beyond themselves? The more I have contemplated the barbarity of the concentration camp system, the more I have admired the power of the desire to live displayed by *any* survivors who emerged from the camps alive. Even taking into account that their privileges gave them a marginally better chance of survival in Birkenau than their fellow prisoners in the women's camp, the strong will to live displayed by the orchestra 'girls' demands to be recognised.

Violette Silberstein freely admitted she was driven by a desire to seek revenge on the man who had denounced her and her parents and which led to their deportation and death.[9] Yvette Assael said how she always prayed in the camp: '"Please God don't let me die here", and that kept me going. Then I was peaceful. I always said my prayers and I knew it would be okay.'[10]

Margot Anzenbacherová, the Czech musician and poet, insisted 'I must survive so that I can bear witness.'[11]

For Hélène Wiernik it was, unusually, the beauty of music that sustained her as well as a deep desire to see her parents again. Having lost her faith in God she tried to lose herself completely in playing well. Occasionally she managed it, 'reaching a moment of forgetting where we were . . . if we really concentrated and then we had to come back to reality'.[12]

Yet in my search to understand why some women survived and what qualities, if any, helped them I know I must resist drawing any conclusions from watching dozens of interviews on my computer screen to see how some survivors, decades later, can recount their story of horrors in a flat, unemotional voice while so many others falter constantly on the verge of tears as they remember the brutality they faced with a quivering voice. I have no sure answers beyond knowing that it is desperately important to hear directly from all those who experienced the camps and wish to speak while remaining aware that for the rest of us, merely trying to frame in words these events risks betraying what was experienced during the Holocaust. 'Don't words make speak-able what is not?' asked the American writer Lore Segal.[13]

As for religious belief being a help, Anita says she could not believe, either then or now, in a God in the traditional sense of 'a man sitting up there making sure everything is okay... how could I when everything was all wrong?'

Pressed in 1996 by the BBC radio interviewer Sue Lawley as to what did then sustain her in Auschwitz, Anita said that her faith was in other people or at least the other people with whom she shared this torment, the ones who looked after each other and bullied each other to watch out in case any of them started giving up, not eating the little they had or not washing... but then she added *sotto voce* 'not that I have so much [faith] in other people'. Anita, eighteen years old when she arrived at Auschwitz in 1943, mostly relied on herself.[14]

And yet, and yet...

There is a telling story in Anita's 1996 memoir *Inherit the Truth* about how she carried a small capsule of cyanide on her, given to her by a friend at the beginning of the war. When she and Renate were first arrested, they decided this was the moment to swallow it and end it all. But when they discovered that the capsule contained white icing sugar, not cyanide, Anita admitted 'our relief at still being alive was enormous'.

As Anita reflected in her memoir: 'The episode proves if nothing else our total ignorance of what the next moment may hold in store for us ... except that in normal life the circumstances might have been rather less extreme.'[15]

When I question Hilde more closely on whether it was religious faith that sustained her in Auschwitz, she tells me, 'I had a profound spiritual belief that I would survive ... which I might call hope.'[16]

She brought with her from Auschwitz via Belsen and on to Israel Alma's diary and a version of *Faust* that she received from a woman in Kanada and used to read on occasion in the music block.

'*Faust* of all things, *Faust* in Auschwitz!' Anita exclaimed in one of our interviews. But yes, *Faust*, of course *Faust*, this dramatic poem considered by many to be the supreme work of German literature written by Goethe over many years and published in two parts in the early nineteenth century, which tells the rich and complex story of a man who sold his soul to the devil in exchange for earthly fulfilment. 'In the tower, he sees the moon and the stars and says: "It is so good to be alive." It helped us to keep our spirits up,' Hilde explained.[17]

Hilde's determination to keep hold of these two books as well as the simple red bag hand-sewn from a pillowcase that her friends in Kanada had given her and which she used to carry around the vital sheet music until the end are, to me, a profound demonstration of Hilde's faith that she would survive the war. All three artefacts, sad tokens of horror, of no practical use unlike food or warm clothes, are now preserved in Jerusalem at Yad Vashem, Israel's memorial and research centre on the Holocaust which stands for all time to remind people of what they were forced to do to survive.

Ruth Kluger, who survived Auschwitz but was not a member of the orchestra, wrote about the role played by hope in her 2001 memoir, *Still Alive: A Holocaust Girlhood Remembered*. She pointed out that the song that many women in the orchestra heard being sung by prisoners on their way to their deaths in the gas chamber, and which subsequently became the Israeli national anthem, was not simply about hope but 'The' hope, Hatikvah, 'as if there were only one which encompasses all other minor ones'.[18] Hatikvah means literally the hope and the lyrics* had been written in 1886, long before the Second World War.

On the other hand, Kluger recognised that while in her case hope was justified as she survived, 'the result did not refute the improbability of such an outcome any more than naming a sweepstake winner refutes the fact that most gamblers lose their stake'.[19] In other words, if hope were a coin, luck is its obverse. One who survived Auschwitz but could not survive life, for survival never guaranteed a happy end, was the Polish non-Jewish writer Tadeusz Borowski. Borowski was so depressed by his experience at Auschwitz, witnessing the Nazi gas chambers, that he gassed himself to death in his own kitchen, aged twenty-nine, in 1953. In his novella, *This Way for the Gas, Ladies and Gentlemen*, he wrote of the negative aspects of hope.

> It is that very hope that makes people go without a murmur to the gas chambers, keeps them from risking a revolt, paralyses them into numb inactivity. It is hope that breaks down family ties, makes mothers renounce their children, or wives sell their bodies for bread, or husbands kill. It is hope that compels man to hold on to one more day of life because that day may be the day of his liberation. Ah, and not even the hope for a different, better world but simply for life, a life of peace and

---

* As long as the Jewish spirit is yearning deep in the heart, With eyes turned toward the East, looking toward Zion, Then our hope – the two-thousand-year-old hope – will not be lost: To be a free people in our land, The land of Zion and Jerusalem.

rest. Never before in the history of mankind has hope been stronger in man, but never also has it done so much harm as it has in this war, in this concentration camp. We were never taught how to give up hope, and this is why today we perish in gas chambers.[20]

Faltering hope stumbled and sputtered alongside varieties of pain in Auschwitz. One reason why the pain experienced by so many of the musicians from the orchestra became so enduring and hard to articulate in the post-war world was because it was tinged with many conflicting emotions which each woman experienced differently, or not at all, including shame, anger, humiliation and guilt. And it manifested itself in different ways, from the apparently minor, such as Regina never again being able to clean shoes, one of her menial tasks in the block, to Fanny who could not eat scrambled eggs because they reminded her of how she had to watch and smell while the Polish girls cooked eggs in the block.

Flora battled myriad issues in trying to adjust to the post-war world. In 1994 she said:

Other than two books, I have nothing at home which reminds me of the war. I still have days that it all comes back. When I go out to a restaurant, I never face a wall. If I move house, then I choose a house with a view. When I return home by car, I park it close to the front door. I no longer dare to cross a dark parking lot at night. I still have a phobia from the time a drunken SS man chased me in Birkenau with a drawn gun.

There are days I don't think about it. I don't suffer from concentration camp syndrome, but I am not liberated. I have tried to suppress it for forty years.

I have never told my grandchildren anything. If they

complained they were hungry I would say: what you experience is not hunger you are just peckish. Two slices of bread a week that's hunger... deep down, without me knowing, that camp is very much alive.[21]

*

In early April 2023 Anita calls me with an urgent request. Why is Hilde not responding to her phone calls and can I check the new number? Every year the orchestra survivors celebrated 15 April together for as long as they could, in whatever way they could, sometimes with cake in person and sometimes long distance with just a phone call. 15 April was, they had decided, their new birth date. Anita and Hilde are, in 2023, the last two survivors of the orchestra but Hilde can no longer get to the phone and needs a carer to bring the phone to her which takes time. Anita, now that she knows Hilde is alive, needs to hear her voice on 15 April and celebrate being alive. The women do eventually make contact not only then but later in the year when Hilde celebrates her centenary with a party on the kibbutz.

I feel deeply fortunate to have met these two women and heard their stories first-hand in addition to hearing the testimony of so many others recorded for posterity on video and audio links as well as in books. Survivor testimony does not need to be treated as sacred. On the other hand, how can it ever be for us, who were not there, to explain, make comments, or judge when it is hard enough to grasp the daily reality of mere survival in the Nazi camps from one day to another.

Dr Jürgen Mathäus, director for the Centre for Advanced Holocaust Studies at the United States Holocaust Memorial Museum USHMM, asked in his book *Approaching an Auschwitz Survivor*, published in 2010, whether it matters to have an account from Zippi Spitzer giving intricate detail about the camp administrative

Hilde Grünbaum Zimche on her 100th birthday in Israel

system to mark new arrivals with colour stripes, triangles and numbers. 'Do we need her matter-of-fact account when we have highly insightful reflections from other Auschwitz survivors, most notably Primo Levi and Jean Amery, who pose profound existential questions? For the historian the answers to these questions are clear: it does matter. Detailed information is essential.

'We can never know enough about what happened at Auschwitz; every voice helps us understand better especially one that speaks on the basis of vast personal experience and deep practical knowledge.'[22]

As Elie Wiesel, the Romanian-born Auschwitz survivor who chaired the US Presidential Commission on the Holocaust, wrote in 1979:

Not to remember the dead now would mean to become accomplices to their murderers.

We must remember not only because of the dead; it is too late for them.

We must remember not only for the survivors; it may even be too late for them.

Our remembering is an act of generosity aimed at saving men and women from apathy to evil, if not from evil itself.[23]

*

There is a sequence in the film *Bach in Auschwitz* where the one-time violinists Helena (Dunicz Niwińska) and Zosia (Zofia Cykowiak), by then two elderly Polish women leaning on sticks, one half blind, wander around the camp trying to remember the layout of Block 12, now just a grass square with some bricks around the edge. More than fifty years on, in 1999, they remember who slept where but have a disagreement over whether Alma entered the main rehearsal room from the right or if that was where Zofia Czajkowska, the block elder, entered. However, on the trauma of having to play when deportees arrived, they are in harmonious if agonised agreement.

The train arrives just over there, in front of our barrack.

We could see it all from a distance as they lined up for the crematorium.

And then they were no longer there. Not a soul. Just the chimney flames glowing.

And we had to play the entire time.

We were deceiving these people.

We were aiding the German deception.

It is a mesmerising scene as Helena and Zosia both say this is the memory that will never leave them. 'I can never escape the look on the Germans' faces. It's the look that haunts me . . . these people who set about with such indifference to their dreadful tasks.'[24]

And it is this scene that I too carry in my head when I visit Auschwitz.

Almost two million tourists and school children from myriad countries visit the camp every year, trampling over what is now, effectively, a mass graveyard with a railway line through its centre. I have visited several other concentration camps and prisons for professional reasons and read many books and seen many films about Auschwitz. But Auschwitz-Birkenau is different from anywhere else. It is hard to know what these tourists expect from a day trip, but they probably cannot form a picture of orchestras playing music in this hellish place. And nor should they.

It is almost impossible to imagine what went on there between 1940 and 1945 and in some ways that is as it should be. The effort of imagining brings with it a danger that, as one tries to understand, or put into words, the process normalises what should remain an outrage beyond explanation. But not beyond remembering and respecting.

As I too wander along the now grassed-over remains of

Auschwitz-Birkenau today

338

Birkenau's Block 12, assailed by bitingly freezing eastern winds even in November, it would be stretching credulity to say I see ghosts, but I wonder if I hear them. For Block 12, the wooden music block, was metres from the infamous ramp alongside the railway lines inside the camp where a flick of a Nazi thumb 'you left – you right' determined life or death and led directly to the crematoria. Block 12 was where at least forty members of the girls' band slept, practised, rehearsed and copied music into something that a motley crew of amateur musicians could play, day in day out, for many months.

In the centre still today is the remains of the small brick oven, granted to Alma Rosé as a necessity to maintain the instruments

All that remains today of Block 12, the musicians' block,
with the central pile of bricks that once provided a stove

and, like so much else in this story, double-edged – a source of both comfort and also argument: who could use it first or who had enough food to use it to heat their meagre rations. It was also where at least one of the girls burned her hand in an effort to keep from freezing. Auschwitz poses endless conundrums. It was a site of fabulous riches as fleeing Jews often brought with them their most precious possessions, as instructed, thinking they were being 'resettled'. But also, a vast plain of desperate need, scarcity, hunger, fear and illness. What possible role could music have in a place of such bestiality?

I realise that merely to speak of cultural life in the camps is a perversion, since this was a world never free of fear and full of crises, coercion, disease and death, all of which automatically destroyed or damaged anything of beauty. Most of the time what the orchestra provided was not in any case beautiful music, but marching tunes used by their oppressors to enforce superficial military discipline while inflicting ferocious damage. Yet at the same time playing Mendelssohn, Chopin or Beethoven, forbidden music on the grounds that the composer was Jewish, Polish or too great for 'inferior' Jewish musicians, in secret, provided occasional moments in the darkest history of the twentieth century when a handful of women showed their defiance of the Nazi system in which they were trapped and made a determined effort to claw back something of what it meant to be human and to feel a surging desire to live.

While the vast majority of prisoners who passed through Auschwitz could derive no benefit whatever from listening to a band of musicians, in fact the reverse, the story of the women's orchestra is a compelling reminder of the power to be derived from overcoming differences with small acts of kindness and gestures of solidarity. At its best, here was female solidarity asserting itself as an immovable force which saved at least forty lives.

PRINCIPAL CHARACTERS

This is a list of the core members of the orchestra between April 1943 and October 1944 under its three principal conductors, Zofia Czajkowska, Alma Rosé and Sonya Winogradowa. There may have been other members who joined briefly and left, and some for whom details are still missing. Several had, in addition to birth names, stage names or pet names, names to differentiate them from others with similar names and, later, married surnames. This list is an attempt to clarify who were the women and girls whose stories feature in the text. If no religion is stated, they were not Jewish. After May 1944 Jewish prisoners had the additional A prefix. Pani is a term of respect given to some of the older women.

Alla Gres, later **Ermilova** (1921–2001 b. Ukraine). Prisoner no. 38116; piano and orchestration

Alma Maria Rosé, later **Přihoda**, then **van Leeuwen Boomkamp** (1906–44 b. Vienna). Prisoner no. 50381; violin and orchestration, 2nd conductor of the orchestra

Anita Lasker, later **Wallfisch** (1925– b. Breslau, Germany, Jewish). Prisoner no. 69388, cello

Bonita Maria Assael, renamed **Yvette** age 6, later **Lennon** (1926–2008, b. Salonika, Greece, Jewish). Prisoner no. 43293; piano, accordion and double bass

Bronia Labuza (1922– b. Ukraine). No number; guitar

341

Carla (or Karla) Wagenberg, later **Tamar Berger** (1923–93
b. Anhalt, Germany, Jewish). Prisoner no. 42020; flute,
recorder and piccolo

(Irma) Charlotte Clara Croner (Tante Croner) (1887–1945
b. Berlin, Germany, d. Belsen, Jewish). Prisoner no. 47511;
flute

Claire Monis, kept surname during marriage to Khan
(1922–67, b. Paris, France, Jewish). No number; singer

Danka/Dani/Danuta Kollak (earlier **Jadwiga Danilowicz**
later **Kollakowa**) (1918–74 b. Ukraine). Prisoner no. 6882;
percussion cymbals

Dora (or Dorys) Wilamowska (engaged to Curt Lewinsky)
(1910–43 b. Gera, Germany, Jewish). Prisoner no. unknown;
singer

Elsa Miller (later **Felstein**) (1923–64 b. Bochum, Germany).
Prisoner no 42490; violin

Esther Loewy (later **Bejarano**) (1924–2021 b. Saarlouis,
Germany). Prisoner no. 41948; recorder, piccolo, accordion,
guitar, voice

Eva Benedek (1921–44 b. Oradea, Hungary/Romania, Jewish).
Prisoner no. 76430; violin

Eva Steiner (later **Forschirm**) (1921–2021 b. Oradea, Hungary/
Romania, Jewish). Prisoner no. A17139; singer

Flora Jacobs (later **Schrijver**) (1923–2013 b. Nimwegen,
Netherlands, Jewish). Prisoner no. 61278; piano and
accordion. Briefly nanny for Josef Kramer

Helena (or Halina and **Halinka) Dunicz** (later **Niwińska**)
(1915–2015 b. Vienna but 'from Lwów'). Prisoner no. 64118;
violin

Hélène Rounder (later **Diatkine**) (1922–72 b. Paris, Jewish).
Prisoner no. 50290; singer

Hélène Wiernik (la Grande Hélène also **Itta** later **Minkowski,**

then **Schepps**) (1927–2006 b. Poland, Jewish). Prisoner no. 51887; violin and concertmaster

Helga (or **Olga**) **Schiessel** (1907–82 b. Germany, Jewish). Prisoner no. 6831; percussion

Henryka Brzozowska (later **Czapla Brzozowska**) (1912–? b. Zawierciere, Poland). Prisoner no. 27578; violin and primary teacher

Hilde (**Hildegard**) **Grünbaum** (later **Zimche**) (1923–2024 b. Berlin, Germany, Jewish). Prisoner no. 41912; violin and orchestration, Friday night reader

(**Pani**) **Irena Lagowska** (1908–80 b. Warsaw, Poland). Prisoner no. 49995; violin

Janina Palmowska (b. Poland); mandolin

Jolanda Steiner, mother of Eva (1891–1976 b. Oradea, Hungary, Jewish). Prisoner no. unknown

Lili Assael (also **Hasid**) (1909–90 b. Salonika, Greece, Jewish). Prisoner no. 43280; accordion

Lily Mathé (stage name previously **Markstein** later **Bernstein**) (1910–1985 b. Eger, Hungary, Jewish). Prisoner no. A17137; violin and some conducting

Margot Anzenbacherová (née **Steinova** later **Větrovcová**) (1915–2007 b. Pilsen, Bohemia, Jewish). Prisoner no. 46155; guitar, poet, language teacher

Maria Langenfeld (**Marylka** later **Langenfeld-Hnyda**) (1920–96 b. Zagorz, Poland). Prisoner no. 42873; violin, mandolin, copyist, room orderly known for her pre-dawn shriek of 'clean your shoes'

Maria Mos (also **Marysia** later **Wdowik**) (1916–2007 b. Będzin, Poland). Prisoner no. 8111; guitar and copyist

Olga Loseva b. **Karelia** (1923–? b. USSR). Prisoner no. 23728 POW; mandolin, occasionally French horn

Rachela Zelmanowicz (later **Olewski**) (1921–87 b. Będzin, Poland, Jewish). Prisoner no. 52816; mandolin, guitar

Regina Kupferberg (also **Rivka** later **Bacia**) (1922–2014 b. Będzin, Poland). Prisoner no. 51095; Alma's personal room orderly

Ruth Basinski (later **Bassin**) (1916–89 b. Rawiz, Poland, Jewish). Prisoner no. 41883; recorder

Sonya Winogradowa (**Soja Alekseevna Vinogradova** later **Tsibulskya**) (1921–? b. Leningrad). Prisoner no. 72319 POW; pianist and 3rd conductor of the orchestra

Stefania Baruch (also known as **Founia** previously **Puchalska**) (1891–? b. Lodz, Poland). Prisoner no. 6877; guitar and mandolin, later room orderly

Sylvia Wagenberg (later **Shulamit Khalif**) (1928–2003 b. Dessau, Germany, Jewish). Prisoner no. 41948; recorder, piccolo

Szura Makarova (later **Nazarova**) (1925–94 b. Vologda, USSR). Prisoner no. 38115 POW; guitarist and nurse

Violette Silberstein (**Fiorica Violette** later **Jacquet**) (1925–2014 b. Romania, childhood in Le Havre, France from age 3). Prisoner no. 51937; singer and violin

Wisia/Jadwiga Zatorska (1916–81 b. Krakow, Poland). Prisoner no. 36243; violin

Zippi (also **Helen**) **Spitzer** (later **Tichauer**) (1918–2018 b. Bratislava, Jewish). Prisoner no. 2286; mandolin and administration

Zofia/Zosha/Zosia Cykowiak (1921–2009 b. Poznań, Poland). Prisoner no. 44327; violin

(**Pani**) **Zofia Czajkowska** (1905–78 b. Tarnów, Poland). Prisoner no. 6873; teacher and 1st conductor of the orchestra

A NOTE ON REPERTOIRE

The women's orchestra had at least 200 pieces of music in its repertoire with only about twelve of these being marches – Schubert's *Marche Militaire*, Strauss's *Radetzky March* and Franz von Suppé's various marches were the most popular. The rest was mostly light music for the Sunday concerts, which were sometimes three hours long and included operatic overtures and operatic duets. The quartet from *Rigoletto*, rescored for four female voices, a medley of Puccini arias from *Madama Butterfly*, or Bizet's *Carmen*, *Cavalleria Rusticana*, Lehár's *The Merry Widow*, and the 'Bell Song' from *Lakmé*, as well as popular tangos including a well-known foxtrot tango called 'Josef, Josef!' featured most often in the performances. Other music played or later referenced by the musicians included the following:

The Chaconne of Bach played by Hélène Wiernik for her audition.

Bel Ami, a popular German song of the day, played by Esther Loewy for her audition.

Anita Lasker played the *Marche Militaire* for her audition and was asked subsequently to play Schumann's *Träumerei* by Josef Kramer. She also spoke about the orchestra repertoire consisting of German hits of the period, Monti's *Czardas*, *Zigeunerweisen*, Peter Kreuder's '12 Minuten', *Blue Danube*, *Tales from the Vienna Woods*, arias from *Rigoletto*, *Carmen* and *Madama Butterfly* as well as 'Dvořákiana' etc.

345

ΑΝΟΤΕΟΝREPERTOIRE

Rachela Zelmanowicz said: 'We used to play Sarasate's *Zigeunerweisen* and Monti's *Czardas* and all kinds ... She [Alma] tried. I remember the last time that she asked us to play *Für Elise* by Beethoven or waltzes. We played waltzes by Strauss so once she said: "No, you will not play like that! You are missing the swing. When you play the waltz of Strauss you must practise more and more and more."'

According to Dr Ella Lingens-Reiner, when the musicians were outside the hospital blocks on Sundays they played light Viennese tunes from Lupi Leopoldi stage shows.

Flora Jacobs spoke of Alma playing Mendelssohn's Violin Concerto in E minor silently and secretly when she was angry and alone. She also gave solo performances accompanied by the orchestra that included Grieg's *Morning Mood*, Fritz Kreisler's *Caprice Viennois* and *Liebeslied*, Schubert's *Legend* and the *Polonaises* of Henryk Wieniawski, a composer of Jewish origin.

Several orchestra members spoke of Chopin's *Tristesse* being played in the barracks with alternative lyrics as well as the attempt to play a quartet transcribed from Beethoven's *Pathétique* sonata.

According to Zofia Cykowiak: 'After about two months, the orchestra, in addition to marches and light music, began to perform works from the more serious repertoire, for example, works or fragments of works by Brahms, Tchaikovsky, Dvořák, Grieg, Lehár, Ravel, Rimsky-Korsakov, Rossini, Sarasate, Schumann, Schubert, Strauss, Verdi and even Chopin. The entire repertoire numbered around 200 items. Alma's solo repertoire included Brahms' *Hungarian Dances*, Monti's *Czardas* and Sarasate's gypsy melodies. Among the light music that featured in the Sunday concert were such popular hits of the day as the tango "Jalousie", "*Komm zurück*" and waltzes by Kalman, Lehár and Strauss and so on.'

BIBLIOGRAPHY

There is a vast library of books about the Holocaust. Below is a short list of some of the books that have been quoted in the text or have informed my thinking.

Adelsberger, Lucie, *A Doctor's Story* (Robson Books, London, 1996)

Adler, H.G., *Theresienstadt 1941–1945 The Face of a Coerced Community* (Cambridge University Press, 2017)

Adlington, Lucy, *The Dressmakers of Auschwitz* (Hodder & Stoughton, London, 2021)

Arendt, Hannah Eichmann in *Jerusalem: A Report on the Banality of Evil* (Viking Press, London 1963)

Borowski, Tadeusz, *This Way for the Gas, Ladies and Gentlemen* (Penguin Modern Classics, revised edition 1992)

Brown, Daniel Patrick, *The Camp Women: The Female Auxiliaries who assisted the SS in running the Nazi concentration camp system* (Schiffer Military History, Atglen PA, 2002)

Brown, Daniel Patrick, *The Beautiful Beast: The Life and Crimes of SS Aufseherin Irma Grese* (Golden West Historical Publications Inc, California, 2004)

Bucheim, Hans, Broszat, Martin and others, *Anatomy of the SS State* (Granada, London, 1970)

Clarke, Comer, *Eichmann: The Man and His Crimes* (Ballantine Books, New York, 1960)

Czech, Danuta, *Auschwitz Chronicle 1939–1945* (Henry Holt and Company, New York, 1997)

Cywinski, Piotr M. A. ed., *Auschwitz-Birkenau: The Place Where You Are Standing* (Auschwitz Birkenau State Museum, 2013)

Delbo, Charlotte, *Auschwitz and After* (Yale University Press, 1995)

Dunicz Niwińska, Helena, *One of the Girls in the Band: The Memoirs of a Violinist from Birkenau* (Auschwitz Birkenau State Museum, 2018)

Eischeid, Susan, *The Truth about Fania Fénelon and the Women's Orchestra of Auschwitz-Birkenau* (Palgrave Macmillan, 2016)

Eischeid, Susan, *Mistress of Life and Death: The Dark Journey of Maria Mandl* (Citadel Press, New York, 2023)

Eyre, Makana, *Sing, Memory: The Remarkable Story of the Man who Saved the Music of the Nazi Camps* (W.W. Norton & Company, New York, 2023)

Fairweather, Jack, *The Volunteer: The True Story of the Resistance Hero Who Infiltrated Auschwitz* (W.H. Allen, London, 2019)

Felstein, Jean-Jacques, *The Violinist of Auschwitz* (Pen & Sword History, Barnsley, 2021)

Fénelon, Fania with Marcelle Routier, *The Musicians of Auschwitz* (Michael Joseph, 1977), also published as *Playing for Time*

Frankl, Viktor, *Man's Search for Meaning: The Classic Tribute to Hope from the Holocaust* (Rider, London, 2008)

Freedland, Jonathan, *The Escape Artist: The Man who Broke out of Auschwitz to Warn the World* (John Murray Press, London, 2022)

Gilbert, Martin, *Never Again: A History of the Holocaust* (Harper Collins, London, 2000)

Gilbert, Martin, *Auschwitz and the Allies* (Holt, Rinehart and Winston, New York, 1981)

Gilbert, Shirli, *Music in the Holocaust: Confronting Life in the Nazi Ghettos and Camps* (Oxford University Press, 2005)

Gutman, Yisrael and Berenbaum, Michael, *Anatomy of the Auschwitz Death Camp* (Indiana University Press, 1998)

Hart-Moxon, Kitty, *Return to Auschwitz: The Remarkable Story of a Girl who Survived the Holocaust* (Sidgwick & Jackson, London, 1981)

Haas, Michael, *Forbidden Music: The Jewish Composers Banned by the Nazis* (Yale University Press, 2013)

Helm, Sarah, *If This Is a Woman: Inside Ravensbrück: Hitler's Concentration Camp for Women* (Little, Brown, London, 2015)

Hillesum, Etty, *An Interrupted Life: The Diaries and Letters of Etty Hillesum 1941–43* (Persephone Books, 1999)

Holden, Wendy with Zuzana Ruzickova, *One Hundred Miracles: Music, Auschwitz, Survival and Love* (Bloomsbury, London, 2019)

Höss, Rudolf, *Death Dealer: Memoirs of the SS Kommandant at Auschwitz* ed. Steven Paskuly (Prometheus Books, NY, 1992)

Jacquet-Silberstein, Violette, *Les Sanglots longs des Violons* (Oskar jeunesse, Paris, 2013)

Karpf, Anne, *The War After: Living with the Holocaust* (William Heinemann, London, 1996)

Kluger, Ruth, *Still Alive: A Holocaust Girlhood Remembered* (Feminist Press, New York, 2001)

Knapp, Gabriele, *Das Frauenorchester in Auschwitz* (von Bockel Verlag, Hamburg, 1996)

Kounio-Amariglio, Erika, *From Thessaloniki to Auschwitz and Back: Memories of a Survivor* (Vallentine Mitchell, Elstree, 2000)

Lachendro, Jacek, 'The Orchestras in KL Auschwitz' in *Auschwitz Studies* 27 (Museum of Auschwitz-Birkenau, 2015)

Laks, Szymon, *Music of Another World* (Northwestern University Press, Evanston, 1989)

Langbein, Hermann, *People in Auschwitz* (University of North Carolina Press, Chapel Hill, 2004)

Lasker-Wallfisch, Anita, *Inherit the Truth 1939–45* (Giles de la Mare, London, 1996)

Lengyel, Olga, *Five Chimneys: A Woman Survivor's True Story of Auschwitz* (Howard Fertig, New York, 1983)

Levi, Primo, *The Drowned and the Saved* (Michael Joseph, London, 1988)

Levi, Primo, *If This Is a Man* and *The Truce* (combined volume, Penguin Books, London, 1979)

Lingens-Reiner, Ella, *Prisoners of Fear: An Account of the Author's Experiences in Auschwitz Concentration Camp* (Victor Gollancz, London, 1948)

Macadam, Heather Dune, *The Nine Hundred: The Extraordinary Young Women of the First Official Jewish Transport to Auschwitz* (Citadel Press, New York, 2020)

Matthäus, Jürgen, ed., *Approaching an Auschwitz Survivor: Holocaust Testimony and its Transformations* (Oxford University Press, 2010)

Mears, Charlotte, *A Social History of the Aufseherinnen of Auschwitz* (Doctoral dissertation Kingston University https://eprints.kingston.ac.uk/id/eprint/50539/1/Mears-C-50539.pdf)

Menasche, Albert, *Birkenau: Auschwitz II: Memoirs of an Eyewitness, How 72,000 Greek Jews Perished* (Isaac Saltiel, New York, 1947)

Miller, Arthur, *Playing for Time* (Nick Hern Books, London, 1985)

Newman, Richard with Kirtley, Karen, *Alma Rosé: Vienna to Auschwitz* (Amadeus Press, Cambridge, 2003)

O'Neil, Robin, *The Mahler Family in the Rise and Fall of the Third Reich* (Memoirs Publishing, Cirencester, 2013)

Perl, Gisella, *I was a Doctor in Auschwitz* (International Universities Press, New York, 1948)

Shuldman, Ken, *Jazz Survivor, The Story of Louis Bannet, Horn Player of Auschwitz* (Vallentine Mitchell, London and Chicago, 2005)

Sington, Derrick, *Belsen Uncovered* (Duckworth, 1946)

Smeed, Suzi with Quinn, Terence, *The Courage to Care* (Connor Court Publishing, Queensland, 2023)

Stone, Dan, *The Liberation of the Camps: The End of the Holocaust and its Aftermath* (Yale University Press, New Haven and London, 2015)

Stone, Dan, *The Holocaust: An Unfinished History* (Penguin Random House, London, 2023)

Stroumsa, Jacques, *Violinist in Auschwitz: From Saloca to Jerusalem 1913–1967* (Hartung-Gorre Verlag, Konstanz, 1996)

Szmaglewska, Seweryna, *Smoke Over Birkenau* (Ksiazka i Wiedza, Warsaw, 2001)

Tedeschi, Giuliana, *There is a Place on Earth: A Woman in Birkenau* (Pantheon Books, 1992)

Verheijen, Mirjam with Schrijver, Flora, *Het meisje met de accordeon* (Uitgerverij Scheffers, Utrecht, 1994)

Wachsmann, Nikolaus, *KL: A History of the Nazi Concentration Camps* (Farrar, Straus, and Giroux, New York, 2015)

Zelmanowicz Olewski, Rachela, *Crying Is Forbidden Here! A Jewish Girl in pre-WW2 Poland* (based on Hebrew Testimony recorded Yad Vashem 21.5.1984, Open University of Israel, 2009)

Zywulska, Krystyna, *I Survived Auschwitz* (Auschwitz-Birkenau Museum, Warsaw, 2006)

Films

We Want the Light: The Jews and German Music, dir.
Christopher Nupen, Allegro Films, 2016, https://www.bbc.
co.uk/programmes/m00109wp

Bach in Auschwitz, dir. Michel Daeron, 1999

Saved by Music: The Wallfisch Family, dir. Mark Kidel, Calliope
Media, 2010

*Music in Nazi Germany: The Maestro and the Cellist of
Auschwitz*, dir. Christian Berger, 2022, https://www.imdb.
com/title/tt23727172/

Playing to Survive, dir. Teresa Smith, BBC, 1996, https://www.
imdb.com/title/tt0939541/

ACKNOWLEDGEMENTS

Any historian who writes about the Holocaust in the twenty-first century owes a large debt of gratitude to those pioneers who assembled the initial documentation and compiled interviews with survivors and witnesses while they could. I happily acknowledge my own debt to those institutions responsible for preserving these collections, especially the Fortunoff Institute at Yale, the USC Shoah Foundation, founded by Steven Spielberg in 1994, Yad Vashem memorial in Jerusalem, and of course the Auschwitz-Birkenau State Museum and Archives.

I also must thank individuals, many of whom are no longer alive, such as the late Sir Martin Gilbert and, in the case of the women's orchestra, Richard Newman, whose biography of Alma Rosé was based on numerous interviews with survivors from the orchestra and was written with a colleague, Karen Kirtley. My thanks to Sara Newman for permission to listen and quote from these. Bruce Colegrove, teacher and holocaust historian, has undertaken years of research into all aspects of the women's orchestra and his generous offer to share his database of documents and archival information has been of incalculable help in writing this book. I thank him wholeheartedly for all his help and support.

A special thank you to the National Archives at Kew for showing me the file of documents, several with my father's signature, detailing his time as a British soldier at Bergen Belsen. My regret at never discussing this with him is overwhelming. Other institutions with valuable archives include the Imperial War Museum in London, with special thanks to Nora Ni Dhomhnaill for pointing me in the right direction, to the London Library whose helpful staff always find the book you need in record time, and the Wiener Library, which holds invaluable resources. My own book has been built on these archives and repositories.

I have also been immensely fortunate to speak to two surviving members of the orchestra, Hilde Grünbaum Zimche and Anita Lasker-Wallfisch. My thanks to them for discussing those years with me are beyond words. Others who have helped in various ways are Jeremy Adler who provided initial avenues to examine and books to read based on his own work in research into his father's writings about Theresienstadt; Sandra Alexander at Jewish Care; Dana Arschin for introducing me to Debbie Assael-Migliori and Peggy Clores, children of orchestra members.

For hospitality in New York and securing a copy of a rare Dutch book, warmest thanks to Joop and Dixie de Koning and to Susanne Lap for translating it so swifty and sensitively; to Mark Kidel, for sowing the seed by showing me his film about the Lasker-Wallfisch family and reading an early draft of the manuscript.

In Poland Jack Fairweather was a source of information and help and introduced me to Katarzyna Chiżyńska who translated some Polish documents held in Auschwitz Birkenau for which I am most grateful; my thanks for guiding me around the site to Renate Koszyk; and to Agnieszka Kita, Jacek Lachendro, Edyta Chowaniec.

I also want to acknowledge Susan Eischeid, Paul French, Tom Gross, Naomi Gryn, Joe Halio, Nina Kaye, Sivanne Cohen Kramer (granddaughter of Regina Kupferberg), Sue Lawley, Rachel Levy, Stephen Ludsin, Raymond Meade, Danielle

Minkowski (daughter of Helene Wiernik), Abraham Mouritz (grandson of Flora Jacobs), Stephen Naron, Arianna Neumann. Arie Olewski (son of Rachela Zelmanowicz Olewski), Murray and Ninette Perahia, Janie Press, founder of Holocaust Music Lost and Found and a constant source of help, David, Yoav and Tsafi Sebba (in Israel), Adam Sisman, Richard Tomlinson, Bret Werb and Ari C. Zev, former member of the senior leadership team of USC Shoah Foundation.

There are no fresh ways to thank those without whose early support and commitment this book would not have been possible: my publishers, agents and family. My immense thanks to Adam, Louise, Amy, Hugh, Imogen and Nora for demonstrating their usual loving interest in my work by offering practical help in myriad ways.

Clare Alexander deserves the biggest thank you for seeing the importance of this story as soon as I first discussed it with her, and being the pillar of constant encouragement every author needs. Several in her team at Aitken Alexander, including Amy St John and Lesley Thorne, also deserve a special thank you.

At Weidenfeld & Nicolson my thanks go to Jenny Lord for her insight, empathy with the story and care with words, as well as to her wonderful team, Lucinda McNeile, Natalie Dawkins, Lily McIlwain and Suzanne Jayes.

And in New York I want to thank the equally supportive team of Charlie Spicer, Hannah Pierdolla and Dori Weintraub who have brought enthusiasm and editorial rigour.

Anne Sebba
London, 2024

NOTES

Introduction: The Women's Orchestra of Auschwitz

1. Zofia (Zosia) Cykowiak testimony Wspomnienia, vol. 141, PMA-B, pp. 6–16 tr thanks to Jack Fairweather and Katarzyna Chiżyńska
2. Anita Lasker-Wallfisch *Inherit the Truth* (ITT) Giles de la Mare publishers 1996 London p.84
3. Richard Newman with Karen Kirtley *Alma Rosé Vienna to Auschwitz* Amadeus Press 2000 Cambridge Mass p.262
4. Charlotte Delbo *Auschwitz and After* tr Rosette C Lamont Yale UP 1995 pp.100–101
5. https://vha.usc.edu/testimony/4103?from=search Pearl Pufeles Interview 19 July 1995
6. https://collections.ushmm.org/search/catalog/vha7832 1995 interview with Irene Zisblatt USC SHOAH Foundation code 7832
7. https://holocaustmusic.ort.org/places/camps/death-camps/birkenau/laksszymono/
8. Anita Lasker-Wallfisch *Inherit the Truth* p.84
9. Helena Dunicz Niwińska *One of the Girls in the Band* tr William Brand Auschwitz-Birkenau State Museum Oświęcim 2018 p.83
10. Dunicz Niwińska *One of the Girls in the Band* p.84
11. Comer Clarke *Eichmann: The Man and His Crimes* Ballantine Books NY 1960 pp. 121–122
12. Dunicz Niwińska to Lasker-Wallfisch unpublished correspondence 1996 courtesy of ALW
13. National Archives, Kew WO 171/4352 Jan-May 1945

Chapter 1: We did not feel pain any more

1. Danuta Czech *Auschwitz Chronicle 1939–1945* Henry Holt 1997 NYC p.146
2. Helen Tichauer (Zippi) to Dr Joan Ringelheim https://collections. ushmm.org/search/catalog/irn508470 USHMM Sept 2000 RG 500300462
3. Ibid.
4. Helen Tichauer interview with David Boder Illinois Institute of Technology https://perspectives.ushmm.org/item/david-boder-interview-with-helen-tichauer 23 September 1946, in the Feldafing Displaced Persons Camp
5. David Boder interview as above
6. Heather Dune Macadam *The Nine Hundred* Hodder & Stoughton 2000 p.115 for further details
7. Ringelheim interview as above USHMM
8. https://perspectives.ushmm.org/item/david-boder-interview-with-helen-tichauer as above
9. Ringelheim interview as above USHMM
10. See https://www.mp.pl/auschwitz/other-publications/313877,infectious-diseases-in-the-auschwitz-birkenau-environment by Karel Ptaszkowski MD
11. *Approaching an Auschwitz Survivor Holocaust Testimony and its Transformations* ed. Jürgen Matthäus OUP 2010 p.110
12. Ringelheim interview as above USHMM
13. *Approaching an Auschwitz Survivor* p.106
14. Ibid.
15. Ringelheim interview as above
16. Ibid.
17. Newman and Kirtley p.22
18. https://jewishcurrents.org/record-keeping-for-the-nazis-and-saving-lives
19. Interview with Katya Singer and Susan Cernyak-Spatz https://jewishcurrents.org/record-keeping-for-the-nazis-and-saving-lives
20. Ibid.
21. Ibid.
22. Ibid.
23. Ringelheim interview as above
24. Szymon Laks *Music of Another World* tr Chester Kisiel Northwestern University Press Illinois 1989 p.52

25. Ringelheim interview as above
26. Danuta Czech as above p.148 citing Rudolf Höss Commandant of Auschwitz 1947
27. Susan Eischeid *Mistress of Life and Death: The Dark Journey of Maria Mandl* Citadel Press NYC 2024 p.13
28. Charlotte Mears https://www.academia.edu/10833241/To_what_extent_does_the_career_of_Maria_Mandel_showcase_the_role_of_women_in_power_during_the_Holocaust quoting prisoner Lina Haag
29. Cited Eischeid *Mistress of Life and Death* p.95
30. Ella Lingens-Reiner *Prisoners of Fear* Victor Gollancz 1948 p.44
31. Ibid. p.29
32. Eischeid *Mistress of Life and Death* p.116
33. Mears as above
34. https://jewishcurrents.org/record-keeping-for-the-nazis-and-saving-lives
35. Ringelheim interview as above
36. Ibid.
37. Ibid.
38. Ella Lingens-Reiner p.78
39. Eischeid *Mistress of Life and Death* p.107
40. Ella Lingens-Reiner p.41
41. Eischeid *Mistress of Life and Death* p.97
42. https://collections.ushmm.org/search/catalog/irn504535 Magda Blau Hellinger interview with Linda Kuzmack 11 June 1990 USHMM tape one access no 1990.408.1 https://collections.ushmm.org/search/catalog/irn504535
43. Ibid.

Chapter 2: Making good music for the SS

1. Helen Tichauer (Zippi) interview Richard Newman 1983 https://collections.ushmm.org/search/catalog/irn558849
2. Jacek Lachendro *Auschwitz Studies* 27 Auschwitz-Birkenau State Museum 2015
3. Lachendro as above p.69 citing Wojciech Kawecki testimony memoirs collection vol. 75 pp.243–244 Auschwitz-Birkenau State Museum

4. Extracted from testimony of unnamed prisoner in BBC documentary *Playing to Survive* https://www.imdb.com/title/tt0939541/

5. Lachendro as above p.68 citing testimony of Janina Janiszewska memoirs collection vol. 95 pp.159–60

6. Lachendro *Auschwitz Studies* 27 p.77

7. Szymon Laks *Music of Another World* p.117

8. Ibid. p.33

9. Oral history interview Helen Tichauer and Dr Joan Ringelheim 2000 https://collections.ushmm.org/search/catalog/irn508470

10. Interview with Dr Joan Ringelheim 2000 as above

11. https://collections.ushmm.org/search/catalog/irn677604 2005 interview with Dr Joan Ringelheim a continuation of previous interviews

12. Interview with Richard Newman https://collections.ushmm.org/search/catalog/irn558849

13. Newman and Kirtley p.231

14. Gabriele Knapp *Das Frauenorchester in Auschwitz* Von Bockel Verlag Hamburg 1996 p.66

15. Cykowiak testimony as above Krakow 2 July 1982

16. Jean-Jacques Felstein *The Violinist of Auschwitz* p.145

17. http://www.auschwitz-prozess-frankfurt.de/index.php?id=97

18. Dunicz Niwińska *One of the Girls in the Band* p.108

19. Zelmanowicz Olewski *Crying Is Forbidden Here!* p.46

20. Newman and Kirtley op. cit. p.231

21. Laks op. cit. p.44

22. Lachendro op. cit. p.92

23. https://baruchfamily.wordpress.com/2018/12/08/hachshara-neuendorf-the-last-youth-hachshara-in-germany

24. William Drozdiak 10 December 1999 'Panel finds Switzerland complicit in Holocaust' *Washington Post*

25. Interview with Inge Franken 2003 http://www.inge-franken.de/fehrbel-liner92/sylvia

26. Ibid.

27. Ibid.

28. Excerpt from the testimony of Shulamit Wagenberg Khalif https://www.yadvashem.org/artifacts/featured/hilde-grunbaum.html

29. Testimony of Esther Bejarano née Loewy Auschwitz-Birkenau Museum Archives 14.1.1995
30. https://ehne.fr/en/encyclopedia/themes/wars-and-memories/violence-war/music-and-torture
31. Szymon Laks *Music of Another World* p.58
32. https://vha.usc.edu/testimony/979?from=search&seg=143%20Shoah%20foundation%201995%20 video interview 1995 with Yvette Assael Lennon USCH Shoah Foundation code 979
33. Ibid.
34. Ibid.
35. Ibid.
36. https://vha.usc.edu/testimony/979?from=search&seg=143%20Shoah%20foundation%201995%20 video interview 1995 interview with Yvette Assael Lennon USC Shoah Foundation code 979
37. Ibid.
38. Ibid.
39. Cykowiak testimony as above Krakow 2 July 1982 Wspomnienia, vol. 141, PMA-B, pp. 6–16.
40. Cited Lachendro p.79
41. Bejarano testimony for Auschwitz-Birkenau Museum Archives as above 14.1.95
42. Newman and Kirtley citing Helena Dunicz Niwińska p.235
43. Felstein *The Violinist of Auschwitz* p.125
44. Ibid.
45. https://vha.usc.edu/testimony/979?from=search&seg=143%20Shoah%20foundation%201995%20 video interview with Yvette Assael Lennon USCH Shoah Foundation 1995

Chapter 3: Something beautiful to listen to

1. Felstein *The Violinist of Auschwitz* p.5
2. Itta W. Holocaust Testimony (HVT-4083) Fortunoff Video Archive for Holocaust Testimonies, Yale University Library
3. Ibid.
4. Ibid.
5. Newman and Kirtley p.233

6. Ibid. (story also told in interview for Fortunoff above)

7. Itta W. Holocaust Testimony (HVT-4083) Fortunoff Video Archive for Holocaust Testimonies, Yale University Library

8. Newman and Kirtley quoting Hélène Wiernik p.233

9. Itta W. Holocaust Testimony (HVT-4083) Fortunoff Video Archive for Holocaust Testimonies, Yale University Library

10. Mali Fritz *Essig Gegen den durst 565 Tage in Auschwitz-Birkenau* Vienna 1986 p.22

11. Lucie Adelsberger *A Doctor's Story* p.38

12. Newman and Kirtley p.231

13. Szymon Laks *Music from Another World* p.45

14. Lachendro *Auschwitz Studies* 27 p.95 citing Auschwitz statements collection vol 129 p.246

15. Newman and Kirtley p.234

16. https://forbiddenmusic.org/2018/01/23/from-crossover-star-to-survivalist-the-unexpected-transformation-of-alma-rose

17. Alma Rosé letter to Leila Pirani 1962 cited Newman and Kirtley p.114

18. https://forbiddenmusic.org/2018/01/23/from-crossover-star-to-survivalist-the-unexpected-transformation-of-alma-rose

19. Testimony of survivors on Convoy 57 Yvette Levy and Gabriel Benichou cited http://garedeportation.bobigny.fr/en/104/the-deportation-stages.html

20. Robin O'Neil *The Mahler Family* Memoirs Publishing, Cirencester 2013 p.457 citing Yad Vashem archives

21. Newman and Kirtley p.221

22. USHM interview https://collections.ushmm.org/oh_findingaids/RG-50.030.0030_trs_en.pdf

23. Magda Hellinger later Blau after her marriage to Bela Blau and post-war life in Melbourne https://wamu.org/story/22/03/15/magda-hellinger-survived-auschwitz-while-saving-her-fellow-prisoners

24. Newman and Kirtley p.223

25. Ibid.

26. Op. cit. p.224

27. Ibid.

28. Newman and Kirtley p.34

29. Ibid.

30. Newman and Kirtley based on various interviews between 1988 and 1999 pp. 234–5

31. Ibid.

32. Ibid.

33. Dunicz Niwińska *One of the Girls in the Band*

34. Itta W. Holocaust Testimony (HVT-4083) Fortunoff Video Archive for Holocaust Testimonies, Yale University Library

35. Kitty Hart-Moxon *Return to Auschwitz* House of Stratus 2000 p.109

36. Itta W. Holocaust Testimony (HVT-4083) Fortunoff Video Archive for Holocaust Testimonies, Yale University Library

37. Lachendro *Auschwitz Studies* 27 p.93 citing *In Birkenau You did not Die Alone* p.71–72

38. Itta W. Holocaust Testimony (HVT-4083) Fortunoff Video Archive for Holocaust Testimonies, Yale University Library

39. Ibid.

40. Newman and Kirtley p.236

41. Lachendro *Auschwitz Studies* 27 p.92

42. Dunicz Niwińska *One of the Girls in the Band* p.112

43. Dr Albert Menasche *Memoirs of an Eyewitness, How 72,000 Greek Jews perished* 1947 pp.65–66

44. Zelmanowicz Olewski *Crying Is Forbidden Here!* English translation based on Hebrew Testimony to Yad Vashem 21.05.1984 p.29

45. Ibid. p.49

46. Cited Sivanne Cohen Kramer based on her private translation from Hebrew of her grandmother Regina Kupferberg's testimony to Yad Vashem

47. As above

Chapter 4: You will be saved

1. Zelmanowicz Olewski *Crying Is Forbidden Here!* p.30

2. Felstein *The Violinist of Auschwitz* p.19

3. Ibid. p.21

4. Ibid.

5. Zelmanowicz Olewski *Crying Is Forbidden Here!* p.39

6. Ibid.

7. Ibid. p.43

8. Dunicz Niwińska *One of the Girls in the Band* p.77

9. Dorys Wilamowska undated newspaper cutting Collection Leo Baeck Institute

10. Zelmanowicz Olewski *Crying Is Forbidden Here!* p.33

11. Flora Jacobs Schrijver with Mirjam Verheijen. *Het meisje met de accordion: de overleving van Flora Schrijver in Auschwitz-Birkenau en Bergen-Belsen.* Uitgeverij Scheffers Utrecht 1994. ISBN 90-5546-011-7 Girl with the Accordion All page numbers approximate p.25 tr into English thanks Susanne Lap

12. Ibid. p.26

13. Newman and Kirtley p.241

14. *Bach in Auschwitz* documentary film by Michel Daeron 1999

15. Newman and Kirtley p.241 based on interview with Flora https://collections.ushmm.org/search/catalog/irn558864

16. Dunicz Niwińska *One of the Girls in the Band* p.35

17. Ibid.

18. Ibid.

19. Newman and Kirtley p.237

20. Op. cit. p.238

21. Ibid.

22. *Bach in Auschwitz* documentary film by Michel Daeron 1999

23. Ibid.

24. Ibid.

25. Lasker-Wallfisch *Inherit the Truth* Preface

26. https://www.hmd.org.uk/resource/anita-lasker-wallfisch

27. Lasker-Wallfisch *Inherit the Truth* p.20

28. Mrs E Lasker to M Lasker Breslau 19 June 1939 IWM archive

29. Mrs E Lasker to M Lasker 26 July 1939 *Inherit the Truth* p.22

30. Lasker-Wallfisch *Inherit the Truth* p.31

31. Ibid.

32. Anita L-W to Marianne Lasker in *Inherit the Truth* p.46

33. Ibid. p.43

34. Ibid. p.53

35. Ibid. p.55

36. Ibid. p.58

37. Ibid. p.71

38. Ibid. p.72
39. Ibid. p.6
40. Ibid. p.80
41. Ibid.

Chapter 5: The orchestra means life

1. Lasker-Wallfisch *Inherit the Truth* p.76
2. Dunicz Niwińska *One of the Girls in the Band* p.101
3. Krystyna Zywulska *I Survived Auschwitz* published in cooperation with Auschwitz-Birkenau State Museum 2004 p.51
4. Newman and Kirtley p.280
5. Ibid. p.282
6. Ibid.
7. Interview as before https://fortunoff.aviaryplatform.com/collections/5/collection_resources/4127
8. Newman and Kirtley p.280
9. Dunicz Niwińska *One of the Girls in the Band* p.101
10. Ibid.
11. ALW interview with author 22.11.2022
12. HDN to ALW private correspondence nd
13. HDN to Anita 4.11.1996 Krakow unpublished correspondence as above
14. Zofia Cykowiak to ALW 16.05.1994 unpublished correspondence
15. Zelmanowicz Olewski *Crying Is Forbidden Here!* 2009 based on her Hebrew testimony at Yad Vashem recorded 21.5.1984
16. Newman and Kirtley p.271
17. Jacques Stroumsa *Violinist in Auschwitz* Hartung-Gorre 1996 p.57
18. Newman and Kirtley p.272
19. Itta W. Holocaust Testimony (HVT-4083) Fortunoff Video Archive for Holocaust Testimonies, Yale University Library
20. Danuta Czech *Auschwitz Chronicle* p.513
21. Dunicz Niwińska *One of the Girls in the Band* p.98
22. *Bach in Auschwitz* documentary film by Michel Daeron
23. Auschwitz testimony as above
24. Itta W. Holocaust Testimony (HVT-4083) Fortunoff Video Archive for Holocaust Testimonies, Yale University Library

25. Newman and Kirtley p.268

26. Cited Lachendro *Auschwitz Studies* 27 p.97 quoting memoirs of Wanda Koprowska

27. Cited Lachendro p.97 from Zarebinska-Broniewska memoirs collection Auschwitz Museum

28. Ibid.

29. Dunicz Niwińska *One of the Girls in the Band* p.77

30. *Bach in Auschwitz* documentary film by Michel Daeron

31. Ibid.

32. Itta W. Holocaust Testimony (HVT-4083) Fortunoff Video Archive for Holocaust Testimonies, Yale University Library

33. Charlotte Delbo *Auschwitz and After* tr Rosette C Lamont Yale UP 1995 pp.100–101

34. Lachendro *Auschwitz Studies* 27 p.103

35. *Bach in Auschwitz* documentary film by Michel Daeron

36. Itta W. Holocaust Testimony (HVT-4083) Fortunoff Video Archive for Holocaust Testimonies, Yale University Library

37. Bejarano Auschwitz Birkenau State Museum testimony as above

38. Zelmanowicz Olewski *Crying Is Forbidden Here!* p.37

39. Ibid.

40. Newman and Kirtley p.271

41. Dunicz Niwińska *One of the Girls in the Band* p.96

42. Cykowiak testimony as above Krakow 2 July 1982 Wspomnienia, vol. 141, PMA-B, pp. 6–16.

43. Cited Sivanne Cohen Kramer based on her private translation from Hebrew of her grandmother Regina Kupferberg's testimony to Yad Vashem testimony 21.5.1984

44. Ibid.

45. Interview with Ruth Bassin https://collections.ushmm.org/search/catalog/irn558875

46. Newman and Kirtley p.289

47. Ibid.

48. Laks *Music of Another World* p.100

49. https://www.nytimes.com/1978/01/07/archives/memories-of-a-nazi-camp-where-a-musical-gift-meant-survival-many.html

50. Interview notes (translated from Hebrew) are from her 1998 USC Shoah video testimonial

51. Information on surnames and prisoner numbers here discovered by orchestra researcher Bruce Colegrove

52. Flora Schrijver with Mirjam Verheijen. *Het meisje met de accordion: de overleving van Flora Schrijver in Auschwitz-Birkenau en Bergen-Belsen.* Uitgeverij Scheffers Utrecht 1994. ISBN 90-5546-011-7 Girl with the Accordion p.25 tr into English thanks Susanne Lap p.44

53. Cykowiak Auschwitz testimony as above vol 141 p.9

54. Newman and Kirtley p.282

55. Ibid. p.275

56. Ibid. p.288

57. Felstein *Violinist of Auschwitz* p.90

58. Zippi Tichauer to Richard Newman tape 1 https://collections.ushmm.org/search/catalog/irn558849

59. European Association for Jewish Studies Congress: Jewish Studies at the Turn of the Twentieth Century: Proceedings of the 6th EAJS Congress, Toledo, July 1998. BRILL, 1999, ISBN 978-90-04-11558-3 p.527

60. Zelmanowicz Olewski *Crying Is Forbidden Here!* p.48.

61. Dunicz Niwińska *One of the Girls in the Band* p.76

62. Cited Newman and Kirtley p.273

63. Ibid.

64. See Dunicz Niwińska *One of the Girls in the Band*

65. Ken Shuldman *Jazz Survivor: The Story of Louis Bannet, Horn Player of Auschwitz* p.35

66. https://collections.ushmm.org/search/catalog/vha49087

67. Felstein *The Violinist of Auschwitz* p.127

68. Lasker-Wallfisch *Inherit the Truth* p.162

69. Newman and Kirtley p.245

70. Dunicz Niwińska *One of the Girls in the Band* pp.92–3

71. See Danuta Czech *Auschwitz Chronicle*

72. *Bach in Auschwitz* documentary film

73. Ibid.

74. Seweryna Szmaglewska *Smoke Over Birkenau* p.230–32

75. Zelmanowicz Olewski *Crying Is Forbidden Here!* p.36

Chapter 6: She gave us hope and courage

1. Itta W. Holocaust Testimony (HVT-4083) Fortunoff Video Archive for Holocaust Testimonies, Yale University Library
2. Ibid.
3. See Felstein p.56 for joke about Sylvia being so small she would not make a very good flame if she were gassed
4. Lasker-Wallfisch *Inherit the Truth* p.84
5. https://collections.ushmm.org/search/catalog/irn558875
6. Hermann Langbein *People in Auschwitz* University of North Carolina Press 2004 p.152
7. Wendy Holden *One Hundred Miracles* Bloomsbury 2019 p.55
8. Hart-Moxon *Return to Auschwitz* p.102
9. https://www.auschwitz.org/en/history/auschwitz-and-shoah/the-unloading-ramps-and-selections
10. Dunicz Niwińska *One of the Girls in the Band* p.104
11. Felstein *The Violinist of Auschwitz* p.89
12. Guido Fackler https://holocaustmusic.ort.org/places/camps/death-camps/auschwitz/camp-orchestras
13. *Bach in Auschwitz* documentary film as before
14. Lachendro *Auschwitz Studies* 27 p.103
15. Ibid.
16. https://collections.ushmm.org/search/catalog/vha25639
17. Hilde Grünbaum testimony to Yad Vashem tr Jessica Ross Bruce Colegrove private archive
18. Cykowiak Auschwitz testimony memoirs book vol. 141, PMA-B, pp. 6–16
19. Newman and Kirtley p.266
20. Yad Vashem Hilde Grünbaum testimony as above
21. Cykowiak Auschwitz testimony memoirs book vol. 141, PMA-B, pp. 6–16
22. Dunicz Niwińska *One of the Girls in the Band* cited Lachendro p.102 *Auschwitz Studies* 27
23. Flora Jacobs Schrijver with Mirjam Verheijen *Girl with the Accordion* tr Susanne Lap p.43.
24. Cited Eischeid, *Mistress of Life and Death*, p.176
25. Newman and Kirtley p.267

26. Flora Jacobs Schrijver with Mirjam Verheijen *Girl with the Accordion* tr Susanne Lap, p.43
27. Itta W. Holocaust Testimony (HVT-4083) Fortunoff Video Archive for Holocaust Testimonies, Yale Univesity Library
28. Dunicz Niwińska *One of the Girls in the Band* p.83
29. Lasker-Wallfisch *Inherit the Truth* Transcript from Trial appendix 4 p.158
30. *The Maestro and the Cellist* film https://www.naxos.com/Catalogue Detail/?id=762808 dir. Christian Berger 2022 ALW has also often spoken of this.
31. BBC Desert Island Discs https://www.bbc.co.uk/programmes/p0093ndt interviewer Sue Lawley
32. ALW interview with author 11.11.2022
33. Danuta Czech *Auschwitz Chronicle* p.562
34. Felstein *The Violinist of Auschwitz* p.92
35. Cykowiak testimony as above Krakow 2 July 1982 Wspomnienia, vol. 141, PMA-B, pp. 6–16 private translation
36. Felstein *The Violinist of Auschwitz* p.92
37. Dunicz Niwińska *One of the Girls in the Band* p.113
38. Ibid. p.110
39. Felstein *Violinist of Auschwitz* p.90
40. Interview with Newman USHMM
41. ALW article on her reaction to Newman's biography of Alma https://www.musicteachers.co.uk/journal/2000-08_laskerwallfisch_3.html from Colegrove private archive
42. Lachendro *Auschwitz Studies* 27 p.93
43. Zelmanowicz Olewski *Crying Is Forbidden Here!* p.33
44. Primo Levi *The Grey Zone* p.37
45. Dunicz Niwińska *One of the Girls in the Band* p.76
46. Lasker-Wallfisch *Inherit the Truth* p.78
47. Ibid.
48. Ibid.
49. Newman and Kirtley p.274
50. Zelmanowicz Olewski *Crying Is Forbidden Here!* p.37
51. ALW interview with author as above
52. Zelmanowicz Olewski *Crying Is Forbidden Here!* p.34

53. Dunicz Niwińska *One of the Girls in the Band* p.84 and https://devilstrillblog.blogspot.com/2018/06/violinist-and-auschwitz-survivor-helena.html
54. Interview with author 26 June 2022
55. Hart-Moxon *Return to Auschwitz* p.103
56. Newman and Kirtley p.268
57. Ibid.
58. Ibid.
59. Seweryna Szmaglewska *Smoke Over Birkenau* p.35–36
60. Lachendro *Auschwitz Studies* 27 p.98
61. Ibid. p.99
62. Newman and Kirtley p.304
63. Felstein *The Violinist of Auschwitz* pp.149–50
64. Newman and Kirtley p.261
65. Zippi Tichauer interview with Richard Newman tape 1 as before
66. Dunicz Niwińska *One of the Girls in the Band* p.103

Chapter 7: I felt the sun on my face

1. Lasker-Wallfisch *Inherit the Truth* p.85
2. Hilde testimony to Yad Vashem tr Jessica Ross with thanks to Bruce Colegrove
3. Ibid.
4. Cykowiak, Zofia, Wspomnienia, vol. 141, PMA-B, pp. 6–16. Kraków, 2 lipca 1982 private translation
5. Giuliana Tedeschi *There is a Place on Earth: A Woman in Birkenau* p.59 Random House 1992
6. 'I too was Eichmann's victim' *News of the World* 23 October 1960
7. Lasker-Wallfisch *Inherit the Truth* p.85
8. *Limburgsche Dagblad* 12 Aug 1937
9. Comer Clarke *Eichmann the Man and His Crimes* pp.121–2
10. Ibid.
11. 'I too was Eichmann's victim' *News of the World* 23 October 1960
12. Ibid.
13. Flora Jacobs Schrijver with Mirjam Verheijen *Girl with the Accordion* p.44
14. *News of the World* as above

NOTES

15. Singapore Free Press 27 Sept 1951 p.4
16. Gabriele Knapp *Das Frauenorchester im Auschwitz* p.130
17. Flora Jacobs Schrijver with Mirjam Verheijen, *Girl with the Accordion* pp 54–55
18. Gisella Perl *I was a Doctor in Auschwitz* 1948 Ayer Co Pub pp 83–84
19. Interview with Volcker Kuhn *They Played for their Life, Cabaret in the face of Death* https://www.aufrichtigs.com/01-Holocaust/00-Otto_Aufrichtig_[Aurich]/Westerbork_Volker_Kuhn.htm
20. Ibid.
21. Ibid.
22. http://www.jewish-theatre.com/visitor/article_display.aspx?articleID=529
23. Flora Jacobs Schrijver with Mirjam Verheijen *Girl with the Accordion* p.42
24. https://brzesko-briegel.pl/en/news/mala-zimetbaum-brzesko-born-heroine-of-auschwitz
25. https://www.latimes.com/archives/la-xpm-1986-10-19-vw-5733-story.html
26. Dunicz Niwińska *One of the Girls in the Band* p.122
27. Zelmanowicz Olewski *Crying Is Forbidden Here!* p.32
28. Ibid. pp.38–9
29. Ibid. p.42
30. Dunicz Niwińska *One of the Girls in the Band* p.105
31. Felstein *The Violinist of Auschwitz* p.56 based on a story told to him by Violette and others
32. Felstein *The Violinist of Auschwitz* p.137
33. Ibid. p.147
34. Ibid. p.148
35. Lasker-Wallfisch *Inherit the Truth* p.86
36. Lily Mathé interview *News of the World* thanks to Bruce Colegrove private archive
37. Lasker-Wallfisch *Inherit the Truth* p.87
38. Bruce Colegrove private archive
39. https://collections.ushmm.org/oh_findingaids/RG-50.005.0009_trs_en.pdf
40. Lasker-Wallfisch *Inherit the Truth* p.87
41. Ibid. p.88
42. Itta W. Holocaust Testimony (HVT-4083) Fortunoff Video Archive for Holocaust Testimonies, Yale University Library

43. Ibid.
44. Ibid.
45. Lasker-Wallfisch *Inherit the Truth* p.90
46. Ibid. p.89
47. Ibid.

Chapter 8: Here you are not going to play

1. Dov Paisikovic Witness Accounts Liberation of KL Auschwitz, Auschwitz-Birkenau Museum
2. Zelmanowicz Olewski *Crying Is Forbidden Here!* p.46
3. Flora Schrijver with Mirjam Verheijen *Girl with the Accordion* p.53
4. Ibid.
5. Ibid. p.59
6. Memories of Violette Silberstein and Hélène Wiernik in BBC documentary film 1996 *Playing to Survive* https://www.imdb.com/title/tt0939541/
7. Fania Fénelon *The Musicians of Auschwitz* p.240
8. 'I too was Eichmann's victim' *News of the World*
9. Lasker-Wallfisch *Inherit the Truth* p.91
10. Hilde Grünbaum Yad Vashem testimony
11. Zelmanowicz Olewski *Crying Is Forbidden Here!* p.48
12. Ibid. p.46
13. Ibid. p.47
14. Felstein *The Violinist of Auschwitz* p.64
15. Flora Jacobs Schrijver with Mirjam Verheijen *Girl with the Accordion* p.60
16. Ibid. p.92
17. Derrick Sington *Belsen Uncovered* Duckworth 1946 p.109
18. Zelmanowicz Olewski *Crying Is Forbidden Here!* p.47
19. Flora Jacobs Schrijver with Mirjam Verheijen *Girl with the Accordion* tr p.61
20. Ibid.
21. Ilse Diament https://collections.ushmm.org/oh_findingaids/RG-50.005.0009_trs_en.pdf
22. Ibid.
23. Itta W. Holocaust Testimony (HVT- 4083) Fortunoff Video Archive for Holocaust Testimonies, Yale University Library

24. Yvette Lennon interview with the USC Shoah Foundation. Visual History Archive, 1995, Interview 979
25. Lasker-Wallfisch *Inherit the Truth* p.93

Chapter 9: I have never seen anything like this

1. Flora Jacobs Schrijver with Mirjam Verheijen *Girl with the Accordion* p.65
2. https://blogs.lse.ac.uk/polis/2020/04/15/75-years-on-richard-dimblebys-bbc-report-on-the-liberation-of-belsen-concentration-camp
3. Lasker-Wallfisch *Inherit the Truth* p.95
4. Ilse Diament https://collections.ushmm.org/oh_findingaids/RG-50.005.0009_trs_en.pdf
5. Flora Jacobs Schrijver with Mirjam Verheijen *Girl with the Accordion* p.65
6. *New York Times* 7 Jan 1978
7. Flora Jacobs Schrijver with Mirjam Verheijen *Girl with the Accordion* p.65
8. *Guardian* 13 Oct 2008 Geoffrey Alderman
9. Article published in the *Middlesex Hospital Journal* July 1945 Gerald Raperport
10. Ibid.
11. 'I too was Eichmann's victim' *News of the World* 23 October 1960
12. Lasker-Wallfisch *Inherit the Truth* p.99
13. Zelmanowicz Olewski *Crying Is Forbidden Here! p.57*
14. Haaretz 'The cellist in Auschwitz who feared the world wouldn't believe her' 1 Mar 2023
15. Lasker-Wallfisch *Inherit the Truth* p.99
16. Ibid. p.101
17. ALW Folder 92/31/1 Imperial War Museum archives
18. ALW to Marianne Lasker IWM archives as above
19. Lasker-Wallfisch *Inherit the Truth* p.112
20. Ibid. p.122
21. Ibid. pp.124–7
22. Ibid. p.130
23. Ibid. p.145
24. Zelmanowicz Olewski *Crying Is Forbidden Here!* p.57
25. Ibid.
26. Ibid.

27. Dunicz Niwińska *One of the Girls in the Band* p.123
28. Ibid. p.125
29. Ibid.
30. Danuta Czech *Auschwitz Chronicle* p.743
31. Dunicz Niwińska *One of the Girls in the Band* p.126
32. https://www.tandfonline.com/doi/abs/10.1080/23256249.2017.1294315
33. Stroumsa, Jacques *Violinist in Auschwitz* p.63
34. Dunicz Niwińska *One of the Girls in the Band* p.129
35. Ibid. p.131
36. Ibid. p.136
37. Ibid. p.144
38. Felstein *The Violinist of Auschwitz* p.144

Chapter 10: Someone three quarters destroyed by her experience

1. Interview with author 15 June 2022
2. Lasker-Wallfisch *Inherit the Truth* p.15
3. Interview with author 22 Nov 2022
4. Newman and Kirtley p.313
5. https://myscena.org/norman-lebrecht/the-true-humanity-of-alma-rose
6. Newman and Kirtley p.313.
7. *Bach in Auschwitz* documentary film by Michel Daeron
8. Hilde's testimony to Yad Vashem as before
9. https://www.sueddeutsche.de/politik/holocaust-esther-bejarano-1.2459943 interview with Esther Bejarano 6 May 2015
10. https://www.theneweuropean.co.uk/esther-bejarano-the-accordionist-of-auschwitz
11. *New York Times* Obituary https://www.nytimes.com/2021/07/15/arts/music/esther-bejarano-dead.html
12. Ibid. https://practisingthepiano.com/remembering-studies-with-peter-wallfisch
13. Ibid.
14. BBC Desert Island Discs https://www.bbc.co.uk/sounds/play/p0093ndt 1996
15. https://www.imdb.com/title/tt0939541/ BBC documentary *Playing to Survive* 1996

16. Interview with Jessica Duchen *Jewish Chronicle* 18 June 2020
17. Interview with author 11 July 2023
18. Desert Island Discs https://www.bbc.co.uk/sounds/play/p0093ndt 1996
19. Ibid.
20. Eischeid *Mistress of Life and Death* p.291
21. Ibid. pp. 297–8
22. Felstein *The Violinist of Auschwitz* p.133
23. Hannah Arendt *Eichmann in Jerusalem: A Report on the Banality of Evil* p.276
24. 'I too was Eichmann's Victim' *News of the World*, 23 October 1960
25. Susan Anderson *New York Times* 'Memories of a Nazi Camp' interview with Fénelon Arceuil, 7 January 1978
26. Fénelon *The Musicians of Auschwitz* p.9
27. Ibid.
28. https://www.nytimes.com/1978/01/07/archives/memories-of-a-nazi-camp-where-a-musical-gift-meant-survival-many.html
29. Gabriele Knapp *Das Frauenorchester in Auschwitz* pp.283–4
30. Fénelon *The Musicians of Auschwitz* p.109
31. Ibid.
32. Eischeid *Mistress of Life and Death* p.36
33. Dunicz Niwińska *One of the Girls in the Band* p.36
34. Eischeid *Mistress of Life and Death* p.37
35. https://www.nytimes.com/2019/01/11/movies/oscars-1978-politics-vanessa-redgrave.html
36. https://www.nytimes.com/1979/08/20/archives/vanessa-redgrave-says-she-wont-quit-tv-role-sparked-sharp-criticism.html https://alchetron.com/Fania-F%C3%A9nelon
37. Itta W. Holocaust Testimony (HVT-4083) Fortunoff Video Archive for Holocaust Testimonies, Yale University Library
38. Lasker-Wallfisch *Inherit the Truth* p.83
39. https://www.czestochowajews.org/wp-content/uploads/Krasner_and_Windman_Families.pdf
40. Lasker-Wallfisch *Inherit the truth* p.84
41. Ibid.
42. Flora Jacobs Schrijver interview with Richard Newman https://collections.ushmm.org/search/catalog/irn558864 e

43. Flora Jacobs Schrijver with Mirjam Verheijen *Girl with the Accordion* 1994 final page
44. Ibid. p.73
45. Ibid. p.81
46. Ibid. introduction
47. Ibid. pp.87–88
48. Dunicz Niwińska *One of the Girls in the Band* p.160
49. Ibid.
50. https://www.sueddeutsche.de/politik/holocaust-esther-bejarano-1.2459943
51. Interview with author 11 September 2023
52. https://www.sfgate.com/bayarea/article/yvette-assael-lennon-survived-holocaust-in-3204554.php
53. Joint Zoom Interview with author 30 April 2023
54. Ibid.
55. Felstein *Violinist in Auschwitz* p.5
56. Ibid. p.68
57. Ibid. p.105
58. Ibid. p.26
59. Ibid. p.29
60. Laks *Music of Another World* p.15
61. Itta W. Holocaust Testimony (HVT-4083) Fortunoff Video Archive for Holocaust Testimonies, Yale University Library
62. Flora Jacobs Schrijver interview with Richard Newman https://collections.ushmm.org/search/catalog/irn558864
63. Lasker-Wallfisch *Inherit the Truth* p.115
64. https://www.bundestag.de/en/documents/textarchive/speech-lasker-wallfisch-542306#:~:text=There%20were%20endless%20difficulties%20to,boundless%20hatred%20of%20anything%20German
65. Lasker-Wallfisch *Inherit the Truth* p.93
66. Lasker-Wallfisch interview with author 18 October 2022

Epilogue: If we forget, we are guilty, we are accomplices

1. Hilde Grünbaum Zimche interview with author 16 January 2023
2. *Bach in Auschwitz* documentary film by Michel Daeron 1999
3. Laks *Music of Another World* p.56

4. Felstein *The Violinist of Auschwitz* p.109

5. Krystyna Zywulska *I Survived Auschwitz* p.105

6. Zelmanowicz Olewski *Crying Is Forbidden Here!* p.34

7. Langbein *People in Auschwitz* p.63

8. Primo Levi *The Drowned and the Saved* p.42

9. Felstein *The Violinist of Auschwitz* p.

10. https://vha.usc.edu/testimony/979?from=search&seg=143%20Shoah%20 foundation%201995%20 video interview 1995 interview with Yvette Assael Lennon USC Shoah Foundation code 979

11. *Bach in Auschwitz* documentary film by Michel Daeron 1999

12. Itta W. Holocaust Testimony (HVT-4083) Fortunoff Video Archive for Holocaust Testimonies, Yale University Library

13. Lore Segal foreword to Ruth Kluger *Still Alive: A Holocaust Girlhood Remembered* Feminist Press NYC 2001 p.11

14. Desert Island Discs https://www.bbc.co.uk/sounds/play/p0093ndt 1996

15. Lasker-Wallfisch *Inherit the Truth* p.52

16. Interview with author 16 January 2023

17. *Bach in Auschwitz* documentary film by Michel Daeron

18. Ruth Kluger *Still Alive* p.88

19. Ibid. p.90

20. Tadeusz Borowski *This Way for the Gas, Ladies and Gentlemen* Penguin Modern Classics 1992

21. Flora Jacobs Schrijver with Mirjam Verheijen *Girl with the Accordion* final page

22. *Approaching an Auschwitz Survivor Holocaust Testimony and its Transformations* ed. Jürgen Matthäus OUP 2010 p.120

23. https://www.ushmm.org/m/pdfs/20050707-pres-commission-79.pdf

24. *Bach in Auschwitz* documentary film by Michel Daeron 1999

PICTURE CREDITS

p.184 Claire Monis (Wikimedia Commons)

p.204 Alma with her father (Gustav Mahler-Alfred Rosé Collection; Archives and Special Collections; Western Libraries; Western University)

p.230 Regina Kupferberg (Sivanne Cohen)

p.260 British Red Cross nurse, Margaret Montgomery (Dumfries & Galloway Arts & Museums, the Stewatry Museum, Kirkcudbright)

p.262 Announcement of a Red Cross concert (Duckworth Books)

p.268 Josef Kramer (Alamy/piemags/ww2archive)

p.272 Hilde Grünbaum, Anita Lasker and Hélène Rounder (Yad Vashem Archives/courtesy Asaf Zimche)

p.294 (Maria Mandel (Alamy/War Archive)

p.298 Lily Mathé (*News of the World*, 23 October 1960)

p.302 The Assael family (Peggy Clores)

p.305 Helena with Anita and Zofia (Helena Dunicz Niwińska, *One of the Girls in the Band* (PMA-B, 2013)

p.311 Lili Assael giving a piano lesson (Peggy Clores)

p.312 Yvette's wedding to Sergeant James Lennon (Peggy Clores)

p.336 Hilde Grünbaum Zimche on her 100th birthday (Asaf Zimche)

p.338 Auschwitz-Birkenau today (Alamy/Eric Nathan)

p.339 The remains of Block 12 (Anne Sebba)

INDEX

Anne Sebba is a historian and one of Britain's most distinguished biographers, who began her career as a Reuters correspondent based in London and Rome. She has written eleven works of non-fiction, mostly about iconic twentieth-century women, which have been translated into several languages, including French, Polish, Czech, Japanese and Chinese. She makes regular television and radio appearances and has presented two BBC radio documentaries about musicians. She is the author of the international bestseller *That Woman*, an acclaimed biography of Wallis Simpson, Duchess of Windsor, and the prize-winning *Les Parisiennes: How the Women of Paris Lived, Loved and Died in the 1940s*. Her most recent book, *Ethel Rosenberg: The Short Life and Great Betrayal of an American Wife and Mother*, was shortlisted for the Wingate Prize. Anne is a Fellow of the Royal Society of Literature, Senior Research Fellow at the Institute of Historical Research and trustee of the National Archives Trust. She lives in London.